The OECD Guidelines for Multinational Enterprises and Labour
Relations 1976–1979

The OECD Guidelines for Multinational Enterprises and Labour Relations 1976–1979

Experience and Review [1]

by Prof. Dr. R. BLANPAIN
University of Leuven, Belgium

Foreword by Prof. Dr. Mark Eyskens
Minister for Development and Co-operation

1979

KLUWER
DEVENTER/BOSTON/LONDON/FRANKFURT/ANTWERP

1. The original English text has been rewritten by MICHAEL JONES, Department Head of the Bishop of Llandaff High School, Cardiff, Wales, UK.

Distribution in the USA:

KLUWER LAW AND TAXATION PUBLISHERS
160 Old Derby Street
Hingham, MA 02043
USA

Library of Congress Cataloging in Publication Data

Blanpain, Roger.
  The OECD guidelines for multinational enterprises
and labour relations, 1976–1979.

  Includes index.
  1. Collective bargaining – International business
enterprises – Europe. 2. Collective bargaining –
International business enterprises. 3. Organization
for Economic Cooperation and Development. 4. Labor
policy – Europe. 5. Labor policy. I. Title.
HD6657.B56   658.31'54   79-26195
ISBN 90 312 0108 1

Cover design: Pieter J. van der Sman
© 1979, Kluwer, Deventer, The Netherlands

4

Contents

Contents

Contents

Conclusions   267

Annexes

Index   307

Foreword

by Professor Dr. Mark EYSKENS
Minister for Development and Co-operation[1]

There is no doubt that the OECD Guidelines correspond to the growing need of the piloting of, international investment and the behaviour of multinational enterprises. They are the expression of far reaching co-operation between Member countries, which is necessary to maintain and even improve a better investment climate; they constitute a positive contribution to the resolving of difficulties, to which the operations of multinational enterprises may give rise, especially in the labour relations area.

Belgium especially, has gained immensely from the positive contributions, which multinational enterprises can make to economic and social progress, could also, from the very moment of their existence, call upon the Guidelines and the competent OECD Committee for help, in order, to solve an important problem concerning the responsibility of the parent company for the (financial) obligations of its subsidiaries.[2] The guidance the Belgian Government received in the framework of the OECD declaration contributed largely to the satisfactory solution of the problem, with which Belgium was confronted. Undoubtedly, other examples could be given, where the Guidelines aided significantly to the creation and maintaining of co-operation between the Government, the enterprise and labour in difficult questions, such as the closing down of a plant. The Report, written by the Committee on International Investment and Multinational Enterprises at the occasion of the 1st review of the Guidelines, testifies to the seriousness and depth with which the Committee has performed its task by creating a reliable and stable framework for the activities of multinational enterprises; it indicates at the same time the Committee's sense for evolution and step by step approach, strengthening especially the use to be made of the Guidelines, what is termed in the Report as the 'follow-up' of the Guidelines. The 1979 Review has indeed revealed the need to strengthen the efforts to make the Guidelines better known by multinational enterprises and by labour; to integrate them in their thinking and practices, so that their impact may steadily increase.

1. M. Eyskens (born 29 April 1933) is Dr. Juris, Dr. in Economy and Baccelaurus in Philosophy, all of the University of Leuven. He also holds an M.A. degree in economics of the Columbia University (USA) and is Professor at the Business School of the University of Leuven and Commissary-General of the Catholic University Leuven-Louvain. He is the Representative of the Leuven area in the Belgian Parliament since 1977, and was in 1976, respectively 1977 appointed as Secretary of State for Flemish Regional Economy and for Budget. He is since 1979 Minister for Development and Co-operation.
2. See Part II, I.

Foreword

The Report recommends Governments, business and labour to undertake further necessary educational activities to make the content of the Guidelines and the manner in which they are to be implemented wider known.

Professor Blanpain's book on the *experience and review of the OECD Guidelines* 1976–1979, may help greatly to foster such a better knowledge and understanding of the Guidelines in operation; what they mean for Governments, business and labour and their potential. Prof. Blanpain, who first undertook on behalf of OECD an inquiry into 'The Industrial Relations and Employment Impacts of Multinational Enterprises' in 1975–1976, has, since 1977, been a Member of the Belgian Delegation to the OECD's International Investment and Multinational Enterprises Committee. Thus, he has had the opportunity to get a firsthand insight of what is going on in the IME Committee. I am grateful for his contribution, which constitutes a unique and balanced report containing basic documents, as well as points of view of all the parties concerned, and personal comments on the importance of Guidelines, and their impact on national and international industrial relations.

List of Abbreviations

AFL–CIO	American Federation of Labor – Congress of Industrial Organizations
ATLAS	Alitalia, Lufthansa, Air France and Sabena
BATCO	British American Tobacco Company
BIAC	Business and Industry Advisory Committee to OECD
CLC	Candian Labour Congress
CNV	Christelijk Nationaal Verbond. Christian National Trade Union Federation. Netherlands
CSC	Confederation of Christian Trade Unions
EEC	European Economic Communities
ETUC	European Trade Union Confederation
FGTB	Fédération Générale du Travail. Confederation of Socialist Trade Unions. Belgium
FIET	International Federation of Commercial, Clerical and Technical Employees
FMTNM	World Federation of Non-Manual Workers
FNV	Federatie van Nederlandse Vakverenigingen. Federation of Dutch Trade Unions
ICEF	International Federation of Chemical, Energy and General Workers Unions
ICFTU	International Confederation of Free Trade Unions
IIME	Committee on International Investment and Multinational Enterprises
ILO	International Labour Organization
IME	Committee on International Investment and Multinational Enterprises
IMF	International Metalworkers Federation
ITF	International Transport Workers' Federation
ITLGWF	International Textile, Garment and Leather Workers' Federation
ITS	International Trade Secretariats
KSSU	KLM, Swissair, SAS, UTA
LO	Confederation of Trade Unions (Denmark, Norway, Sweden)
MNE	Multinational Enterprise
NV	Limited liability company
OCDE	Organization de Coopération et de Développement Economique
OECD	Organization for Economic Co-operation and Development
OEEC	Organization for European Economic Co-operation

13

List of Abbreviations

TCO	Central Organization of Salaried Employees – Sweden
TUAC	Trade Union Advisory Committee to OECD
TUC	Trade Union Congress (Great-Britain)
UN	United Nations
USS	Union Syndicale Suisse – Switzerland
WCL	World Confederation of Labour
WFTU	World Federation of Trade unions

Introduction

1. There is no doubt that multinational enterprises have an important impact on employment and industrial relations in our industrialized market economies.

Impact on Employment

2. In 1976, so an EC survey showed, 5.087 multinationals in 21 most important OECD countries employed not less than 45,923,858 employees.

In Belgium, to give one example, 78 per cent of more than 1,000 enterprises, employing more than 1,000 employees were multinationals. In the industrial sector not less than 48 per cent of the workers in Belgium are employed by multinationals.

Although the impact on the net overall employment position remains an open question, most countries seem to have benefitted from foreign investment or at least have experienced no negative effects. Such a statement may, however, conceal the fact that the export or import of certain kinds of jobs may create structural problems, which may impose a heavy burden upon workers in particular industries or localities, as well as creating problems for governments. A recent survey, again in Belgium, shows that during the recent years of the crisis, less jobs have been lost in multinationals, compared to national enterprises.

Impact and Industrial Relations

3. Research undertaken in the framework of the International Labour Organization, OECD and the EEC have demonstrated that multinationals adapted to the local industrial relations rules and to the local climate.

A study undertaken by experts, appointed by the International Institute for Labour Studies, Geneva, on behalf of the European Commission concluded 'that the national industrial relations norms condition labour-management relations, particularly as regards information disclosure, consultation and negotiation, in transnational enterprises to a greater degree than their transnational character'.[1]

1. *Pilot-study on relations between management of transnational enterprises and employee representatives in E.C. countries*, Report submitted to the Commission of the European Communities, 1977, p. 62.

Another ILO study comments comparisons that have been made for developed countries 'indicate that while, in general, these firms (the multinationals) adapt their wage and salary levels to those of the countries where they operate, they often rank among the better-paying employers'.[2] Regarding working conditions, those multinationals were in line or compared favourably with those of large national employers.[3]

Another, recent ILO study concerning the 'social and labour practices of multinational enterprises in the petroleum industry' concluded: 'that there was little or no evidence . . . to substantiate charges of malpractices or unfavourable conditions of employment in multinational petroleum-enterprises, e.g. that "in order to reduce labour costs, multinational enterprises choose for their operations countries where wages were lowest, trade-unions paralysed or forbidden, governments most amenable to their demands, and regulations or environmental and workers' protection the least strict", or that "petroleum monopolies" pursued anti-trade-union policies and were generally hostile to the application of international labour standards'.[4]

The same study continued as follows: 'On the contrary, the bulk of information . . . – and which is not entirely onesided – tends to corroborate the view that the petroleum industry generally, and the multinational enterprises in particular, hold a position of leadership at national and international levels in comparison with other sectors of industry, particularly in respect of wages, fringe benefits and other conditions of employment, training and occupational health and safety. Nor . . . can the record in the field of industrial relations be considered – with a few isolated exceptions – as below par, at least in the context of the local or national situation. . . .'[5]

Why Then the Need for Codes?

4. If the multinationals have had such an overall beneficial impact on employment; have in general adapted to the local labour relations system and are as good as nationals, or even better employers, regarding wages and conditions, where then is the problem?

Why all the complaints? Why the need for Guidelines, and Codes of conduct, which have been or are being drawn up in so many international organizations.

Balance of Power – Central Decision Making

5. The reasons are, I believe, rather obvious: the multinational enterprises may through central decision making change the balance of power between labour and management and thus affect the hard core of the industrial rela-

2. ILO, *Multinationals in Western Europe: the Industrial Relations Experience*, Geneva, 1975, p. 32.
3. ILO, *Wages and working conditions in multinational enterprises*, Geneva, 1975, p. 50.
4. Geneva, 1977, p. 90.
5. *Idem.*

16

tions, which are in essence power relations in the sense that industrial relations concern the decision making power of the employers, which is countered by the display of power by employees through, for example, strikes, sitting on boards of companies and the like.

Central decision making, which, as I said, may affect the balance of power between management and labour, is at the heart of the multinational enterprise. In the OECD Guidelines for MNE's we can read that 'these usually comprise companies or other entities . . . established in different countries and are so linked that one or more of them may be able to exercise a significant influence over the activities of others . . .

Although the degree of central control differs considerably from one enterprise to another, it is widely accepted that most multinational enterprises have a centralized decision making process covering investment and technology. Pension funds are often centrally controlled and in many cases there is significant central intervention when subsidiaries are engaged in industrial conflict.

Some multinationals have also laid down broad principles concerning labour-management relations and the setting of wages and working conditions; others have developed uniform practices or standard policies over the years (e.g. on dealing with international trade secretariats, or the introduction of check-off clauses and the like). As an ILO study observes, 'there is also the fact that a certain type of behaviour is expected of the members of local top management who are generally selected and appointed by headquarters'. In some enterprises local managers will be allowed to negotiate only within certain financial limits.

It must be recognized that national industrial relations systems and legal rules often leave a lot of flexibility for a company to conduct its own industrial relations policy, which may make it more difficult for the trade union or the representatives of the employees to operate effectively if it differs significantly from established local custom and practice.

From these considerations the following conclusion can be drawn: centralized decision-making, especially in respect of decisions affecting employment in the broad sense, the organization of work, the introduction of a central company philosophy into industrial relations, which may be foreign and alien to local customs and consequently, in some cases, the lack of an 'interlocuteur valable' can undoubtedly affect the balance of power between management and labour; multinationals thus escape the national social network and may become, or seem to become, unaccessible to the local partners.

The balance of power can also be affected by the size of a multinational enterprise. The size of a firm, whether national or multinational is an important element in its power. Although small firms can also be powerful, there is no doubt that the larger enterprises, as measured by the number of workers employed, or the amount of the invested capital, command more resources and thus generally possess more power in the sense that they have more courses open to them and have greater endurance under pressure than smaller ones. Some unions express the fear 'that a particular operation of a multinational enterprise constitutes so small a part of the company's worldwide operations that it can be treated almost casually. As a consequence, the parent company can close down a given subsidiary in reprisal for a strike or what the company deems unreasonable labour conditions . . .'[6]

The Notorious Exceptions

6. Although multinationals in general are in the forefront of industrial relations and wages and working conditions there are some exceptions which because of the importance of the firm, became so notorious in their magnitude that they have thrown a damaging shadow on the behaviour of others.

Some multinationals in particular have had a bad press and were labelled as new forms of colonialism, accused of toppling democratic governments, of flirting with dictators; of bribing government officials . . . and the like. These charges have undoubtedly heavily impressed public opinion.

Countries

7. Moreover, small and even bigger countries feel that the multinational enterprises escape them and want to instaure to a certain degree sovereignty over the multinationals.

They fear the possible abuses of multinationals 'in the facilities they have to allocate their functions (such as production, research, financing and exportation) geographically, to distribute costs and profits between affiliates and to respond with greater freedom than domestic enterprises to policy objectives of home and host countries'.

But on their own, small and even bigger countries cannot do so much. They need the investment, especially the technology and know that national measures will scare multinationals away: so they strive in general, for international rules; which may also be necessary to help to solve disputes, which may arise between home and host countries. Most countries want especially to safeguard an 'open and stable environment for international investment', emphasizing that the basic orientation towards international investment should be promoted since these increase general welfare.

Trade-Unions

8. The greatest demand for Guidelines obviously comes from the trade-unions. In trying to restore the balance of power and in order to be able to influence decisions taken at headquarters, there are basically two ways for the trade union movement to confront the multinationals:
1. To strengthen the international trade union movement, especially the industrial internationals, and coerce multinational headquarters on the basis of that strength to hold meetings, leading to collective bargaining and (or)

6. ILO, *Multinationals in Western Europe: The Industrial Relations Experience*, op. cit., p. 20.

2. Appeal to political power by getting the help of governments and (or) international organizations in order to impose upon the multinational enterprises rules favourable for labour.

9. Some international trade unions, like the International Federation of Chemical Energy and General Workers' Union (ICEF) categorically reject any political help and (or) collaboration with international organizations like the UN, ILO, OECD, EEC. This position is, however, rather exceptional, especially given the *failure* of the international trade union movement to build a powerful structure at international level, which would be capable of getting the multinationals to talk with the international unions, let alone bargain with them. In fact, only exceptionally have meetings between international unions and headquarters taken place; those meetings are much sought after by the unions, but as a general rule they are refused. The world councils, which have been set up by and are composed of unions, organizing employees of the same multinational operating in different countries, have been mainly talking to themselves. As a general rule no bargaining at international level has taken place; international solidarity of workers, bans on overtime and the like, have proved to be the exception and not of a caliber to greatly influence managerial decision-making.

10. The reasons for this failure are manifold, and essentially I believe, they are structural in nature. These reasons are well known by now: ideological diversity, organizational conflicts, financial weakness and, above all, a conflict of interest between the unions themselves.

11. First of all there is the *ideological diversity* between the WFTU (communists), ICFTU (social democrats) and the WCL (former christians). The 'rapprochement' within the framework of overall 'detente' between some European and Communist Unions caused the American AFL-CIO to withdraw from ICFTU in 1969, although the American Unions are still active in the International Trade Secretariats and are associated with ICFTU through the Latin American Regional Organization of ICFTU (ORIT).
Even in the so-called 'same ideological groups' there are tensions which tend to paralyse the international movement. Tensions between national and international unions: national unions do not want to lose too much autonomy to European or International Organizations, especially in the area of collective bargaining.[7] There may be jurisdictional conflicts between the European Industrial Committees and the International Trade Secretariats. There is the special relationship between ICFTU and ETUC, which organizes both christian and communist unions; the ETUC is, for example, fundamentally divided over certain issues such as workers' participation; German and Scandinavian unions opting for codetermination and other unions, such as the Belgian and

---

7. See Blanpain R., Etty T., Gladstone A., Günter H., *Pilot Study on Relations between Management of Transnational Enterprises and Employee Representatives in EC Countries*, Report submitted to the Commission of the EC, 1977, 70 p. + annexes.

French socialists rejecting any 'integration' in the capitalistic system and opting for workers' control and (or) self government.

12. The international trade union movement is, next to structural problems, confronted with lack of *financial* means. Inflation has also cut into the unions' budget. ICFTU (budget 3,000,000 $ in 1974) at its latest Congress in Mexico in October 1975 increased the dues by 30 per cent, so that the national union centres have to pay almost US $ 80 per 1,000 members, which means about 30 per cent of the TUC's total income, many unions pay only partly or not at all. The same financial weakness characterizes the ETUC and most international trade secretariats, which consequently lack the necessary manpower.

13. The most important factor of weakness is the *conflict of interest* between the different unions fighting for the same jobs within the framework of a shrinking world economy in crisis and a new division of labour between North and South. It is German workers and their unions opposing Volkswagen to invest in the USA; American workers putting pressure on Japanese workers to export less cars to the USA market; American Unions opposing export of jobs and even export of technology; Belgian Volvo workers asking for a greater share of the overall Volvo production . . . and the like . . . which amount to lack of real solidarity between workers across the boundaries of different countries.

14. Most unions want to compensate this lack of trade union strength by putting pressure upon their national governments to do something at the international level, and here the relationships between trade unions and political parties are obviously of the utmost interest. These relationships are of particular importance in the European Countries; but also at this level safeguards are built in: countries do not want to harm their own multinationals by hard and fast rules.

15. The overall point is, however, that the trade union movement has to pressurize international organizations to adopt measures to control multinational enterprises as a means to build up trade union strength.[8] Unions try to get more grip on multinational enterprises by the establishment of international rules governing, for example,
– outward conditions on investment;[9]
– recognition of trade unions and collective bargaining;
– information;[10]
– access to headquarters and real decision-makers;
– consultation on investment decisions;
– countering of run away firms;

8. See the ICFTU's 'Charter of Trade Union Demands for the Legislative Control of Multinational Companies', (Mexico, 1975), *Bulletin of Comparative Labour Relations*, no. 7, 1976, p. 405–450.
9. Trade unions express concern about investment in countries which do not respect human and trade union rights.
10. Information on the multinational as a whole, and information in advance. See further OECD, *The industrial relations and employment impacts of multinational enterprises. An inquiry into the issues*, (1977), by A. Morgan and R. Blanpain.

– legalization of international trade union action and
– the making of a legally binding code.

Multinationals

16. It is not only governments and unions – be it for different reasons or not –
which favour the adoption of certain guidelines or rules concerning international investment, but also many multinationals, weary of what they consider to
be unjustified, and often conflicting criticism, and consequently not always sure
themselves of what course of action is indicated from the overall societal point
of view, support the idea of Guidelines, which, if lived up to, would lift their
conduct above the level of undue criticism. The condition that the Guidelines
are constructive; that they also recognize the positive contribution of multinational enterprises; they are consistent with international law and do not
discriminate between multinational and national enterprises.

OECD – ILO

17. Endeavours to draw up a code of good conduct, or guidelines, or a
declaration of principles concerning multinational enterprises and social policy
were recently undertaken by the UN, ILO, OECD and the EC. OECD was the
first to promulgate its 'Guidelines for Multinational Enterprises', on June 21,
1976.[11]
The ILO governing body adopted in November 1977 a declaration of principles, the status of which has yet to be determined.[12]
On September 20, 1977 the Governments of the nine Member States of the
European Communities adopted a Code of Conduct for Companies with
interests in South Africa.[13]
The Guidelines for OECD will be the most important! Why? OECD, the
richmen's club is of the right size: most of the multinationals are located in one
of the 24 member countries of OECD, which is an organization of countries
with industrialized market economies including USA, UK, Japan, Canada,
Germany . . . , the 9 EC countries, the Scandinavian countries and those which
are committed to promote free commerce and the free flow of investment over
the boundaries: the neo-capitalists. The European Communities may simply
not be large enough to develop effectively and uphold a set of rules for parent
companies, which are located outside their territory.
The UN and the ILO are of course big enough, but they may lack the right
climate to make the Guidelines work and have a major bearing on reality.

11. See S. Niklasson, 'Multinational Enterprises, Industrial Relations and Codes of Conduct.
United-Nations', in: *Bulletin for Comparative Labour Relations*, no. 10, 1979, pp. 49–58.
12. H. Günter, 'International Labour Office', *Ibidem*, pp. 59–84.
13. R. Smith, 'Labour Policies and Apartheid: The Role of Employment Codes in South Africa',
Ibidem, pp. 93–123.

International Guidelines can only work if governments can cooperate closely towards that end. Such a relationship between countries is self-evidently easier between countries, which share to a certain extent common political, economic and social views and structures. Such a co-operation, which is absolutely necessary if Guidelines are to be a living reality, may obviously be more difficult to realize within the framework of let us say, the ILO – especially since the USA left on November 5, 1977 – or in the UN where this community of interest is not always as obvious as in the OECD.

The OECD Guidelines and Labour Relations

18. There is no doubt that industrial relations during the 1976–1979 period were the centre of attention of the IME Committee which was set up in 1975 to strengthen co-operation between Member countries on issues pertaining to international investment and the activities of multinational enterprises. The clarifications of the scope and the meaning of the Guidelines given by the Committee in 1979, and consequently, the experience with the follow-up procedures and the ensuing developments in that area were largely inspired by these discussions concerning industrial relations issues.

One can speculate about the reasons for this focus on industrial relations. Obviously, the fact, that one of the two advisory bodies, namely the Trade Union Advisory Committee (TUAC) has its main interests in that area. TUAC clearly wants to augment the impact of the Guidelines on multinational enterprises and has taken a number of important initiatives in this field; such as the introduction of cases and issues for interpretation. The IME Committee and the Levy working group have devoted much of their time discussing these cases and formulating clarifications of issues, which these cases brought up. Students of international labour relations have to follow these developments closely.

The Aims

19. In this book I try to evaluate the impact of the OECD Guidelines on labour relations. The time to make such a first evaluation is right. A first phase has indeed been concluded. In 1979, a review of the Guidelines took place, as well as the publication of the first report of the IME Committee to the Council of Ministers. At the occasion of the review only one change was made to the Guidelines; the follow-up of the Guidelines and the way to strengthen their use, was greatly improved.

The IME report contains, moreover, a number of important clarifications of the Guidelines, thus giving an answer to the questions for interpretation put to the Committee by governments, as well as by business and labour. A first period of experience under the Guidelines, namely from 1976 to 1979 is thus concluded, and it is time to reflect upon what has happened and the way it came about.

There is also, I believe, a definite need for more documentation on this subject.

Not so much is known about the role of the IME Committee, the way it functions, its relationship with the advisory organs, BIAC and TUAC . . . the different clarifications, which are contained in the IME report are the result of cases and issues introduced by Governments and unions. What were these cases? What were the facts as presented to the Committee and what were the points of view of business and labour on the issues involved? In this book I want to answer this need and provide the necessary background information, which, I believe, is absolutely necessary for the understanding of the Guidelines and of the remarkable evolutionary process which has taken place in the OECD. At the same time I obviously want to expand on the nature of the exercise; the character of the Guidelines and speculate about further developments.

20. In the writing of this book, I have a unique advantage. Since Minister Mark Eyskens appointed me as his adviser for the Badger Case[14] I have been a member of the Belgian delegation to the OECD's IME Committee and have participated in the discussions leading to the IME report and the 1979 review. Thus, I have the privilege of a first hand insight. Everyone will, however, understand that a delicate balance has to be respected between the academic vocation and desire for communication on the one hand and the limitations imposed by confidentiality and discretion on the other hand.

Method and Presentation

21. In trying to give the necessary background information, insight and evaluation, I start with a rather long *prologue*, in which I give descriptions of the OECD; of the IME Committee; of the advisory bodies, BIAC and TUAC and of the International Trade Union Movement. This prologue is concluded with a general examination of the Guidelines, their genesis, their content, of the (non) definition of the multinational enterprise and of the nature and binding character of the Guidelines.

22. The book contains a further three parts. Part I deals with the *action under the Guidelines and the 1976 decisions*. I first examine the action by Member Governments (I) then the action by the IME Committee (II) and by the advisory bodies, BIAC and TUAC (their attitudes, activities and the way in which the consultations with the IME Committee and its Working Party took place) (III). In Part II I *evaluate the impact of the Guidelines*, with the help of the cases and issues, which were brought up in the IME Committee and the clarifications given in the IME report. For each of the twelve issues raised, I first give the relevant text of the Guidelines, or its introduction, then formulate 'the issue'; at the same time I publish the documentation concerning the case as put forward to the IME Committee, as well as the relevant part of the report of the IME Committee, which contains the clarification of the issue. I finally conclude the discussion of each issue with some personal comments on the

14. *The Badger Case and the OECD Guidelines for Multinational Enterprises*, Kluwer, Deventer, 1977, 210 p.

clarification given by the IME Committee and their significance from the industrial relations point of view.
The following issues are discussed:
– the co-responsibility of the parent company and subsidiaries;
– access to real decision makers;
– the closedown of an allegedly profitable subsidiary;
– the rights of employees to be represented;
– the status of international trade secretariats;
– international collective bargaining;
– participation in international trade union seminars;
– provision of information for collective bargaining;
– 'reasonable notice' in case of major change;
– comparable standards of employment;
– transfer of employees in case of a labour dispute;
– definition of a multinational.

Part III discusses the *follow-up procedures*, especially the strengthening of those procedures under the 1979 review. In this part of the book I pay attention, first to the preparation of the review, then to *reporting*, by the multinational enterprises, as well as by Governments and the IME Committee (I) to *problem solving*, at national and at international levels. Here I discuss the (new) role of the IME Committee and the format of the forthcoming contracts between the Committee and BIAC and TUAC as well as the new opportunities for individual enterprises to present their points of view to the Committee (II). I then take a look at the forthcoming review at the latest in 1984 (III).
Finally, I present the overall *conclusions* on the nature of the Guidelines; the importance and the meaning of the clarifications given by the IME Committee, on the new follow-up procedures, on the role of the IME Committee and of the exercise as a whole.

23. In the annexes, the revised OECD Declaration of 21st June, 1976 on International Investment and Multinational Enterprise (I) are reproduced. A press release by OECD, April 11, 1978 (II), one of the cases, introduced by IMF (III)[15] and a case which was not considered relevant by the IME Committee (IV). Finally, an index is published.

15 July 1979

15. For reasons of presentation.

Prologue

I. The Organization for Economic Co-operation and Development

24. OECD is an instrument for intergovernmental co-operation among 24 industrialized countries on matters relevant to economic and social policy, set up under a Convention, signed in Paris on 14 December 1960. Its basic premises are:
– a high degree of international economic interdependence is beneficial for economic growth and social progress
– intergovernmental co-operation among 'like-minded' market-economy industrialized countries can help to solve the problems that they are facing together and those that confront them in their relations with each other and with the outside world.
OECD is neither regional – though historically it arose from an association of European countries receiving Marshall Plan Aid – nor world-wide, though its membership includes countries from four continents. Rather its members are linked by a community of interests, by a similarity of economic structures and levels of development, by strong historic ties and – because of their combined economic weight – by common responsibilities to the outside world.
Members of OECD are: Australia, Austria, Belgium, Canada, Denmark, Finland, France, the Federal Republic of Germany, Greece, Iceland, Ireland, Italy, Japan, Luxembourg, The Netherlands, New Zealand, Norway, Portugal, Spain, Sweden, Switzerland, Turkey, the United Kingdom and the United States. Limited participants are the Commission of the European Communities and Yugoslavia.[1]

25. Providing a broad framework for economic co-operation, OECD is not limited to specific tasks but rather is designed to respond to the changing needs of participating governments.
The Organization's activities are geared to two main objectives:
1. to help Member countries promote economic growth, employment and improved standards of living
2. to help promote the sound and harmonious development of the world economy and improve the lot of the developing countries, particularly the poorest.

1. *The OECD*, Paris, OECD, s.d., 254 p.; *L'OCDE à l'oeuvre*, 1969, Paris, OCDE, 160 p.; *OCDE Historique. Objectifs. Structure.*, Paris OCDE, s.d., 59 p.; *OECD*, Paris, OECD, s.d., 28 p.

A PROFILE OF OECD MEMBER COUNTRIES*

	AREA 1,000 sq. km	POPULATION thousands	FULL-TIME SCHOOL ENROLMENT for children aged 15–19 percentage of age group 1975	GDP PER CAPITA at 1976 prices and exchange rates USA	GDP AVERAGE ANNUAL VOLUME CHANGE: 1970–1976 %
AUSTRALIA	7,686.8	13,916	46.1	6,760	3.8
AUSTRIA	83.1	7,513	37.0	5,410	4.1
BELGIUM	30.5	9,818	61.3	6,710	3.3
CANADA	9,976.1	23,025	66.4	8,410	5.0
DENMARK	43.1	5,073	62.1	7,590	2.5
FINLAND	337.0	4,729	60.8	5,950	3.5
FRANCE	549.1	52,927	51.3	6,550	4.3
GERMANY	248.6	61,531	51.3	7,250	2.5
GREECE	132.0	9,167	45.4	2,400	5.2
ICELAND	103.0	220	..	6,610	5.1
IRELAND	70.3	3,162	47.1	2,510	3.1
ITALY	301.2	56,156	40.8	3,040	2.9
JAPAN	372.3	112,768	76.3	4,920	5.5
LUXEMBOURG	2.6	356	33.5	6,280	2.0
NETHERLANDS	40.8	13,770	57.5	6,500	3.6
NEW ZEALAND	268.7	3,116	43.2	4,130	3.3
NORWAY	324.2	4,027	63.4	7,770	4.8
PORTUGAL	92.1	9,694	29.6	1,630	4.6
SPAIN	504.8	36,240	34.5	2,890	4.9
SWEDEN	450.0	8,219	57.1	9,030	2.2
SWITZERLAND	41.3	6,346	51.6	8,870	0.3
TURKEY	780.6	41,039	12.7	1,000	7.6
UNITED KINGDOM	244.0	55,959	43.9	3,910	2.0
UNITED STATES	9,363.4	215,142	72.0	7,910	2.9

Unless otherwise indicated these statistics are for the year 1976.
(a) Fiscal year starting 1st April.
(b) Includes some or all expenditures on the social Sciences and/or humanities.
(c) 70 per cent of total energy requirements (more than double the OECD average) are consumed by the industry sector mainly for export.
.. Not available

GROSS FIXED CAPITAL FORMATION % of GDP	CURRENT GOVERNMENT EXPENDITURE % of GDP	GROSS DOMESTIC EXPENDITURE ON R & D in natural sciences and engineering: % of GDP 1975	OFFICIAL DEVELOPMENT ASSISTANCE AS % OF GNP net disbursements	PER CAPITA ENERGY CONSUMPTION total primary energy requirements in tons of oil equivalent
23.7	28.6 1975–76	..	0.42	4.69
26.0	33.9 1975	..	0.12	3.22
20.6	41.6 1975	..	0.51	4.55
23.1	36.4	1.1 1975–76	0.46	8.51
21.5	42.8	1.1 b	0.56	3.82
27.0	34.7	0.9	0.18	4.77
23.1	40.0	1.8	0.62	3.36
20.7	41.7 1975	2.1	0.31	4.23
21.5	27.7	..	..	1.45
29.5	24.9 1968	0.9	..	4.86
24.5	34.8 1973	0.8	..	2.26
20.3	40.6	1.0	0.13	2.42
29.6	21.6	1.7 1975–76	0.20	3.09
28.2	42.1 1975	..	..	11.48c
19.7	52.2	2.0	0.82	4.73
25.2a	..	..	0.41	3.37
36.3	43.2	1.1 1974	0.70	5.16
23.9	27.2 1975	..	..	0.87
22.9	23.4	0.3 1974	..	1.81
20.6	49.8	1.8	0.82	6.11
20.7	31.1	2.2b	0.19	3.49
17.9 1973	18.0 1972	..	..	0.71
19.2	41.5	..	0.38	3.69
16.2	33.0	2.3b	0.25	8.10

STRUCTURE OF OECD

* *Committee on International Investment and Multinational Enterprises*, Committee for Invisible Transactions, Payments Committee, Insurance Committee, Committee on Financial Markets, Committee on Fiscal Affairs, Committee of Experts on Restrictive Practices, Committee on Consumer Policy, Maritime Transport Committee, Tourism Committee, Consortium for Turkey.
** Educational Building, Co-operation in Road Research, Club du Sahel.

26. Since OECD is by its very nature an organization which deals with changing problems and changing realities, its *structure* and *working* methods must be flexible. And both have in fact undergone considerable change since the Organization was established in 1961. But the basic means of achieving results has not changed: combining the available technical expertise with inter-government consultation so that policy discussions can take into account the international dimension and analysis be translated into concrete action.

The focus of the Organization and its central body is the *Council*, composed of permanent representatives of all 24 Member countries[2] and chaired by the Secretary General. It is within the Council that governments come together to take action on matters of substance. The Council is also the governing body of OECD and as such directs the work of its other bodies, co-ordinates their action and approves the programme of work and budget of the Organization. Through frequent meetings of the Council at ambassadorial level, day-to-day guidance is thus given to the Organization by Member governments.

2. Yugoslavia, is not a member of OECD, but has a special status within the Organization and participates in Council meetings and many of the activities without having the right to vote. A supplementary protocol to the OECD Convention provides for the Commission of the European Communities to 'take part in the work' of the Organization, and it is represented in the Council and most other OECD bodies.

28

The Council also meets at Ministerial level, normally once a year, to review the most urgent current problems and give political impetus to the coming year's work; each year a different country takes the chairmanship for this meeting. To prepare the Council's work, an *Executive Committee* has been created under the chairmanship of one Ambassador; at present it has fourteen members.

Since 1972, the framework of the Executive Committee has been used to organize special sessions, attended by senior officials in charge of international economic relations, to discuss matters which clearly cut across traditional lines: North-South and East-West relations and inter-related trade and investment issues are current examples.

The Council is also assisted by *specialized committees* (see chart) which cover macro-economic problems, development co-operation, industry, agriculture and fisheries, trade, energy, manpower and social affairs, science, education, environment and various financial and fiscal matters. The committees are composed of policy makers in their respective fields who come from capitals to attend OECD meetings. The key Economic Policy Committee, for example, includes economic advisers and senior officials from Finance and Economic Ministries who meet two or three times a year to evaluate the overall economic situation and the policy response of individual countries. But since problems confronting OECD governments are increasingly complex some of the newer committees are problem-oriented rather than sectoral in coverage, for example the Committee on International Investment and Multinational Enterprises.

Committees may also meet at Ministerial level and increasingly have been doing so: Ministers of Science have met intermittently since 1963; Ministers of Development, Agriculture, Industry, the Environment and Labour have also met at OECD to discuss common problems in their particular fields of responsibility.

Many of these committees have expert groups or working parties (there are roughly 200) which undertake more specialized tasks; some of them have assumed considerable importance on their own, the most notable example being 'Working Party Three' of the Economic Policy Committee which, with high-level representatives from ten of OECD's 24 members, closely monitors the balance-of-payments adjustment process.

In order to provide the necessary flexibility, both in membership and action, a third organizational category has emerged which includes *semi-autonomous institutions, limited membership activities and specially financed projects*.

– One of these, the *Nuclear Energy Agency*, predates the OECD itself having been formed under the Organization's predecessor, the OEEC (in 1958 with 18 European countries) to further the development of nuclear energy for peaceful purposes. Since then the membership has enlarged to include 23 OECD countries and its emphasis has shifted to helping them, through international co-operation, evaluate the nuclear option and solve the safety, regulatory, technical and economic problems involved in bringing nuclear energy on line.

–The *OECD Development Centre*, created in 1962, fulfills four main functions: research on development issues, liaison and co-operation with specialized training and research institutes, dissemination of information, exchange of development experience and contacts at technical level with experts of the Third World.

- The *Centre for Educational and Innovation* (created in 1968) explores forward-looking educational concepts – recurrent education, closer integration of schools into the community, educational financing – and promotes experimentation with new ideas.

- A *Road Research Programme* also set up in 1968 provides Member governments with the scientific and technological basis needed to solve the problems of road safety, traffic and construction.

- The *International Energy Agency* was created in November 1974, in the wake of the oil crisis, to implement an international agreement on an International Energy Program. It is a policy-oriented and operational body within the framework of the OECD, committed to improving the future balance of energy supply and demand. With 19 participating countries, the IEA has its own Governing Board compromised of senior energy-policy-making officials which also meets at Ministerial level. Its Executive Director is elected by the Governing Board with the concurrence of OECD's Secretary General, and the Agency has its own voting rules including the provision for majority voting.

- The *Interfutures* project in which eighteen countries participate was set up in 1976 to analyse in systematic fashion the broad spectrum of long-term problems facing the industrial societies, to examine their policy implications and to build up alternative scenarios for a harmonious evolution of the world economy.

This complex intergovernmental structure is serviced by an *international secretariat* – a professional staff of economists and experts in other disciplines drawn from the 24 Member countries. It constitutes a body of international civil servants, independent of Member governments. The permanent staff is supplemented as necessary by specialized consultants for projects requiring particular kinds of expertise. At the head of the secretariat is the Secretary General who is also Chairman of the Council and is appointed by Member governments for a period of five years to manage the Organization, co-ordinate its activities and represent the OECD in its relations with non-member countries and other international organizations. The Secretary General is assisted by two Deputy Secretaries General. The secretariat is divided into directorates, specializing in the various areas with which the Organization is concerned.

27. The rules of Procedure of the Organization, in execution of the Convention of 1960, indicate the *different categories of acts* which the Council may adopt.

The most formal is a *Decision* of the Council, which is legally binding on governments.[3] More common, however, is voluntary action in the form of a Council *Recommendation* addressed to Member countries. Although not legally binding, a Recommendation carries with it a strong *moral obligation*. It has

3. Since OECD is an inter-governmental organization, Council decisions must be put into effect by each government in accordance with appropriate national procedures.

been much used within OECD and has given impetus to specific measures on the part of Member countries. Thus, for example, a Recommendation to follow an active manpower policy made by the Council in 1968 – and reinforced in 1976 – has been cited in several national manpower laws. Recommendations have also been common in the nuclear energy and environmental fields. Usually a Recommendation is accompanied by specific follow-up procedures: countries agree to notify OECD of measures taken (before or after they come into effect), to consult with other Members, and to report back on progress made or obstacles encountered.

In addition, new kinds of action have recently emerged such as *Declarations* by Ministers which are expressions of political will on the part of governments and hence carry considerable weight. Examples are the Trade Pledge first made in 1974 and an agreement to abide by certain guidelines on multinational enterprises and international investment. OECD's Council encourages their implementation by establishing consultations or other follow-up procedures. Finally, some or all Member governments may, within the framework of OECD, negotiate an *international treaty*, such as a Convention, now in force in 12 Member countries, on liability in the event of a nuclear energy accident. Another example is the agreement on an international Energy Program.

28. Only Governments are members of OECD, unlike the ILO, which is tripartite and equally composed of Governments, employers' associations and trade union organizations. Business and labour have at the OECD a consultative status only.

II. The Committee on International Investment and Multinational Enterprises

1. The Establishment of the Committee: 1975

29. At its 8th Special Session on 25th and 26th November, 1974, the Executive Committee discussed proposals submitted by OECD's Secretary-General, E. Van Lennep, aimed at strengthening co-operation betweem Member countries on issues pertaining to international investment and the activities of multinational enterprises. The Executive Committee proposed that a Committee on International Investment and Multinational Enterprises should be set up to carry out this programme.

On 21st January, 1975, the Council adopted a Resolution establishing a Committee on International Investment and Multinational Enterprises (IME), and setting forth its mandate. The Council instructed the Committee to prepare a number of action proposals aimed at developing improved exchange of information and harmonized statistics in respect of the activities of enterprises engaged in international investment, and at working out uniform standards of behaviour applicable to multinational enterprises, as well as intergovernmental procedures for dealing with their implementation. Recommendations on these matters were to be made to the Council by the end of 1975; this date was subsequently extended to 30th June, 1976.

This Resolution reads as follows:

«The Council . . . decides:

1. A committee on International Investment and Multinational Enterprises (thereinafter called the 'Committee') is hereby established with the purpose of strengthening co-operation in the field of international investment and the activities of multinational enterprises aimed at making progress in these fields in a generally balanced way.

2. The Committee shall,

a. consider with regard to issues pertaining to the activities of multinational enterprises and enterprises engaged in international investment, as a stage in a continuing process in developing the Organization's procedures in this field, the preparation of action proposals for Member governments aimed at developing:
    (i)   improved exchange of information,
    (ii) improved and harmonized statistics,
    (iii) uniform standards of behaviour applicable to the enterprises,
    (iv) intergovernmental procedures for dealing with possible complaints;

b. consider in connection with a further review of issues pertaining to international investment, the organizing of consultations, in particular regarding:
    (i) official investment incentives or disincentives,
    (ii) national treatment for enterprises under foreign control;

c. make recommendations concerning (a) and (b) above to the Council at an early date and no later than the end of 1975.

3. The Committee shall also exchange views on work concerning the activities of multinational enterprises in other international organizations.

4. The Committee shall carry out its activities in co-operation with other committees concerned, as appropriate which would report to the Council through the Committee on International Investment and Multinational Enterprises on the future progress of this work.

5. The Committee shall be established on a provisional basis until the end of 1976, or until the Council, on the proposal of the Executive Committee in Special Session, as appropriate, decides to maintain or to review its terms of reference, whichever is the earliest.»

30. In opening the first meeting of the new Committee OECD's Secretary General, drew attention to some of the main problem areas:

«Multinational enterprises have been the object of a great deal of comment in recent years, but the discussion has often been emotionally charged and hampered by a lack of qualitative and quantitative information or of agreement on the real political nature of the problem.

The rise of multinational enterprises and the increasing foreign involvement of business have been deplored by some as likely to limit substantial elements of national sovereignty. Others have hailed multinational enterprises as agents for the establishment of a pattern of international economic relations characterized by an optimum allocation of resources.

One should certainly not lose sight of the positive contribution made by multinational enterprises to the welfare of both the countries in which they operate and those in which they are based. The rapid growth in the number of these firms over the last decade, however, their increased size and scope, as well as the discrepancies which may exist between the transnational structures of these enterprises and the national character of governments have given rise to concern.

How to deal with these problems? First, there is of course a clear need for improved exchange of quantitive and qualitative information which should be translated, however, in a fairly short time into recommendations for *action*. Two approaches to the reduction of tensions between multinational enterprises and national sovereignty can be envisaged: first, multinational enterprises themselves can agree on some sort of principles of conduct on a purely self-regulatory basis without involving governmental action. Second, governments can agree on some sort of *standards of behaviour* applicable to the enterprises – as necessary on a regional basis – and *guidelines* which could serve as a basis for governmental action and also, as appropriate, *intergovernmental consultation procedures* as a stage in a continuing process aiming at the harmonization of national laws and administrative procedures. Without dismissing the idea that self-regulation may be useful, the Council of OECD has instructed the new Committee to follow the second approach: to prepare at this stage action proposals aimed at developing uniform standards of behaviour applicable to the enterprises and to develop intergovernmental procedures for dealing with possible complaints. In the long run, however, the objectives will be strengthening intergovernmental co-operation through harmonizing national laws and procedures and possibly even establishing equitable international rules – if possible in a wider context than the OECD area. For, unless fast progress is made in adapting the *political* structures to modern reality by strengthening intergovernmental co-operation, governments might on the one hand be unable to take the measures necessary to safeguard the public interest and welfare; on the other hand multinational enterprises might find themselves increasingly harassed by unnecessary obstacles and restrictions that could seriously reduce their potential and therefore hinder them from making an optimum contribution to the welfare of nations.

There is therefore a clear need for action-oriented co-operation in this field. Such action, however, should not impair the level of liberalization which OECD Member countries have already been able to achieve in the field of international investment. The second major area with which the Committee will have to deal, therefore, is encompassed in the phrase *issues pertaining to international investment*. In this field, the Committee, according to its mandate, will first have to consider the organizing of *consultations* regarding the reduction of harmful effects on Member countries' economies which may result from the use of investment incentives and disincentives in other countries. Second, the Committee will have to consider the possibility of implementing the principle of national treatment of enterprises under foreign control.»[4]

4. *The OECD Observer*, 1975, no. 74, pp. 14–15.

2. The 1976 Mandate

31. In 1976 the negotiations in the Committee were concluded and the Council of Ministers adopted the Declaration, to which the Guidelines for Multinational Enterprises and the Decisions are attached[5] and in which the governments of Member countries set forth, in summary, the following main points:
  (i) that they jointly recommended to multinational enterprises operating in their territories the observance of the Guidelines;
  (ii) that Member countries should, subject to certain conditions, accord to foreign enterprises operating in their territories treatment no less favourable than that accorded in like situations to domestic enterprises ('National Treatment');
  (iii) that they recognized the need to strengthen their co-operation by giving due weight to the interests of Member countries affected by specific measures providing incentives and disincentives to international direct investment;
  (iv) that they were prepared to consult one another on the matters set forth above in conformity with the procedures laid down by the Council in its Decisions taken on the same day;
  (v) that they would review all these matters within three years with a view to improving the effectiveness of their co-operation on issues relating to international investment and multinational enterprises.

32. The IME Committee was put in charge of these consultation procedures. In the framework of the consultations on matters related to the Guidelines, the IME Committee was also instructed to invite periodically the Business and Industry Advisory Committee (BIAC) and the Trade Union Advisory Committee (TUAC) to express their views. In addition, a Member country may propose to the Committee that it should give the opportunity to individual enterprises to express their views concerning the application of the Guidelines. An individual enterprise, however, is in no way bound to accept such an invitation and the consultations are not designed to lead the Committee to reach conclusions on the conduct of individual enterprises.

Having regard to the 1976 Declaration and Decisions, the Committee received by Resolution of the Council of 22nd December 1976 a new mandate instructing it to carry out the tasks assigned to it by virtue of the Declaration and the Decisions of 21st June, 1976 in respect of international investment and multinational enterprises. These tasks encompass two main elements: the first is to gather experience from the application of the Guidelines, 'National Treatment' and the Decision on International Investment Incentives and Disincentives during the initial three-year period; the second is to develop and strengthen further co-operation among Member countries in this field.

This reference to further co-operation was inter alia, related to the fact that governments declared to consider their agreement of 21st June, 1976 as the

5. See Annex I.

conclusion of the initial phase of their continuing co-operation programme. Further endeavours within the OECD may lead to complementary arrangements and agreements in the field of international investment and multinational enterprises. The task of the Committee would therefore be to monitor this programme and prepare, when the occasion arises, new proposals for the Council. In addition, the Committee was instructed to keep itself informed of activities carried out in other international bodies in the field of international investment and multinational enterprises and to provide a forum for Member countries jointly to consider these activities and to take account of them in its own work.

In order to fulfil its task effectively, the Committee promoted the co-ordination of all work on international investment carried out by existing committees and working parties in the OECD. These specialized committees, during the negotiations, have assisted the IME Committee to formulate particular sections of the Guidelines and have continued to work on certain aspects of international investment and multinational enterprises.

The new mandate, contained in the resolution of 22nd December 1976, reads as follows:
«The Council. . . .
DECIDES:
I. TERMS OF REFERENCE OF THE COMMITTEE ON
   INTERNATIONAL INVESTMENT AND MULTINATIONAL
   ENTERPRISES

1. The Committee on International Investment and Multinational Enterprises (hereinafter called the 'Committee') shall have the task of further developing and strengthening co-operation among Member countries in the field of international investment and multinational enterprises.
2. The Committee shall carry out the tasks assigned to it by virtue of the Declaration of OECD Member countries of 21st June, 1976 and by the Decisions of the Council of 21st June, 1976 referred to above.
3. The Committee shall be responsible for monitoring and promoting co-ordination of all work carried out within the Organization in the field of international investment and multinational enterprises, and for presenting proposals for this purpose to the Council or to other committees. Other committees concerned will report to the Council through the Committee on the progress of their work.
4. The Committee shall keep itself informed of activities carried out in other international bodies in the field of international investment and multinational enterprises and shall provide a forum for Member countries to consider their views in respect of issues raised in such bodies, and take account thereof, as appropriate in its own work.
5. The terms of reference provided for in the Resolution of the Council of 21st January, 1975 referred to above are repealed.
6. These terms of reference are established for a period of three years from the date of the present Resolution.»

35

33. The IME Committee at the occasion of its meeting of July 7–8th, 1977, decided to create an ad hoc Working Group, with the mandate to have an exchange of views and further informal contacts with BIAC and TUAC on the Guidelines to which reference was made at the occasion of the introduction of cases in the IME Committee on March 30th, 1977.

3. THE NEW MANDATE AFTER THE 1979 REVIEW

34. Under its new mandate, which was negotiated at the occasion of the 1979 review of the Guidelines and which we discuss in detail in Part III of this book, the IME Committee got far reaching competences, but which can be summarized as follows:[6]
1. Exchange of views a) between Governments, b) with BIAC and TUAC and c) individual enterprises;
2. Clarification of the Guidelines;
3. Bi-annual reporting to the Council;
4. Proposals for review at the latest in a period of five years.[7]

III. The Advisory Bodies: BIAC and TUAC

1. BIAC

35. The Business and Industry Advisory Committee (BIAC)[8] was constituted on March 9, 1962, as an independent organization officially recognized by the Organization for Economic Co-operation and Development. Its task is to represent business and industry in the work of OECD and to express opinions on questions of common interest.
To fulfill its role, BIAC – through consultations with the OECD Committee for Liaison with Non-governmental Organizations; through meetings with representatives of various OECD Committees, and through on-going contacts with the OECD Secretariat – gives OECD and its Member Governments the benefit of comments based on the experience of the business community. By exercising its influence in a practical way, BIAC tries to contribute to the aims of the OECD, which are directed mainly to the promotion of balanced economic growth and social progress.

36. Inasmuch as BIAC brings together the industrial and employers' organizations of the 24 OECD Member countries, it is thus representative of *private enterprise* as a whole in the industrialized world. BIAC does not, however,

---

6. For the text of the relevant decisions by the Council, see Annex I.
7. See further Part III, II.
8. *Annual report of activities, 1978.*

represent all enterprises to which the Guidelines apply, in conformity with paragraph 8 of the introduction, which reads: . . . These usually comprise companies or other entities, whose ownership is private, state or mixed . . . On a number of occasions BIAC has indicated that this constitutes a problem, since when considering the compliance with the Guidelines a number of companies escape BIAC's jurisdiction and involve more the responsibility of the Governments, especially when state-owned enterprises are concerned.

Member Organizations of BIAC are:

Australia	Confederation of Australian Industry
Austria	Vereinigung Österreichischer Industrieller
	(Federation of Austrian Industrialists)
Belgium	Fédération des Entreprises de Belgique
	(Federation of Belgian Enterprises)
Canada	Canadian Business and Industry Advisory Committee for the OECD
Denmark	Industriraadet
	(Federation of Danish Industries)
	Densk Arbejdsgiverforening
	(Danish Employers' Confederation)
Finland	Suomen Teollisuuden Keskusvaliokunta
	(Council of Finnish Industries)
France	Conseil National du Patronat Français
	(National Council of French Employers)
Germany	Bundesverband der Deutschen Industrie e.V.
	(Federation of German Industries)
	Bundesvereinigung der Deutschen Arbeitgeberverbände
	(Confederation of German Employers' Associations)
Greece	Syndesmos Ellinon Viomichanon
	(Federation of Greek Industries)
Iceland	Felag Islenzkra Idnrekenda
	(Federation of Icelandic Industries)
	Vinnuveitendasamband Islands
	(Confederation of Icelandic Employers)
Ireland	Confederation of Irish Industry
	The Federated Union of Employers
Italy	Confederazione Generale dell'Industria Italiana
	(General Confederation of Italian Industry)
Japan	Japanese Business and Industry Advisory Committee to the OECD
Luxemburg	Fédération des Industriels Luxembourgeois
	(Federation of Luxemburg Industrialists)
Netherlands	Raad van Nederlandse Werkgeversverbonden
	(Council of Netherlands Industrial Federations)
New Zealand	New Zealand Employers Federation

37

Norway	Norges Industriforbund (Federation of Norwegian Industries) Norsk Arbeidsgiverforening (Norwegian Employers' Confederation)
Portugal	Associaçao Industrial Portuguesa (Portuguese Industrial Association)
Spain	Confederación Española de Organizaciones Empresariales (Spanish Confederation of Business Organizations)
Sweden	Sveriges Industriförbund (Federation of Swedish Industries) Svenska Arbetsgivareföreningen (Swedish Employers' Confederation)
Switzerland	'Vorort' des Schweizerischen Handels- und Industrie-Vereins ('Vorort' of the Swiss Federation of Commerce and Industry) Union Centrale des Associations Patronales Suisses (Central Union of Swiss Employers Associations)
Turkey	Turkiye Ticaret Odalari, Sanayi Odalari Ve Ticaret Borsalari Birligi (Union of Chambers of Commerce, Industry and Commodity Exchanges of Turkey)
United Kingdom	Confederation of British Industry
United States	USA Business and Industry Advisory Committee to the OECD

37. BIAC's organization is shown in the following chart.

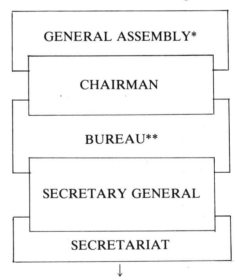

↑

COMMITTEES AND WORKING GROUPS
- · International Investment and Multinational Enterprises
- · Economic Policy
- · Energy and Raw Materials
- · Capital Movements and Capital Markets
- · Taxation and Fiscal Policy
- · – Working Party on Taxation of Multinational Enterprises
- · Restrictive Business Practices
- · Technology
- · Manpower and Social Affairs
- · Education
- · Environment
- · – Chemicals
- · Private Investment and Development Aid
- · Trade

---

* Composed of delegates from all Member Organizations
** Composed of the Chairman, Four Vice-Chairmen, Treasurer (ex officio), and Secretary General (ex officio).

38. The General Assembly normally meets in full session once a year to review and establish policies and to set general priorities. The Bureau is the executive arm of the General Assembly, overseeing the implementation of the policies established. Various specialist working groups, drawn from member organizations and private industry, study the real problems arising within their field with the object of formulating a common viewpoint. The Secretariat, consisting of the Secretary General and a small staff, is located near OECD, in Paris. Its chief functions are to maintain close contact with OECD, keep Members informed of developments and to organize and to co-ordinate the activities of the working groups.

39. Because of the nature of its relationship with OECD, BIAC's range of activities naturally corresponds broadly with that of OECD itself. However, in addition to responding to the requirements of OECD, BIAC is at liberty to take up new problems on its own initiative.
Areas covered vary according to changing trends and circumstances but can broadly be classified as follows: economic policy, financial, trade, manpower and social affairs, development aid and investment and multinational enterprises. Views are exchanged with OECD, formally and informally, at all levels, both on policy matters and technical questions. The Bureau normally meets OECD's Liaison Committee for Non-Governmental Organizations once a year for policy discussions, while other high-level discussions are held when necessary. BIAC's working groups meet OECD representatives throughout the year; at staff level, there is almost daily contact.
Under these main headings, examples of study and consultation include such diversified topics as the problems of employment and manpower policies for full employment; vocational education; obstacles to free trade; transfer of technology; structural adjustment; guidelines for MNE's; energy conserva-

tion; transfer; pricing; the removal of obstacles to capital flows and fiscal anomalies, improvement of the investment climate in developing countries and the protection of the Government.

BIAC COMMITTEES AND GROUPS OF EXPERTS

Committee on International Investment and Multinational Enterprises
    Chairman: Mr. G. A. Wagner (The Netherlands)
Committee on Economic Policy
    Chairman: Dr. H. G. Sohl (Germany)
  Vice-Chairmen: Mr. P. Combin (France)
                 Mr. T. Yamada (Japan)
Committee on Energy and Raw Materials
    Chairman: Mr. E. G. Collado (United States)
  Vice-Chairmen: Mr. F. Lindsay (United States)
                 Mr. P. Hatry (Belgium)
Group of Experts on Capital Movements and Capital Markets
    Chairman: Mr. V. H. Grigg (United States)
Group of Experts on Taxation and Fiscal Policy
    Chairman: Prof. D. Helmers (Sweden)
Working Party on Taxation of Multinational Enterprises
    Chairman: Prof. D. Helmers (Sweden)
Group of Experts on Restrictive Business Practices
    Chairman: Dr. F. Hermanns (Germany)
Group of Experts on Technology
    Chairman: Mr. H. Ledin (Sweden)
Group of Experts on Trade
    Chairman: Mr. Y. Aubin (France)
Group of Experts on Manpower and Social Affairs
    Chairman: Dr. W. Lindner (Germany)
Group of Experts on Education
    Chairman: Mr. F. Haldén (Sweden)
Group of Experts on Environment
    Chairman: Dr. F. Brandi (Germany)
Chemicals Sub-Group
    Chairman: Drs. P. L. de Reeder (The Netherlands)
Standing Group on Development Aid and Private Investment
    Chairman: Mr. T. J. Bata (Canada)

2. TUAC

40. In an information sheet TUAC (Trade Union Advisory Committee to OECD) describes itself as an integral part of the international trade union movement. Essentially, it serves to inform members of OECD activity and to present its members' views to the OECD so as to best influence the latter's policies and activities. One of the oldest international trade union groupings with direct consultative status with an inter-governmental organization, the Trade Union Advisory Committee was founded in 1948 to allow European unions to play a full and vital role in the administration of the Marshall Plan by the OEEC (Organisation for European Economic Co-operation) and vis-à-vis the European Recovery Program.

With the creation in 1961 of the OEEC's successor, the OECD, TUAC was officially accredited with consultative status by the OECD, representing the organized workers of member countries.

A further development of particular importance to the international trade union movement took place in January 1971 with the creation of a single TUAC Secretariat, thus bringing together for the first time both ICFTU (International Confederation of Free Trade Unions) and WCL (World Confederation of Labour) affiliates, together with some union centres having no international affiliation. The present membership of 38 organizations from 22 countries gives TUAC a membership of 50 million trade unionists. International Trade Secretariats also participate in TUAC work, contributing to it their particular experience of various industrial sectors.

41. TUAC describes its structure, working and priorities as follows:

«The *structure* of TUAC is relatively flexible. There is some unclarity as to the level on which statements coming from the organization are to be made. This reflects the day-to-day realities in contacts with the OECD which sometimes gives documents for comments only a few days before TUAC is consulted – if, indeed, such documents are given at all. In these circumstances, it is impossible to set off an elaborate decision making process.

However, in matters involving a basic and principal attitude of the TUAC affiliates on certain questions, the decision making process is clear. Decisions are made by the *Plenary Session*, which consists of all 38 affiliates and representatives of the international organizations (ICFTU, WCL, ETUC, NFS) as well as the ITS's. They are generally prepared – especially insofar as draft texts are concerned – by the *Working Groups*, established by the Plenary Session.

The role of the *Administrative Committee* has been to prepare decisions for the Plenary Session on such matters as the budget, membership fees, personnel questions and requests for affiliation. There have been cases (i.e. before the submission of the trade union views in June, 1978, to the OECD Ministerial Council) when the Administrative Committee has discussed substantive questions. In the case referred to above, the motivation was that during one half year, three Plenary Sessions had already taken place and a fourth one was approaching. As an *ad hoc* solution, representatives of the international organizations were invited to the meeting.

TUAC has currently three permanent Working Groups: on Economic Policy, on Multinational Enterprises, and on Education. *Ad hoc* groups have been convened for consultations on a given subject which is not dealt with by a Working Group. In practical terms it has been necessary, on a number of occasions, to prepare not only a draft but also the final presentation in the Working Groups without a meeting of the Plenary. One example was the presentation of TUAC views to the Education Committee which met on Ministerial Level in October, 1978. Documents on basis of which the views could be defined were made available only 10 days before the consultations themselves, and OECD had requested both written and oral comments.

In this connection it has to be underlined that the invitations to meetings of the Working Groups are sent to all organizations: affiliates, international organizations, and the ITS's. Thus, the composition of the Working Groups is the same as that of the TUAC Plenary Session. Of course working groups tend to be more composed of experts that the Plenary – but on occasions, e.g. prior to consultations with the Committee for International Investment and Multinational Enterprises, in April, 1978, the Plenary Session did not essentially differ from the Working Group on Multinational Enterprises, due to the subject matter discussed.

The Working Groups also report on their activities to the Plenary Session which is to adopt the reports.

Decisions in all these bodies have, as a rule, been made on the basis of consensus. The same principle applies to the decision making of the OECD as well.

42. There are no written *rules of procedure* for TUAC with the exception of the necessary documentation given to French authorities in connection with the recognition of TUAC as an international non-governmental organization. The status of TUAC is one of a non-governmental organization, recognized as a consultative body by the OECD. (An updated list of the 38 central organizations making up the organization has just been delivered to the OECD, at the request of its Secretary-General.)

There has recently been discussion among the affiliated organizations of the lack of rules of procedure. The main reason to have such rules would be to have a clear division of labour established between the Plenary, the Administrative Committee, and the Working Groups. If rules of procedure are to be drawn up, the following elements could be included: (a) tasks; (b) membership; (c) decision making procedure; (d) division of labour between the various bodies; (e) modalities of work; (f) meeting procedure; (g) determining of the affiliation fee; and (h) co-operation with other international organizations.

In establishing rules of procedure, the question of competence between the Plenary Session and the Working Groups is crucial. It might be possible to either leave the responsibility for the preparation *and presentation* of TUAC views to the Working Groups entirely or to ask the TUAC Secretariat to prepare a first draft and then solicit the views of all member organizations before presenting the TUAC position by a delegation specially composed for the consultations concerned. A combination of these two is also feasible. (It is necessary to underline that consultations involve a relatively free exchange of views between TUAC on one hand and the government representatives as well as those from the OECD Secretariat on the other hand. Written submissions are thus only one element in the consultations. It might be useful to establish rules for the composition of TUAC delegations for consultations as well.)

The alternatives in the preceding paragraph do not take the Plenary Session into account. They are based on a hypothesis of a 'permanent lack of time', due to the timing of OECD and the possibilities of receiving documents for consultations. The Plenary Session cannot be called in on a short notice without risking both the quantity and quality of participation. The role of the Plenary Session would be to establish the main orientations of TUAC activities and to approve the reports of the Working Groups. In the case of important decisions, also documents of major significance, these should be approved by the Plenary as well. (A concrete example could be that while statements to Summit Meetings or the Ministerial Council would be discussed and approved by the Plenary whereas e.g. statements to various OECD Committees on multinational enterprises or adjustment policies would be prepared and presented by the relevant Working Groups.) The Plenary Session could be held regularly twice a year, for some 2 days, once in the Spring and once in the Autumn, with the possibility of special sessions for approving major documents.

With fewer – and timewise more fixed – Plenary Sessions and an enlarged role for the Working Groups, the functions of the Administrative Committee could also be revised. One possibility is to develop it into some kind of a general purposes committee which could prepare all items for the Plenary Sessions. It could also make decisions if the Working Groups' competence would not seem to be enough but if it would be impractical to call a full meeting of the Plenary. In this connection the composition of the committee should also be discussed.

In the immediate future, it might be appropriate to prepare a document on these questions for the TUAC Plenary. The Plenary could, for instance, establish an *ad hoc* group to discuss rules of procedure for the organization.

43. The *priorities* established by the Plenary Session are at present the following: (a) economic policy and employment questions; (b) multinational enterprises; (c) energy; and (d) education. Three of them are covered by activities of Working Groups, energy being dealt with on an *ad hoc* basis. These priorities are conditioned by the work programme of the OECD. There would seem to be little need to change, let alone omit any of these priorities. On each of them, the consultative arrangements are being developed with the OECD.

However, they are – especially regarding the first one – very broad and can be overlapping. Under priority (a) the following activities have taken place during the past year: the statement to the Bonn Summit Meeting, the statement to the Ministerial Council, a set of consultations on adjustment policies, an informal meeting with the Chairman of the OECD Economic Policy Committee, and continued work on youth unemployment. Under priority (b), apart from consultations with the relevant OECD Committee, three specific areas for consultations have emerged, viz. transfer pricing, accounting standards, and tax evasion.»

MEMBER ORGANIZATIONS

1. Australian Council of Trade Unions ACTU
2. American Federation of Labor – Congress of Industrial Organizations AFL–CIO
3. Confederation of Islandic Trade Unions ASI
4. Confédération Française Démocratique du Travail CFDT, France

5. Confédération Générale des Cadres CGC, France
6. Confédération Générale du Travail – Force Ouvrière CGT–FO, France
7. Confédération Générale du Travail du Luxembourg CGT–Lg
8. Confederazione Italiana Sindacati Lavoratori CISL
9. Canadian Labour Congress CLC
10. Confédération des Syndicats Chrétiens de la Suisse CSC
11. Christelijk Nationaal Vakverbond (Christian National Trade Union Federation) CNV, Netherlands
12. Confédération des Syndicats Chrétiens de Belgique CSC
13. Confédération des Syndicats Nationaux CSN, Canada
14. Deutscher Gewerkschaftsbund (German Federation of Trade Unions) DBG, Germany
15. Japanese Confederation of Labour DOMEI
16. Fédération de l'Education Nationale FEN, France
17. Fédération Générale du Travail de Belgique FGTB
18. Federation of Danish Salaried Employees FTF
19. Greek General Confederation of Labour GSEE
20. Irish Trades Union Congress ICTU
21. Confédération des Syndicats Chrétiens de Luxembourg LCGB
22. Confederation of Danish Trade Unions LO
23. Confederation of Norwegian Trade Unions LO
24. Confederation of Swedish Trade Unions LO
25. Nederlands Katholiek Vakverbond (Catholic Trade Union Federation of the Netherlands) NKV(*)
26. Nederlands Verbond van Vakverenigingen (Federation of Dutch Trade Unions) NVV(*)
27. Central Organisation of Finnish Trade Unions SAK
28. The General Council of Trade Unions of Japan SOHYO
29. Solidarity of Basque Workers, STV, Spain
30. Association Suisse des Salariés Evangéliques ASSE (SVEA)
31. Confederation of Salaried Employees TCO, Sweden
32. Trades Union Congress TUC, Great Britain
33. Confederation of Turkish Trade Unions TURK–IS
34. Confederation of Salaried Employees in Finland TVK
35. Union General de Trabajadores UGT, Spain
36. Unione Italiana des Lavoro UIL
37. Union Syndicale Suisse USS
38. Osterreichischer Gewerkschaftsbund (Federation of Austrian Trade Unions)

ADMINISTRATIVE COMMITTEE

The TUAC Administrative Committee is composed of representatives of the following Member organizations:
LO–Denmark, Chairman of TUAC: Svend Bache Vognbjerg, Secretary of LO
CSC Belgium, Vice-Chairman of TUAC: Jozef Houthuys, President of CSC
TUC, representative to TUAC Administrative Committee: Lord Allen

AFL–CIO, representative: Irving Brown
DBG, representative: Aloïs Pfeiffer
CGT–FO, representative: Antoine Laval
CFDT, representative: Jean Bourhis
General Secretary of TUAC: Kari Tapiola

IV. The International Trade Union Movement

44. According to Professor J. Windmuller, the international trade union movement can be grouped into four categories: 1) global 2) regional 3) industrial and 4) specialized internationals.[9]

The term *global internationals* refers to organizations seeking world wide affiliation with national trade union centres. Actually, there are three global organizations: the International Confederation of Free Trade Unions (ICFTU), the World Federation of Trade Unions (WFTU) and the World Confederation of Labour (WCL).

ICFTU dominates the trade union scene in the industrialized market economies. 60 per cent of its almost 52 million members belong to European Confederations, since the American AFL-CIO left ICFTU in 1969.

Most of the Confederations, which are members of the WFTU, belong to communist countries, although the major unions in France and Italy are also communist inspired. WFTU claims 190 million members. A much smaller organization is (former christian) WCL, which has its most important affiliates in Belgium and the Netherlands.

The European Trade Union Confederation is undoubtedly the most important of the different *regional internationals*. Although most of its members are confederations, which adhere to ICFTU, ETUC is also affiliated to WFTU and WCL and now claims some 39 million members.

A third category of trade unions is the *industrial internationals*, which organize unions of different countries whose members are employees of the same industry or profession. These operate within the framework of each global international. The most important are those associated with the ICFTU. Some are very large organizations: the International Metalworkers Federation (IMF), for example, *e.g.* organizes some 13,500,000 members, while the International Federation of Commercial, Clerical and Technical Employees (FIET) claims some 6 million members. Within the framework of the European Trade Union Confederation *industry committees* operate. So far six of these committees have been established; one of which is the European Regional Organization of the International Federation of Commercial, Clerical and Technical Employees (Euro-Fiet).

A fourth category of international trade union organizations consists of *specialized groups* which have been established to represent the trade union movement towards an International Organization. The Trade Union Advisory Committee (TUAC) to the OECD, is such a specialized agency.

9. *International Trade Union Movement*, in: International Encyclopaedia for Labour Law and Industrial Relations, [R. Blanpain], Deventer, 1978, 172 p.

45. *International Trade Secretariats*[10]

	Head-quarters	Number of Members	Number of Affiliates	Number of Countries	Year
International Federation of Building and Woodworkers (IFBWW)	Geneva Switzerland	3,000,000	100	50	1976
International Federation of Chemical, Energy, and General Workers' Unions (ICEF)	Geneva Switzerland	5,500,000	110	66	1978
International Federation of Commercial, Clerical and Technical Employees (FIET)	Geneva Switzerland	6,400,000	171	77	1978
Universal Alliance of Diamond Workers (UADW)	Antwerp Belgium	10,000	4	4	1974
International Secretariat of Entertainment Trade Unions (ISETU)	London England	500,000	50	33	1976
International Union of Food and Allied Workers' Associations (IUF)	Geneva Switzerland	2,000,000	155	61	1977
International Graphical Federation (IGF)	Berne Switzerland	810,000	34	25	1976
International Federation of Journalists (IFJ)	Brussels Belgium	83,000	28	25	1978

46

45. *International Trade Secretariats*[10]—*contd.*

	Head-quarters	Number of Members	Number of Affiliates	Number of Countries	Year
International Metalworkers' Federation (IMF)	Geneva Switzerland	13,500,000	145	69	1977
Miners' International Federation (MIF)	London England	1,000,000	34	32	1977
International Federation of Plantation, Agricultural and Allied Workers (IFPAAW)	Geneva Switzerland	1,600,000	76	50	1977
Postal, Telegraph, and Telephone International (PTTI)	Geneva Switzerland	3,300,000	174	86	1978
Public Services International (PSI)	Feltham England	5,000,000	155	60	1977
International Federation of Free Teachers' Unions (IFTU)	Brussels Belgium	2,500,000	48	43	1976
International Textile, Garment and Leather Workers' Federation (ITGLWF)	Brussels Belgium	5,250,000	100	60	1976
International Transport Workers Federation (ITF)	London England	4,400,000	378	81	1976

10. Windmuller J., *o.c.*, p. 165.

V. The Guidelines for Multinational Enterprises

1. THE GENESIS OF THE GUIDELINES AND OF THE 1976 DECLARATION

46. «After a year and a half of intensive negotiations to reconcile positions which were at the outset markedly divergent, governments of OECD Member countries have agreed to take measures designed to improve the investment climate and have recommended that multinational enterprises should abide by certain standards of behaviour set forth in a series of guidelines. This agreement took the form of a Declaration adopted by governments on the occasion of an OECD Council meeting at ministerial level.[11]
The problems of international investment in the Seventies are complex and OECD's action does not attempt to deal with all of them. First, investment has been growing in volume which means that inhabitants in one country are more and more affected – as consumers, employers, investors and suppliers of services such as banking and insurance – by decisions made in another. Second, the source of these flows has shifted: although OECD countries as a group are still the world's largest exporter of capital, there are increasing flows from the oil producers. Third, the multinationals have come to the forefront of public attention as they have increasingly come to be seen by governments as able to circumvent certain national or local policies. Finally the trend of liberalization which characterized the Sixties has shown signs of reversing as a number of countries have put up barriers against the influx of private capital or taken measures that discriminated against foreign companies.
The role of the OECD area in this network of problems is a key one, not only because it is a source of capital and by far the largest base for multinational corporations but also because of its important role as importer of capital and host country for multinationals.
But individual Member countries have very different positions. A few such as Germany have a rough balance between incoming and outgoing investment. Others are primarily 'importers' of investment. For small countries particularly this imported capital can have an important impact on the functioning of the national economy. The U.S. is home base for the greatest number of multinationals, while certain other countries have special problems i.e. Canada where U.S. investment accounts for more than 50 per cent of total foreign investment.
In view of this diversity and the complexity of the problems involved, OECD set itself a relatively limited task – to get political agreement in a short time on some basic principles governing investment relations among OECD countries. The emphasis was on voluntary action and a pragmatic rather than an overly legalistic approach to the problems, with an emphasis on procedures which would bring possible questions to the OECD for consultation and further clarification. Within three years the Declaration (and the accompanying decisions) will be looked at again with an eye to revision. Thus it is seen as a first

---

11. The government of Turkey did not participate in the Declaration.

step in an evolutionary process. But it is also *the* first step since agreement on many of these matters has not previously been reached in any international forum.

The main problem, says Helga Steeg of Germany, Chairman of OECD's Committee on International Investment and Multinational Enterprises which saw the Declaration through its negotiation stage, was to achieve a balance between the two main elements:

– what, in the legal terminology is called 'national treatment' i.e. the principle that governments shall not discriminate against foreign firms in relation to national firms
– the recommendation to multinationals that they observe certain guidelines in their dealings with governments, groups or individuals in the country where they operate.

A third point was also included in the package – a provision on incentives and disincentives offered by governments to international direct investment.

The pragmatic approach of OECD to this subject is perhaps most evident in what is not included in the guidelines: no attempt is made to define what a multinational corporation is since there is substantial divergence as to the precise definition (differences focus on such questions as how much autonomy the affiliates may enjoy, and what the percentage of domestic versus foreign holdings is). Agreement not to insist on definition made it possible to reach an accord without protracted arguments between experts. The same holds true for much of the content of the eight items included in the agreement: general policies, disclosure of information, competition, financing, taxation, employment, industrial relations and science and technology. Technical questions could be raised on each point, and many of them are being studied by OECD's technical committees and other groups. But in view of the differences between countries' taxation and industrial relations systems and the lack of any international antitrust law or competition policy, more precise formulation of the problems would be a long-range task. This more precise definition is expected to come about in the course of the consultation procedures which are allied to the Declaration.»[12]

«The IME Committee met 10 times (23 days of negotiation) between March 1975 and mid-May 1976 under the chairmanship of Mrs. Helga Steeg, Bundeswirtschaftsministerium, Bonn. Vice chairman was Mr. Sten Niklasson, head of the Swedish delegation. Usually all (24) member-countries were represented in the meetings.

The Committee was assisted by a drafting group in which the heads of the most interested (about 8) delegations, according to the subjects under discussion, participated. The drafting group was chaired by professor Theo Vogelaar, Special Consultant to the Secretary General on matters related to International Investment and Multinational Enterprises. In this group negotiations took place and texts were elaborated on the basis of the general indications given by IME Committee.

The Special Consultant co-ordinated the work of the relevant technical com-

12. *The OECD Observer*, 1976, no. 82, pp. 12–13.

mittees and of the Secretariat and he kept close contact with BIAC and TUAC. He supplied, as the representative of the Secretary General, proposals and alternatives, often after consultation with leading delegations and the chairman of IME Committee.»[13]

47. Ms Helga Steeg indicated that there were three major issues on which accord was the most difficult:
«–Consultative machinery. Some thought it was too soon to describe in detail what should happen, and there was a difference as to whether the companies should participate.
– Disclosure. Most companies do not now publish their balance sheets on a consolidated basis. One achievement is that now if a company has operations in several countries, it has to publish information not only on the operation of one entity, subsidiary or parent company, but on the enterprise as a whole broken down by individual countries or groups of countries, leaving it to the multinational enterprise to decide what procedures suit it best.
– Industrial relations. One important issue was whether the guidelines should prescribe that, in collective bargaining, multinational enterprises should bargain with trade unions on a multilateral basis or not. The guidelines have left the question open. Practically speaking, multilateral collective bargaining will probably meet with unsurmountable difficulties in the foreseeable future in view of the unharmonized labour organization and labour relations systems in Member countries. What the guidelines do provide is the right to information for bargainers; they also say that trade unions should be able to bargain with the people who have the authority.[14]
In OECD's Ministerial meeting there was consensus that agreement on the guidelines was an important political act. Some speakers indicated that they would like this agreement to be the first step towards more binding rules. Others preferred the voluntary approach. The opinion was expressed that the multinationals would in fact observe the guidelines, that it would be useful to have in the OECD a forum in which these matters could be kept under review and that, after the three-year experimental period, improvements could be made in the precise content of international co-operation on this issue.»[15]

48. BIAC and TUAC had the opportunity to comment on the draft guidelines at several stages and their comments influenced the final shape of the Guidelines.[16]
«Although their views were presented in separate meetings, BIAC and TUAC had similar reactions on several points. They agreed on the need for stringent guidelines on bribery and political manipulation which have at times damaged the image of multinational enterprises. Both organizations wish to take part in

13. Vogelaar Th., 'The OECD Guidelines, philosophy, history, nature, implementation-procedure and review' (Symposium, University of Bielefeld, July 1979).
14. *The OECD Observer*, 1976, no. 82, p. 15.
15. *The OECD Observer*, 1976, no. 82, p. 13.
16. *Idem.*

the intergovernmental consultations through which the guidelines will be interpreted and developed.

BIAC, in its discussions, stressed that the guidelines should not introduce discrimination against multinational enterprises vis-à-vis domestic ones; nor should they allow multinationals to become the victim of conflicting national policies.

TUAC favoured stronger guidelines on the disclosure of information to unions and other workers' representatives and a clearer recognition of workers' rights to representation by unions than appears in the draft guidelines. They also made a number of specific proposals on employment and industrial relations.»

49. On the occasion of publication of the guidelines BIAC issued following statement:

«The Business and Industry Advisory Committee to OECD welcomes the positive efforts made by Member governments to coordinate their attitude towards international investment and multinational enterprises: it draws attention to the OECD's recognition in the preamble of the positive contributions which international investment makes to the economic and social progress of Member countries and OECD's constructive attitude towards multinational enterprises. It notes the significance of the provisions for protection of investment.

BIAC stresses the importance of the OECD Governments having recognized their responsibility to treat enterprises equitably and in accordance with international law and their contractual obligations.

BIAC is confident that the Guidelines will be respected by individual enterprises. It particularly welcomes the fact that the Guidelines seek to eliminate discrimination between national and multinational, and between state-owned and private enterprises. They embody standards which, where relevant, reflect good practice for all enterprises.

BIAC fully accepts the Guidelines on general policy and is glad to note that its own recommendation on strengthening the clause dealing with bribery has at least been partially accepted but recommends further work on this subject. While welcoming the Guidelines dealing with disclosure of information, which it hopes will add to the public understanding of multinational operations, it draws attention to the difficulty and cost of assembling all the figures, particularly for widely spread enterprises and in countries where the recommendations of the Guidelines go beyond current practice. Moreover, comparisons of information from different enterprises in areas where conditions are widely dissimilar can be misleading and may confuse rather than enlighten.

On competition, BIAC notes that difficulties may arise when the application of the Guidelines and national law impose conflicting requirements but that procedures are laid down for resolving these.

BIAC fully accepts that multinational enterprises should observe good employment and industrial relations practices in the countries where they operate and should deal with them in the national context: conflicts between national interest would certainly arise if there were any move towards collective bar-

51

gaining on an international basis. BIAC notes that the Guidelines do not alter each state's rights to provide the conditions under which enterprises operate within its national jurisdiction. Given the range and divergency of law and regulation in OECD Member countries, BIAC supports this effort to apply the Guidelines consistently with the rights and duties of an entity under the law of the country in which it is located.

BIAC welcomes the opportunity to express its views periodically to OECD in the review of the Guidelines. This is important when operating in a new field, so as to allow practical experience to be taken into account. It is also important that in specific circumstances individual enterprises may have an opportunity to state their side of a case. Future experience will enable the international community to assess the true value of the Guidelines.»

50. On the occasion of the promulgation of the Guidelines in 1976 TUAC issued following statement:

«The trade union movement in the OECD Member countries grouped within the Trade Union Advisory Committee to the OECD actively contributed to the work and negotiations at the OECD in an effort to establish guidelines for multinational enterprises. The trade unions consider the Declaration and the Decisions which the OECD adopted on the 21st June 1976 in the field of international investment and multinational enterprises, as *a first result* of these endeavours.

In March 1975, TUAC submitted its own concept and proposals for the regulation of the activities of multinational enterprises. TUAC notes that the governments of the OECD have followed a certain number of the suggestions made by its member national unions and the associated international trade union organizations, ICFTU, WCL and International Trade Secretariats. TUAC particularly points to the fact that the OECD Guidelines recognize for the first time the right of negotiations on collective bargaining and labour relations to be conducted with the authorized level of management, including that of the international management of the enterprise as a whole; recognize the necessity of appropriate disclosure of information on the activities of the enterprise as a whole; and the necessity of forbidding bribery and other types of misconduct, including the restriction of freedom of association and negotiation; and condemn the use of the threat to transfer abroad the activities of a subsidiary during a labour dispute.

Certainly the present OECD Guidelines constitute only a first step towards solving the many problems related to the activities of the multinational enterprises which are leading to the abuse of economic power and to growing conflicts with the governments and working people. TUAC's positive reaction on this *first step*, is, therefore, based on the recognition by the OECD Ministers that 'continuing endeavours may lead to further international arrangements and agreements', i.e. binding rules, and that the Declaration itself provides for the review of the present texts within three years. TUAC believes that such binding regulations at the international level will prove essential and should deal in particular with full disclosure of the worldwide operations of multinational corporations on a country by country basis, their pricing and taxation practices, and the abuse of strong market positions jeopardizing free competition.

TUAC member organizations appeal to national authorities to implement rapidly and effectively at the national level the principles embodied in the OECD Guidelines and to introduce whatever new legislation and regulations or changes in governmental administrative practices are necessary. For their part the workers' organizations will endeavour to take all action necessary to this effect and are determined to use the facility provided to them through TUAC, as specified in the OECD's consultation procedures, to take part in the periodic reviews undertaken by the OECD on the implementation of the Guidelines.»

51. Mr. T. Vogelaar, OECD Consultant on International Investment and Multinational Enterprises, who played a major role in the negotiating and the drafting of the Guidelines, declared as follows:
«I think it is extremely important that Western countries have laid down amongst themselves a certain philosophy for the phenomenon of international investment; that they have confirmed their belief in a liberal investment climate; that they speak of the positive contributions multinational enterprises may make to the economic and social development of the OECD area and the world as a whole and that they are willing to co-operate with efforts elsewhere.»[17]

2. CONTENT OF THE DECLARATION AND THE GUIDELINES

a. Content and Nature of the Declaration

52. The Declaration contains:
1. A *recommendation to multinational enterprises* operating in their territories *to observe the Guidelines* for Multinational Enterprises;
2. The principle of *National Treatment*, namely the accordance by Member countries to enterprises operating in their territories and owned, or controlled, directly or indirectly, by nationals of another Member country (Foreign-Controlled Enterprises). These enterprises should respect the laws, regulations and administrative practices of the Member countries consistent with international law and no less favourable than that accorded in like situations to domestic enterprises;
3. A statement on *International Investment Incentives and Disincentives*. Member governments recognize the need to strengthen their co-operation in the field of international direct investment; they thus recognize the need to give due weight to the interests of Member countries affected by specific laws, regulations and administrative practices in this field (measures) providing official incentives and disincentives to international direct invest-

17. *The OECD Observer*, 1975, no. 78, p. 17.

ment; Member countries will endeavour to make such measures as *clear* as possible, so that their importance and purpose can be ascertained and that information on them can be readily available;
4. *Consultation procedures*, namely that the governments are prepared to consult one another on the above matters in conformity with the relevant Decisions;
5. A statement on the *Review of the Declaration*. The Governments will review the above matters within three years with a view to improving the effectiveness of international economic co-operation among Member countries on issues relating to international investment and multinational enterprises.

«As the decisions and recommendations of the Organization can only be addressed to member countries and not to private bodies like MNE's, the governments of the OECD member countries were bound to select the DECLARATION form.

Generally, declarations constitute a solemn form of understanding on principles, without stipulating strict commitments for the participating parties. Depending on their formulation they are to be situated somewhere in between decisions and non-binding recommendations.

The 21st June, 1976 Declaration is an act of governments acting together in the framework of the OECD and not an act of the Organization; in other words, the Ministers who issued the Declaration acted as representatives of their governments and not as members of the Council.

In OECD decisions and recommendations are taken or made by mutual agreement of all Members. Although abstentions do not invalidate them, the risk of vetoing is not negligible. Declarations, on the other hand, offer a flexible means for majority actions, as they cannot be voted down.

Usually, an OECD Declaration adopted by the governments is brought to the attention of the Council immediately after its adoption. The Council thereupon restores the link with the Organization by deciding to entrust its implementation to the OECD by setting in force the substance of the Declaration. Thus the Declaration becomes integrated in the normal structure of the Organization. By this procedure the same effect is achieved as by real Council decisions.

The declaration form equally permitted the linking of the three domains in which the OECD wanted to go forward (national treatment, incentives and the Guidelines for multinationals) in one act underlining their interconnection. Further, it introduced the integration of these actions in the consultation mechanism of the Organization necessary for their implementation.

The Declaration constitutes an agreement (source of international law) on basic principles of investment policy and on proceedings on how to materialize these. The appeal to the social responsibility of MNE's to contribute – complementarily to the actions undertaken by governments – to the improvement of the investment climate both in their own interests and in the public interest of the member countries forms part of these policy principles.

In the Declaration the governments 'jointly recommend to MNE's the observance of the guidelines' on which they reached agreement. The Guidelines could have been incorporated in the Declaration itself, but this would have upset the optical balance in their favour. For this reason they were *annexed* to the Declaration.

As OECD Council, the governments decided to establish consultation procedures including the review of such procedures in conformity with the aims and timing laid down for the review of the Declaration.

The skillful combination of voluntary guidelines for MNE's and government agreements on their implementation confers on the guidelines the highest possible degree of government backing and authority.»[18]

b. Content of the Guidelines

53. The Guidelines[19] contain, in addition to an introduction, which constitutes an integral part of them, seven sections, namely:
1. General policies;
2. Disclosure of information;
3. Competition;
4. Financing;
5. Taxation;
6. Employment and Industrial Relations;
7. Science and Technology

From the labour relations point of view the Introduction and the chapters on disclosure of information and self-evidently employment and industrial relations are of particular importance

54. In the introduction the Member governments give the general framework, the underlying philosophy and the tone of the Guidelines. They first concentrate on the importance of the contribution of multinational enterprises and the problems to which their operations may give rise as follows:

«Multinational enterprises now play an important part in the economics of Member countries and in international economic relations, which is of increasing interest to governments. Through international direct investment, such enterprises can bring substantial benefits to home and host countries by contributing to the efficient utilization of capital, technology and human resources between countries and can thus fulfil an important role in the promotion of economic and social welfare. But the advances made by multinational enterprises in organizing their operations beyond the national framework may lead to abuse of concentrations of economic power and to conflicts with national policy objectives. In addition, the complexity of these multinational enterprises and the difficulty of clearly perceiving their diverse structures, operations and policies sometimes give rise to concern» (paragraph 1).

In paragraph 2 governments indicated their goals:

«The common aim of the Member countries is to encourage the positive contributions which multinational enterprises can make to economic and social

18. Vogelaar Th., *Ibidem*.
19. See Annex I.

progress and to minimize and resolve the difficulties to which their various operations may give rise. In view of the transnational structure of such enterprises, this aim will be furthered by co-operation among the OECD countries where the headquarters of most of the multinational enterprises are established and which are the location of a substantial part of their operations. The guidelines set out hereafter are designed to assist in the achievement of this common aim and to contribute to improving the foreign investment climate.»
The introduction also deals, among others, with the nature and the binding character of the Guidelines, their relationship to national law, a (non) definition of the multinational enterprise, the relevance of the Guidelines for national enterprises and the use of dispute settlement machinery, which we will examine further on in this prologue.

55. Multinational enterprises are asked to provide quite detailed *information on the enterprise as a whole*, as the following:

«*Disclosure of Information*
Enterprises should, having due regard to their nature and relative size in the economic context of their operations and to requirements of business confidentiality and to cost, publish in a form suited to improve public understanding a sufficient body of factual information on the structure, activities and policies of the enterprise as a whole, as a supplement, in so far as is necessary for this purpose, to information to be disclosed under the national law of the individual countries in which they operate. To this end, they should publish within reasonable time limits, on a regular basis, but at least annually, financial statements and other pertinent information relating to the enterprise as a whole, comprising in particular:

   (i) the structure of the enterprise, showing the name and location of the parent company, its main affiliates, its percentage ownership, direct and indirect, in these affiliates, including shareholdings between them;
  (ii) the geographical areas[20] where operations are carried out and the principal activities carried on therein by the parent company and the main affiliates;
 (iii) the operating results and sales by geographical area and the sales in the major lines of business for the enterprise as a whole;
 (iv) significant new capital investment by geographical area and, as far as practicable, by major lines of business for the enterprise as a whole;
  (v) a statement of the sources and uses of funds by the enterprise as a whole;
 (vi) the average number of employees in each geographical area;
(vii) research and development expenditure for the enterprise as a whole;

20. For the purpose of the guideline on disclosure of information the term 'geographical area' means groups of countries or individual countries as each enterprise determines it appropriate in its particular circumstances. While no single method of grouping is appropriate for all enterprises, or for all purposes, the factors to be considered by an enterprise would include the significance of operations carried out in individual countries or areas as well as the effects on its competitiveness, geographic proximity, economic affinity, similarities in business environments and the nature, scale and degree of interrelationship of the enterprises' operations in the various countries.

(viii) the policies followed in respect of intra-group pricing;
 (ix) the accounting policies, including those on consolidation, observed in compiling the published information.»

56. As far as *employment and industrial relations* are concerned, the Guidelines cover following points:
– freedom of organization and collective bargaining;
– information to employees;
– standards of employment and industrial relations;
– training and employment of the local labour force;
– reasonable notice and consultation in case of major charges in their operations;
– discrimination in employment;
– unfair influence in bona fide negotiations with employees;
– access to real decisionmakers.

The Chapter on Employment and Industrial Relations expands on these points as follows:
«Enterprises should within the framework of law, regulations and prevailing labour relations and employment practices, in each of the countries in which they operate,
1. respect the right of their employees to be represented by trade unions and other bona fide organizations of employees, and engage in constructive negotiations, either individually or through employers' associations, with such employee organizations with a view to reaching agreements on employment conditions, which should include provisions for dealing with disputes arising over the interpretation of such agreements, and for ensuring mutually respected rights and responsibilities;
2. a. provide such facilities to representatives of the employees as may be necessary to assist in the development of effective collective agreements;
   b. provide to representatives of employees information which is needed for meaningful negotiations on conditions of employment;
3. provide to representatives of employees where this accords with local law and practice, information which enables them to obtain a true and fair view of the performance of the entity or, where appropriate, the enterprise as a whole;
4. observe standards of employment and industrial relations not less favourable than those observed by comparable employers in the host country;
5. in their operations, to the greatest extent practicable, utilize, train and prepare for upgrading members of the local labour force in co-operation with representatives of their employees and, where appropriate, the relevant governmental authorities;
6. in considering changes in their operations which would have major effects upon the livelihood of their employees, in particular in the case of the closure of an entity involving collective lay-offs or dismissals; provide reasonable notice of such changes to representatives of their employees, and where appropriate to the relevant governmental authorities, and co-

operate with the employee representative and appropriate governmental authorities so as to mitigate to the maximum extent practicable adverse effects;

7. implement their employment policies including hiring, discharge, pay, promotion and training without discrimination unless selectivity in respect of employee characteristics is in furtherance of established governmental policies which specifically promote greater equality of employment opportunity;

8. in the context of bona fide negotiations[21] with representatives of employees on conditions of employment or while employees are exercising a right to organize, not threaten to utilize a capacity to transfer the whole or part of an operating unit from the country concerned in order to influence unfairly those negotiations or to hinder the exercise of a right to organize;

9. enable authorized representatives of their employees to conduct negotiations on collective bargaining or labour management relations issues with representatives of management who are authorized to take decisions on the matters under negotiation.»

57. The Guidelines 1, 2, 3, 4, 6, 8 and 9 were quite extensively debated during the exchange of views which took place in the IME Committee 1976–1979 as Part II of our book shows.

3. THE (NON) DEFINITION OF THE MULTINATIONAL ENTERPRISE

58. The Guidelines indicate in paragraph 8 of the introduction that a precise legal definition of multinational enterprises is not required for the purpose of the Guidelines. In fact, paragraph 8 contains a definition and one which is particularly appropriate from the point of view of labour relations where, *power* constitutes the essence of those relations[22]; paragraph 8 defines the multinational as follows:

«These usually comprise companies or other entities whose ownership is *private, state or mixed, established in different countries* and so linked that one or more of them may be able to exercise a significant influence over the activities of others and, in particular, to share knowledge and resources with the others. The degree of autonomy of each entity in relation to the others varies widely from one multinational enterprise to another, depending on the nature of the links between such entities and the fields of activity concerned» and concludes:

«The word 'enterprise' as used in these guidelines refers to these various entities in accordance with their responsibilities.»

---

21. Bona fide negotiations may include labour disputes as part of the process of negotiation. Whether or not labour disputes are so included will be determined by the law and prevailing employment practices of particular countries.
Guideline 8 was amended in the course of the 1979 review. See further no. 195.
22. See Blanpain R., *The Badger Case and the OECD Guidelines for Multinational Enterprises,* Deventer, 1977, pp. 16–17.

The essential element in the definition is found in the words 'to exercise a *significant influence*', which refers to the element of central control, centralized decision making, which constitutes in my opinion the backbone of the multi-national enterprise.[23]

4. NATURE AND BINDING CHARACTER OF THE GUIDELINES

59. The Guidelines contain *rules of conduct* for multinational enterprises; they lay down *standards* for the activities of these enterprises, the introduction says (no. 6).

60. Observance of the Guidelines is *'voluntary* and *not legally enforceable'*. On the voluntary character of the Guidelines, Mr. Theodore Vogelaar, then Special Consultant to OECD's Secretary General on International Investment and Multinational Enterprises, rightly observes 'is not so much a matter of principle as of judicial necessity'. «In our democracies the power to bind citizens and corporations is reserved to Parliaments who may act, of course, by ratifying and giving effect to international treaties or conventions. In the case of a mandatory code covering items like disclosure of information, taxation, company law, social- and anti-trust laws, providing for separate obligations for multinational enterprises as distinct from others, the legislative work involved would be a tremendous, life-time, undertaking requiring utmost care and precision. In addition, questions of uniform interpretation, non-discriminatory implementation and comparable enforcement would arise. In the present state of our diffused world of 146 countries, yes even amongst the 24 OECD's parallel orientated, free, countries, any attempt to establish a binding code is, I am afraid, doomed to remain illusory.»[24]

Voluntary does not mean that multinational enterprises are free to choose, whether they accept the Guidelines or not. The Guidelines constitute recommended behaviour, since they are recommendations jointly addressed by Member countries to the multinational enterprises. The Guidelines carry that weight and represent a firm expectation of Governments for MNE behaviour.[25] Both business and labour have accepted the Guidelines as 'the' behaviour to expect from enterprises and means that the Guidelines constitute 'the' rules of conduct which society as a whole requires the multinational enterprises to live up to. In this sense they are *'morally'* binding; they indeed relate to societal

23. *Idem.*
24. Speech, December 13, 1976.
25. Report of the IME Committee, para 37. BIAC defended another point of view. At the occasion of the 1979 review BIAC declared . . . 'From the fact that the Guidelines are voluntary it follows that it is for the enterprises to whom they are addressed to decide at a particular point in time whether they wish to support the Guidelines and to choose the manner in which this should be expressed. Enterprises also have the option not to endorse the Guidelines. BIAC believes it is important for enterprises to be encouraged to give their support to the Guidelines while action should be avoided which discourages them from doing so. Even though the Guidelines are not "legally enforceable" BIAC believes that once enterprises have decided to support them, they will feel morally bound to honour their undertaking.'

principles of right and wrong in behaviour, which constitutes the essence of morality. Whether an enterprise has accepted to follow the Guidelines or not is in fact irrelevant.[26]

On the contrary, the Guidelines are not legally enforceable, which means that they can not as such be sanctioned by the courts, although they could acquire in the course of time the legal character of a custom and become 'as customs' legally enforceable.

61. Difficult questions arise concerning the relationship between these moral obligations and the legal obligations under the law of the land. Paragraph 7 of the introduction states, and this is self-evident, that 'the entities of a multinational enterprise located in various countries are subject to the laws of these countries'. The Guidelines should indeed help to ensure 'that the operations of these enterprises are in harmony with national policies of the countries where they operate' (no. 6, introduction). National law then comes first, confirming

26. «Nevertheless they constitute a source of law in a domain not covered so far by positive rules of law. As a source of law they may have a wider impact on the solution of problems arising from the activities of MNE's than their voluntary nature at first view seems to indicate. Although phrased in broad and non legal terms, they formulate some notions of law presently emerging in this field.

The fact alone that 23 governments of civilized nations in the Western world, after serious consideration, have adopted them, accords to the Guidelines a legal authority.

Nothing in the Guidelines may be construed to urge MNE's not to apply national law. The respect of law and practice in each of the countries in which they operate has first priority, but the governments sometimes invite MNE's to go further, to undertake vaster responsibility than the law requires. Their role is to introduce supplementary standards of behaviour of a non legal character, in particular with respect to the international scope of operations of these enterprises.

Consequently, the Guidelines are independent of or complementary to positive law and are to be used to fill the gaps where national or international law does not give an answer.

The OECD Governments have certainly recognized the validity of the aims and problems of corporations desirous to carry out their business activities across borders and anxious to maintain the coherence of their group in an international pluralistic environment. They have been equally aware of the need for their legal security. However, in the fear of the factual limitations of national and international law-making in this field they could not take another course than setting voluntary rules as a first step to a more solid regime.

By doing this the OECD governments have started a classic process of law-making.

Starting from recognized principles and a common concept of what is just and fair behaviour the law has been gradually evolved in every country, resulting in the end in the definition and settlement of legal relations between States, between States and private bodies and between private bodies.

The Guidelines, therefore, constitute a source of law that means a method to detect and determine rules of law as a positive factor in the process of law creation. Their role in preventing or resolving conflicts is to indicate, in the absence of express rules decisive on particular cases, how to find an equitable solution.

In order to qualify as a source of law, the Guidelines must enjoy general acceptance. Their validity depends on whether in reality they reflect a generally accepted concept of what is just and fair. Their unanimous adoption, without any reservations or unilateral interpretations manifests at least that the governments share this concept. But the Guidelines concern other parties as well. The positive reaction and support by BIAC and TUAC, Management and Unions – being the main interested private users – publicly given at the time the Guidelines were promulgated, evidences further and complements this general acceptance. A last requirement, however, is that continuous use will be made of them in the daily practice of either board meetings, corporate decisions, disclosure, demands by labour unions, consumers or others, public authorities, legislators, jurisdictions, arbitrators or literature.» (Vogelaar Th., *Ibidem*).

the sovereignty of the State; and consequently, the Guidelines can not enforce the enterprises to do anything which would be in conflict with national law. However, the Guidelines do place obligations on multinationals which go beyond what is strictly required by law. This again is self-evident. If the Guidelines only said that the multinationals must respect local applicable law, they would be superfluous. The Guidelines are necessary since national law does not suffice to regulate the 'transnational' character of the multinational phenomenon; this constitutes the very 'raison d'être' of the Guidelines. Consequently, the Guidelines may add obligations and are thus supplementary to national law. This is even so for the so-called 'chapeau' of the Chapter on Employment and Industrial Relations which reads 'Enterprises should, within the framework of law, regulations and prevailing labour relations and employment practices, in each of the countries in which they operate. . .'. The expression 'within the framework of . . .' means taking the national system into account. Indeed, it is not sufficient under the Guidelines to apply national law; only the Guidelines can and do go further, if, e.g. they state that, as in Guideline 6 of the Employment and Industrial Relations Chapter, a reasonable term of notice of important changes must be given to employees, when such a notice would not be obligatory under national law.

62. The Guidelines are addressed to the multinational enterprises *'operating in the territories of OECD Member countries'* and are meant to guide *'the activities of multinationals in the different Member countries'*, as no. 6 of the introduction indicates. This then means that the Guidelines apply to the entities of multinationals which operate in OECD Member countries, except in Turkey;[27] they only concern multinationals with headquarters in OECD countries for their subsidiaries activities in these countries and for multinational enterprises with headquarters outside OECD countries, for their entities activities in OECD countries.

63. The Guidelines are also relevant for *domestic enterprises*. They indeed, as paragraph 9 of the introduction indicates, 'reflect good practice for all. Accordingly, multinational and domestic enterprises are subject to the same expectations in respect of their conduct whenever the Guidelines are relevant to both'. Consequently, the Guidelines do contain moral obligations for national enterprises, namely those Guidelines, which taking the domestic character of the national enterprises into account, applying to them – e.g. national enterprises as well as multinationals, are expected to give, reasonable notice to employees in the case of major change in their operations, as required in Guideline 6 of the Employment and Industrial Relations Chapter. This rule of equal treatment is inspired by a strong political will not to discriminate between national and multinational enterprises. The employers especially have insisted on equal treatment and this has resulted in a Decision of the Council on National Treatment, as indicated (See Annex I).

64. The IME report reminds us that the introductory part of the Guidelines-

27. Since Turkey did not participate in the Declaration and abstained from the Decisions.

forms, as stated in Section I of the 1976 Declaration, an integral part of the Guidelines and are necessary for a proper comprehension of the nature of the whole exercise (paragraph 36).

65. Let us finally indicate, that the Guidelines recommend the use of appropriate *international dispute settlement* mechanisms, including arbitration, as a means of facilitating the resolution of problems arising between enterprises and Member countries (no. 10 of the Introduction) and that the Member Countries have accepted the obligation to fulfil their responsibilities *to treat enterprises equitably* in accordance with international law and international agreements, as well as contractual obligations to which they have subscribed. The question arises whether there is a duty upon States to implement the guidelines? The minimum one can say is that there is certainly a duty not to frustrate the guidelines.[28]

28. See Baade, H.W., 'The Legal Effects of Codes of Conduct for MNE's', Symposium University of Bielefeld, July 1979.

Part I. The Action under the Guidelines

I. The Action by Member Governments

A. Survey of Measures Taken by Member Governments to Promote the Guidelines[1]

66. «This survey has been prepared on the basis of reports by Member countries on promotional action taken since the adoption of the Guidelines. The promotional efforts reported to the Organization can be classified into four main categories; dissemination of the Guidelines, promotion in private circles, discussions between officials and the interested parties, and use of the Guidelines in the context of national policies.

1. Dissemination of the Guidelines

67. In most countries, the Guidelines have been widely distributed to all ministries and public organizations concerned. The Declaration of 1976 has been brought to the knowledge of the general public by means of official press releases or press briefings in Australia, Canada, Denmark, Japan, Norway, Sweden, Germany and the United States and/or through its insertion in official publications. In the United Kingdom, the Guidelines were published in a white paper with a foreword by the Secretary of State for Industry. In Portugal the Declaration and the Decisions were published in the Official Gazette. In the United States the Declaration and Secretary Kissinger's statement before the OECD Council were published in the July 1976 edition of the Department of State Bulletin. In Switzerland the Declaration was published in the Official Gazette as an annex to the 7th Report of the Federal Council on Foreign Economic Policy, submitted to Parliament in August 1976. In Sweden, the Government notified the Declaration and Decisions by means of an ordinance published in the Swedish Book of Statutes. In Australia, the 1977 Report of the Foreign Investment Review Board as well as the government's revised foreign investment policy issued in 1978 drew attention to the Guidelines and issued the Declaration in full as an attachment.

1. Report of the IME Committee, Annex I.

63

2. Promotion of the Guidelines in private circles

68. In all Member countries, the Guidelines have been extensively distributed to the business community, labour unions, professional federations, chambers of commerce, individual companies (for instance in Japan, 5,000 private enterprises received the Guidelines from the Government which distributed ten thousand pamphlets explaining the Guidelines in detail), either in the OECD version (English or French) or translated into a foreign language (Danish, Dutch, Finnish, German, Japanese, Norwegian and Swedish). The booklet was often accompanied by an official foreword requesting the parties to bring the contents of the Guidelines to the attention of those of its members which are multinational enterprises and urged their observance of the Guidelines or stressing the need for the enterprises to comply with the Guidelines. Finally, some Member countries sent letters to individual enterprises informing them of the Declaration and commending the Guidelines to them. In the United States, such a letter, jointly written by the Secretaries of State, Treasury and Commerce, has been sent to more than 800 chief executive officers of major U.S. corporations. In Germany, the Federal Minister of Economics sent a communication to the business organizations and unions concerned. This communication was also published. In Austria, the same addresses received a letter from the Federal Minister of Trade, Commerce and Industry. In the United Kingdom, the Secretary of State for Trade has written to the Heads of the major City institutions, such as the Stock Exchange.
Some Member countries have taken steps to bring the Guidelines to the attention of their enterprises operating abroad through official or non-official channels. In Denmark, the Declaration has been distributed to all embassies and missions abroad. In Italy, the Declaration and Decisions have been sent to all members (more than 5000) of the Italian Section of the International Chamber of Commerce. In Japan, the Government has taken necessary steps to communicate the instruments to the embassies in the countries where Japanese companies are operating. The United States Ambassador to the OECD undertook an intensive programme to brief United States businessmen in OECD countries.

3. Discussions with the Interested Parties

69. Among the Member countries which have arrangements for regular discussions with the interested parties on matters relating to the Guidelines may be mentioned the following: the Canadian Government has had exchanges of views from time to time with the Canadian business and labour communities on the application of the 1976 instruments. In the United States, the Department of State has a Public Advisory Committee on Transnational Enterprises in which issues arising under the instruments are discussed. In Sweden, Norway and Finland, Interministerial Groups with the participation of business and labour organizations have been established to co-ordinate the participation of each of these countries in the OECD work on Multinational Enterprises;

representatives of MNEs operating in Norway and Sweden have been invited to participate in these discussions. In Australia, the Foreign Investment Review Board held discussions about the Guidelines with some of the major organizations representing foreign enterprises in Australia. In the Netherlands, an inter-ministerial group discusses regularly with business and labour organizations all relevant matters with respect to the 1976 instruments. In Germany, officials hold regular exchanges of views with the business community on the same matters. In Switzerland, regular contacts were established between the federal authorities and the interested parties in the course of the negotiations on the 1976 instruments; these contacts have been pursued with respect to the application of the instruments. In Austria, the Federal Minister for Trade, Commerce and Industry has made contact with the Federal Chamber of Trade and Industry and employees and workers' organizations with a view to providing the OECD in due course with information on the Austrian experience in applying the Guidelines. In the United Kingdom, the Divisions of the Department of Industry responsible for individual sectors of industry are discussing the Guidelines with companies in the normal course of their dealings with them. In Japan, Government officials have also held meetings and conferences to provide further clarifications of the Guidelines and to answer any questions which groups or individuals may have.

4. Use of the Guidelines in the Context of National Policies

70. Some Member governments have used one or more of the Guidelines in the context of national policies. The American and the Swedish Governments have referred to the Guidelines on competition policy when dealing with restrictive business practices involving activities of multinational companies in other countries. The Netherlands Government has on various occasions stated that it takes into account the relevant Guidelines when determining its policies. The Australian Government has incorporated the Guidelines as an integral part of its policy on inward foreign investment, has indicated publicly it wishes foreign interests operating in Australia to observe them, and uses them as points of reference in the examination of applications submitted to the Government under its foreign investment policy.»

B. INTRODUCTION OF CASES

71. Three Governments have introduced cases to the IME Committee. The Belgian Government introduced the Badger Case in order to obtain a clarification of paragraph 8 of the Introduction to the Guidelines and Guideline 6 of the Employment and Industrial Relations Chapter. The most important problem in this case involved the responsibility of the parent company for financial obligations of its subsidiaries. The Danish Government introduced the Hertz case in order to obtain an amendment of Guideline 8 of the Employment and Industrial Relations Chapter. The issue in this case related to the temporary

65

transfer of workers from a foreign branch during negotiations, including labour disputes, in order to influence (unfairly) those negotiations. The Dutch Government introduced the BATCO care, which relates to the closure of an allegedly *profitable* company.

II. The Action by the IME Committee

A. COMPOSITION AND WORKING OF THE IME COMMITTEE AND THE AD HOC WORKING GROUP

72. The IME Committee is composed of representatives of Member Governments. Most of them are civil servants representing the competent national ministers. The delegates represent the Ministries of Economic Affairs, or Industry, or Trade, or Foreign Affairs, or Finance. A number of them belong to the permanent delegation of their country to OECD. The EEC is also represented by a number of delegates. The secretariat is also present with a number of civil servants, belonging to the OECD staff. It is remarkable in a sense that Departments of Labour were not more involved since, as indicated practically, all cases and issues, which were discussed in the IME Committee since the promulgation of the Guidelines, related to labour and industrial relations problems.
Quite a number of persons attend the meetings with the consequence that the IME Committee is a sizable group. At the occasion of its eighteenth meeting, held on the 30th –31st October 1978, to give one example, no less than 64 persons (1 Chairman, 53 delegates, 4 representatives of the EEC and 6 members of the OECD secretariat) attended the meeting.

73. Since its establishment, a delegate of the Federal Republic of Germany has chaired the IME Committee. The first chairperson was Ms Helga Steeg, who was then succeeded by Mr. H. Abramowski. The present chairman is Mr. W. von Dewitz and the Vice-chairman is Mr. S. Niklasson (Norway).[2]

74. At the occasion of the meeting of 7–8th July 1977 the IME Committee decided to create an *ad hoc Working Group*, in order to examine the material submitted by Member Governments, BIAC and TUAC. This Group, often named the Levy Group,[3] is an informal working party, open to all delegations. Informal means that the positions Governments take are not official. The Levy group is usually composed of a large number of persons. The meeting of January 29th 1979, to give an example, was composed of 41 persons (1 Chairman, 34 delegates, 2 representatives of the EEC, and 4 civil servants of the OECD staff).

2. Mr. Niklasson is also Chairman of the United Nations Intergovernmental Working Group on a Code of Conduct.
3. Mr. P. Levy, heads the Swiss delegation to the IME Committee.

75. *Working languages* of the OECD are French and English. Obviously English is the language most used. The Committee and Working Group *used to meet* three to four times a year for several days.

76. The Committee holds exchanges of views on the basis of submissions by Governments, BIAC and TUAC. Governments are often asked to submit reports on particular problems, e.g. national law and the practice concerning the responsibility of the parent company for their subsidiaries and the like. On the basis of these reports the Secretariat may draft comparative studies which aliment the discussion and also makes summary reports of the meetings. The Secretariat tries in particular to distillate out of the different discussions possible common views and proposes drafting language which then serves as a basis for further negotiations until, hopefully, a consensus in the committee is reached. Different drafts of the IME report to the Council of Ministers were discussed and each time rewritten before a consensus could be reached. Those drafts were also communicated to BIAC and TUAC who then had the opportunity to make comments and suggestions and thus have an imput on the final wording of the report.

B. The Review – the IME Report to the Council of Ministers

77. The report of the Committee reflects the action which the IME Committee has undertaken since the Guidelines were promulgated and the Committee's approach to the whole exercise.
The report, in fact, presents the work of the Committee and achieves different aims. As far as *content* is concerned, the report contains
1. a clarification as to the scope and the meaning of the Guidelines;
2. proposals for change of the Guidelines and the Decisions.
Since the report is to be published, *public* understanding of the Guidelines and the approach taken by the OECD Governments, through the IME Committee will be improved.

78. A long and often difficult debate has taken place concerning content and destination of the report. A number of countries defended the opinion that the Committee's task was limited to exchange of views and reporting to the Council of Ministers with the sole aim of finding out whether the 1976 instruments needed to be changed or not. Others thought that the Committee's role was an evolving one and that the Committee was responsible in giving guidance to those it asked to live up to the Guidelines, interpreting the Guidelines and make these interpretations public. It was the latter view that prevailed.
Only one proposal for amending the Guidelines was retained. It was accepted by most that the 1976 deal constitutes a fragile package, with a delicate balance, which had to be maintained. The credibility of the Guidelines, BIAC pleaded, could not permit, that after such a short period of less than three years, changes would be made to the Guidelines. TUAC of course, asked, as will

67

appear in full detail later on for quite a number of changes.[4] These clarifications as well as the amendment are discussed in Part II.

A number of additional proposals for future follow-up procedures were submitted and retained. These follow-up procedures are further examined in Part III.

79. The Report carries the following title: *Review of the 1976 Declaration and Decisions on International Investment and Multinational Enterprises* (Report by the Committee on International Investment and Multinational Enterprises to the Council). The report contains the following content:

4. See further TUAC statements or the occasion of the review no. 207–208.

III. The Action by Business and Labour

80. Paragraph 2 of the 1976 Decision of the Council on Inter-Governmental Consultation Procedures on the Guidelines for Multinational Enterprises foresees that the IME committee 'shall periodically invite the Business and Industry Advisory Committee to OECD (BIAC) and the Trade Union Advisory Committee to OECD (TUAC) to express their views on matters related to the Guidelines and shall take account of such views in its reports to the Council'.

In execution of that decision, formal and informal consultations with BIAC and TUAC have been held. The formal consultations were held with the IME committee and the informal with the Levy Working Group,[5] an ad hoc working party, created at the IME meeting of July 7–8th 1977, with the mandate to discuss the principles relating to the Guidelines involved in the different cases which were brought up by TUAC. This working party was open to all delegations and being informal, meant that the positions Governments may take are not official and, consequently, ad referendum.[6]

Meetings between the IME committee and the consultative organizations took place on March 30, 1977; April 11, 1978; February 26, 1979; and with the Levy group on October 20 and 23, 1978, and January 29, 1979.

5. Named after the Chairman of the Group, Philippe Levy, Head of the Swiss delegation in the IME committee.
6. There were also informal consultations between the Secretariats of OECD and BIAC and TUAC.

81. Those consultations were certainly not tripartite, since OECD, unlike the ILO, is not a tripartite organization; however, and in conformity with the OECD decision, representatives of all consultative organizations were – with one exception – always present at the consultations with the other organizations. In general, no tripartite talks developed, since the representatives of the other body, acted merely as observers.

These consultations proved to be very constructive and rewarding since they performed a number of important functions, which, in fact, went beyond 'the expression of views of the parties' as indicated in the decision; this development, however, corresponds to the intention of the founding fathers of the Guidelines, since the exercise was from the beginning seen as – and proved to be – an evolutionary process.

During the contacts with IME and the Levy group, TUAC and BIAC not only expressed their 'views' on matters related to the Guidelines within the framework of the review of the 1976 package in 1979; business and labour took the opportunity to indicate their general philosophy toward the Guidelines, their expectance, their support for the Guidelines and the difficulties in implementing them. TUAC introduced, as already indicated, a number of cases and the issues which led to far reaching discussions of the Guidelines, which in turn resulted in a better understanding and clarification of the Guidelines and also an amendment of them with a substantial change in the follow-up procedures.

A. BIAC[7]

1. BIAC's Report of Activities: 1976, 1977, 1978

82. Part IV of BIAC's annual report of activities of 1976 reads as follows: «Following the adoption by the OECD Council, in June 1976, of the Declaration on International Investment and Multinational Enterprises, of the Guidelines for Multinational Enterprises and of the related decisions on Inter-governmental Consultation Procedures on the Guidelines, National Treatment and International Investment Incentives and Disincentives, the OECD Committee on International Investment and Multinational Enterprises (IIME Committee) was given a new mandate for the next phase of OECD's activities in this field. These new terms of reference were adopted in December 1976 and they will remain in force for a period of three years.

According to this new mandate, the OECD IIME Committee: 1 shall have the task of further developing and strengthening co-operation among Member Countries in the field of International Investment and Multinational Enterprises; 2 it shall be responsible for monitoring and promoting co-ordination of all work carried out contributions which international investment makes to the economic and social progress of Member countries and its constructive attitude towards multinational enterprises.

7. J. Coates, 'Multinational Enterprises, Industrial Relations and Codes of Conduct. The Employer's Point of View', *Bulletin for comparative Relations*, no. 10, 1979, pp. 125–129.

In its immediate response to the publication of the Guidelines, following their adoption, BIAC stressed the importance of the OECD Governments having recognised their responsibility to treat enterprises equitably and in accordance with international law and their contractual obligation. BIAC expressed confidence that the Guidelines would be respected by individual enterprises. It particularly welcomed the fact that the Guidelines sought to eliminate discrimination between national and multinational and between state-owned and private enterprises, and embodied standards which, where relevant, reflected good practice for all enterprises.

BIAC was fully able to accept the Guidelines on general policy and was pleased to note that its own recommendation on strengthening the clause dealing with bribery had been accepted but recommended further work on this subject. Whilst welcoming the Guidelines dealing with disclosure of information, which it was hoped would add to the public understanding of multinational operations, it drew attention to the difficulty and cost of assembling all the figures, particularly for widely spread enterprises and in countries where the recommendations of the Guidelines went beyond current practice. Moreover comparisons of information from different enterprises in areas where conditions were widely dissimilar could be misleading and might confuse rather than enlighten.

On competition, BIAC noted that difficulties might arise when the application of the Guidelines and national law imposed conflicting requirements but that procedures were laid down for resolving these.

BIAC fully accepted that multinational enterprises should observe good employment and industrial relations practices in the countries where they operated and should deal with them in the national context: conflicts between national interest would certainly arise if there were any move towards collective bargaining on an international basis. BIAC noted that the Guidelines did not alter each state's rights to provide the conditions under which enterprises operated within its national jurisdiction. Given the range and divergency of law and regulation in OECD Member countries, BIAC supported this effort to apply the Guidelines consistently with the rights and duties of an entity under the law of the country in which it is located. Finally, BIAC welcomed the opportunity to express its view periodically to OECD in the review of the Guidelines. This is felt to be particularly important when operating in a new field so as to allow practical experience to be taken into account. It was also considered important that in specific circumstances individual enterprises might have an opportunity to state their side of a case. It would only be future experience that would enable the international community to assess the true value of the Guidelines.

Following the adoption by the OECD Council of the Declaration on International Investment and Multinational Enterprises and of the accompanying Decisions of Consultation procedures on the Guidelines, on national treatment and on international investment incentives and disincentives, the Council invited the Secretary General to propose a new mandate for the OECD Committee on International Investment and Multinational Enterprises, for the next phase of the OECD's activities in this field.

These new terms of reference were adopted by the OECD Council at its meeting on December 22nd, 1976 and they will remain in force for a period of three years. On the basis of this new mandate the future activities of the OECD Committee for International Investment and Multinational Enterprises can generally be described as falling into two categories: the gathering of experience in the implementation of the package, in particular the Guidelines, through consultation procedures; and secondly, the setting up and the implementation of a pragmatic, balanced and continuous programme which may lead to arrangements and agreements complementary to the package adopted in June and covering new fields of action. BIAC and TUAC will be consulted on these matters. The Committee will also keep itself informed of activities carried out in other international bodies in the field of international investment and multinational enterprises and shall provide a forum for member countries to consider their views in respect of issues raised in such bodies. It shall also monitor and promote co-ordination of the work carried out in this field by other existing committees of the Organization.

During a meeting of the OECD's IME Committee in November, it was decided that pursuant to the relevant decision of the OECD Council, BIAC and TUAC should be invited to express their views on matters relating to the Guidelines. Accordingly, arrangements were made for a consultation between the OECD Committee and the BIAC Committee on Multinational Enterprises on March 30, 1977. A separate meeting was also arranged with TUAC.

In preparation for this consultation, written statements were requested from BIAC and TUAC to be made available to members of the OECD Committee in advance.

In order to assist Sir Michael Clapham and his Committee in the elaboration of BIAC's statement, Member Organisations were invited to report on the situation in their countries since the publication of the Guidelines. In particular information was sought on: the guidance given by Governments to industry on their expectations on the observance of the Guidelines; questions raised by individual companies on the interpretations of the Guidelines or problems encountered which should be brought to the attention of OECD; formal public statements made by companies on their attitude to the observance of the Guidelines; and any disputes between companies and governments which have been referred to the OECD Committee on International Investment and Multinational Enterprises. In addition to taking stock of what has happened since the publication of the Guidelines, the BIAC statement should also express clear views on the shape of future OECD activities arising from the Guidelines.

Since it is clear that there will be a continuing role for BIAC vis-à-vis the OECD Committee on International Investment and Multinational Enterprises, and in view of the anticipated work involved in preparing views on the operation of the Guidelines, it was decided that the BIAC Committee on International Investment and Multinational Enterprises, which has been ultimately responsible for the work on the response to the Guidelines, should be reconstituted to undertake this new task. Accordingly a new mandate was prepared and considered by the Adminstrative Committee in December, and the membership of the Committee is being reviewed.

Finally, following a request from the UN Centre on Transnational Corporations for BIAC's comments on a Code of Conduct for Multinational Enterprises to be elaborated by the Centre, it was decided to associate BIAC's comments with those made by the International Chamber of Commerce, rather than to duplicate work, it being recognized that the ICC was the appropriate business organisation to respond to the UN. However, BIAC did make clear in its response to Mr. Sahlgren, Director of the Centre on Transnational Corporations, that, as the accredited advisory body to the OECD, it has supported the OECD's work on the Guidelines for multinational enterprises and related decisions and therefore wished to emphasize the need to avoid conflict between the OECD Guidelines which have been agreed and applied by 23 Member governments, and any Code to be developed by the UN Centre.»

83. The 1977 report commented on multinational enterprises as follows:
«The major event in this field was the adoption, by the OECD Council meeting at Ministerial level on June 21, of a Declaration on International Investment and Multinational Enterprises together with the Guidelines for Multinational Enterprises and Decisions on Intergovernmental Consultation Procedures on the Guidelines, National Treatment and International Investment Incentives and Disincentives.

After many months of negotiations these measures were adopted with the intention of improving the investment climate and recommending certain standards of behaviour to multinational enterprises. It was of course essential that industry had its views taken into consideration during the formulation of the Guidelines and accordingly representations were made both through the BIAC and through national channels. In this way industry was able to influence the outcome of the inter-governmental deliberations. Consequently, BIAC was able to welcome the positive efforts made by member Governments to co-ordinate their attitudes towards international investment and multinational enterprises and in particular OECD's recognition of the positive within the Organization in this area and for presenting proposals for this purpose to the Council, and 3) it shall keep itself informed of activities carried out in other international bodies and shall provide a forum for Member Countries to consider their views in respect of the issues raised in such bodies and take account thereof as appropriate to its own work.

It can generally be said therefore that the new mandate of the OECD IIME Committee concentrates on two main functions: the gathering of experience related to the implementation and application of the Council Declaration, with particular emphasis on the Guidelines, through consultation procedures; and the implementation of a balanced on-going programme whose work may result in arrangements and/or agreements relevant to the Council Declaration as well as extending the work into new fields of activity.

Since the publication of the Guidelines, there has been one formal meeting of consultation of the OECD IIME Committee with TUAC and BIAC separately. These meetings took place on March 30, 1977.

73

In its written presentation, and at the meeting itself, at which BIAC observers were present, the TUAC emphasized the need for the 'surveillance of the application of the Guidelines; the adoption of adequate measures and procedures to be followed in the event of disputes' on matters covered by the Guidelines. In addition, TUAC submitted a series of cases of alleged violations of the Guidelines for the purpose of information and illustration of areas where the Guidelines would need clarification or improvement.

For its part, the BIAC Committee on International Investment and Multinational Enterprises outlined the initiatives and actions which had already been taken by various Governments and national business organisations in order to publicize, explain and encourage observance of the Guidelines. This work took a variety of forms including letters of Guidelines support to the principal officers of corporations, meetings and seminars to explain the implications of the Guidelines as well as studies of specific sections of the Guidelines. Although it was as emphasized that it was too early to monitor the response of individual enterprises, general reference was made to formal declarations of Guidelines observance by many large corporations as well as the intentions of a number of others to include a statement of support within their 1977 Annual Reports. The BIAC Committee suggested that the OECD should promote work towards the harmonization of accounting standards and reporting requirements since many corporations were faced with contradictory national requirements. This would help to avoid problems of data interpretation as well as unnecessary costs. BIAC also stated that it would be important to have the collective experience of the OECD countries injected into the related activities of other international organizations, such as the United Nations, while coordinating their views with Member Governments.

Finally, BIAC expressed regret that TUAC had chosen to submit a series of cases of alleged violations of the Guidelines by individual companies, of which only one had been formally presented to the OECD IIME Committee by a Member Government. The need was expressed for the development by OECD of a process which would confine all future contributions relating to the problems associated with implementing the Guidelines to points of principle rather than specific cases. Otherwise, it was felt that the OECD Committee would be transformed into a tribunal, a function for which it was not originally created.

As a result of this Consultation and of the orientation of the OECD's work in the area of multinational enterprises, it was felt that BIAC had entered into a new phase of its relationship with the OECD in this field. This phase would be more 'operational' by nature and necessitate on our part continued attention and certainly further work. These circumstances have therefore induced the Chairman of BIAC to convene on October 13, 1977, an Extraordinary Meeting of the BIAC Administrative Committee in order to evaluate and reassess BIAC's policy in this area and to develop a new strategy to direct our future work. It was finally agreed at this meeting that BIAC's aims and objectives in the immediate future should be;

– to establish and reinforce the credibility of the OECD Guidelines by illustrating both their acceptance and implementation by industry;

– to maintain the voluntary character of the Guidelines;
– to hold Governments to these undertakings regarding the issue of National Treatment.

The programme developed by the Administrative Committee to achieve these goals is two-fold: information/promotion and analysis.

The information/promotion phase requires a firm commitment on the part of all BIAC Member Organizations, as well as their contributions in order to collect all possible data concerning cases of enterprises which have accepted the Guidelines and are publicising and applying them. This collection of information should provide the BIAC Committee on International Investment and Multinational Enterprises with part of the necessary background material in preparation for its next formal consultation with the OECD IIME Committee scheduled for April 1978.

The analysis work will involve a close scrutiny of the procedures followed by the OECD IIME Committee in considering the issues arising from the allegations submitted by the Trade Unions. In this respect, it is worth recalling that the OECD Council's decision of 1976 lays down that 'the OECD IIME Committee shall periodically invite BIAC and TUAC to express their views on matters related to the Guidelines and shall take account of such views in its report to the Council'; 'the Committee shall not reach conclusions on the conduct of individual enterprises'; 'Member countries may request that consultations be held in the Committee on any problem arising from the fact that multinational enterprises are made subject to conflicting requirements.' In conformity with these decisions, the OECD IIME Committee is analysing the material presented by TUAC with a view to gaining experience of the practical problems that arise in connection with the Guidelines and this in the context of the review of the Guidelines to be undertaken by OECD Member Governments in 1979.

On the subject of National Treatment the OECD IIME Committee is engaged in a review of the different categories of exceptions. For the time being it seems that Member Governments have been asked to establish contacts with their business circles on a national level to obtain their views. BIAC as such might however be called upon at some state to contribute in this field.»

84. The 1978 annual report comments on BIAC's activities as follows:
«The BIAC Committee on International Investment and Multinational Enterprises was a most active one during 1978 with eight Committee meetings involving two major consultations, one with its counterpart OECD Committee and the other with the Working Party on the Guidelines (the Levy Group).

After the resignation of Sir Michael Clapham, Mr. Gerrit Wagner accepted the chairmanship of the Committee and chaired the first meeting on March 1. At that meeting, and at a second one held on April 10, the Committee members finalized both a *Progress Report on Support for the OECD Guidelines for Multinational Enterprises*, which reflected the activities of business organizations to encourage support for the Guidelines and the response by enterprises, as well as an oral statement to be made by the Committee Chairman on April

11 at a *consultation with the OECD Committee on International Investment and Multinational Enterprises (CIME)*.
At the April 11 consultation, the discussion concentrated on four areas: Disclosure of Information, Employment and Industrial Relations, Responsibility of Parent Companies, and Consultation Procedures. On the issue of disclosure, BIAC agreed to provide CIME by late 1978 with a survey on the degree to which 1977 Annual Reports of corporations had taken the Guidelines into account. On consultation procedure, which was discussed at the request of the CIME chairman, BIAC's position was that all national possibilities for settling disputes in specific cases should be exhausted before the relevant issues are referred by the government involved to CIME for discussion.
BIAC stated its view that disclosure could be facilitated by work on harmonization of accounting standards, which could render various company reports more comparable and could ameliorate problems associated with enterprises being subjected to conflicting national requirements. This suggestion was well-received by the CIME which later established a Working Party on Accounting Standards for which BIAC contributed suggestions for terms of reference. A BIAC accounting expert has been invited to participate in the activities of that Working Group in the coming year.
At a meeting in June, the BIAC Committee decided to send a letter to OECD clarifying BIAC's position on the consultation procedure, since it was felt that the OECD record of the April Consultation was less than clear on this point. At this same meeting the Committee established the procedure for the *survey of implementation of the Disclosure Guidelines* which had been promised the OECD the end of 1978.
In September the Committee assembled for preparations for a consultation with the CIME's Working Party on the Guidelines (Levy Group) scheduled for October. BIAC's Group of Experts on Manpower had prepared a statement on the employment and industrial relations section of the Guidelines, which formed the basis for the discussion in which the chairman of the Manpower Group participated. (See also section H, below.)
On October 20, the Committee had *informal discussions with the Levy Group* on issues arising with regard to application of the Guidelines. Among other things, the BIAC representatives recognized that the issue of 'strikebreaking' had not been covered by the Guidelines; they also responded to several questions by government delegates regarding the prerogative of management to transfer production abroad and the relevance of 'profitability' to such decisions. BIAC informed the Levy Group members of the survey underway on implementation of the Disclosure Guidelines, a report of which would be provided OECD around the end of the year. BIAC urged governments to realize that providing required information is very costly to business and to limit their disclosure requirements to really useful information. On the situation with regard to disclosure to employees, BIAC had earlier provided several country studies, for which the Levy Group expressed their appreciation.
At a plenary session of CIME later in October, dates and procedures for the 1979 Review of the Declaration and Guidelines were established. BIAC was

requested to meet with the Levy Group (Working Group on the Guidelines) early in 1979 to be followed shortly by a meeting with the full Committee. Those two meetings were envisaged as the only ones to be scheduled on the Review, and BIAC was asked to provide any written statement and the results of the Disclosure Survey by the end of the year if possible. In order to meet the deadlines requested and to fulfill commitments previously made, a December 19 meeting of the BIAC Committee was held. At this meeting discussion centred around a *statement of BIAC on the Review* and a draft *report of the results of the Disclosure Survey*. The statement was subsequently submitted to the OECD in late December and the Report on the Survey, which was augmented to include a brief outline of efforts of the business community to propagate and support the Guidelines, was submitted shortly thereafter. In addition to consultations mentioned already, there were several conferences between the BIAC Secretariat, the chairman of the BIAC Committee and members of the OECD Secretariat.»

The Manpower and Social Affairs Committee of BIAC also dealt with the OECD Guidelines. Indeed, as part of the preparation for the overall BIAC statement concerning the 1979 Review of the OECD Guidelines for Multi-national Enterprises, a meeting of the BIAC Group of Experts on Manpower and Social Affairs took place on September 6, at Noordwijk, Netherlands, in order to make a contribution and to be able to offer comments and advice to the BIAC Committee on International Investment and Multinational Enterprises. The Group concentrated on the section of the Guidelines concerning Industrial Relations. Accordingly, the discussion dealt in particular with the 'right of employees to be represented by trade unions'; the transfer of workers, production, facilities and products from foreign affiliates in the context of negotiations or organizational activities; the concept of 'reasonable notice'; and the information to be provided to employees and governments in the context of the disclosure Guidelines on employment and industrial relations. As a result of the debate, a draft statement was prepared and sent to the BIAC Committee on International Investment and Multinational Enterprises, as a contribution to the preparation of its informal meeting with the 'Levy Group' (the Working Party of the OECD CIME Committee) held on October 20.

2. Contacts with the IME Committee and the Levy Group: BIAC's Points of View

85. In these contacts BIAC expanded on:
1. the unreserved welcome of the Guidelines by the business community and its expectations;
2. the support of business of the OECD Guidelines;
3. the difficulties concerning the disclosure of information and compliance;
4. the different cases introduced by TUAC.

a. BIAC's Welcome of the Guidelines and its Expectations

86. This welcome of the Guidelines has been reaffirmed over and over again by BIAC, for example, in the introduction to the written statement BIAC had forwarded to OECD, on March 2nd, on 'OECD Guidelines for Multinational Enterprises and Related Undertakings of Governments', in preparation of the first formal consultation on March, 30, 1977.
This introduction reads as follows:

«1. As representatives of business and industry in OECD countries we welcomed unreservedly the action of member governments in strengthening a liberal system of international investment through the declaration and decisions adopted by the Council of Ministers on 21 June 1976. We recognize that the prosperity of OECD countries, and indeed of the world as a whole, depends on the efficient application of private investment. We share the view expressed in the Preamble that international investment has considerably contributed to the development of OECD countries and that multinational enterprises play an important role in this process.

2. It is our hope that we shall not merely be able to collaborate with OECD in their periodic review of the Guidelines but also to contribute positively to achieving their aims of stimulating economic and social progress through international investment. We look forward to assisting in any measure which will resolve any problems which are seen to arise from multinational operations, and so improving the climate for investment.»

87. At the occasion of the consultations with the IME committee, on April 11, 1978, BIAC put forward its *expectations* regarding the Guidelines and their implementation toward multinational enterprises as follows:
«In closing, it is perhaps worth singling out those parts of the preamble to the Guidelines which BIAC believes are fundamental principles for any international endeavour which purports to enhance the international flow of capital and technology and the maintenance of stable and equitable investment conditions. One is that Governments 'will fulfil their responsibilities to treat enterprises equitably and in accordance with international law and international agreements, as well as contractual obligations to which they have subscribed'. The second (in paragraph 11) is that Governments 'will endeavour to resolve problems of conflicting requirements to which multinational enterprises may be subject'. The last (in paragraph 9) is that Governments, 'in promulgating the Guidelines, were not aiming at introducing differences of treatment between multinational enterprises and domestic enterprises since wherever relevant they reflect good practice for all; and that accordingly, they are subject to the same expectations in respect of their conduct wherever the Guidelines are relevant to both'.»

b. Support of the Guidelines

88. To assist the consultation with the IME committee on April 11, 1978,

BIAC submitted a progress report and made a verbal statement. The BIAC statement outlined the action taken by Member Federations to publicize the Guidelines and the response of the multinational enterprises. The statement also included discussion of some specific issues arising from some of the Guidelines such as disclosure of Information and Employment and Industrial Relations.

89. The progress report on support for the OECD Guidelines (of March 20, 1978) reads as follows:

«Progress Report on Support for the OECD Guidelines
(for the consultation with the OECD IIME Committee on April 11, 1978)

I. Introduction

Following the first consultation between BIAC representatives and the OECD IIME Committee on 30th March, 1977, the Committee re-affirmed in its letter of 19th April to BIAC its desire to receive further information on the general acceptance of the Guidelines and the application of the section on disclosure of information. The first part of this paper is, therefore, a progress report reflecting the current response to the Guidelines based on studies conducted by BIAC Member Organisations, the second highlights a number of other areas where BIAC is anxious to co-operate further with the Committee.

A. *BIAC Member Organizations' Information Programmes on the OECD Guidelines*

The *Australian* Council of Employers' Federations and the Associated Chambers of Manufactures of Australia, through the Central Industrial Secretariat (CIS) had been considering the question of adoption of their own guidelines prior to 1976. They eventually adopted their own guidelines in October 1976 after noting that they were in essence consistent with the OECD Guidelines promulgated in June 1976. The CIS Guidelines (together with the OECD Guidelines) were published and widely distributed among member organisations and among individual enterprises.

The Federation of *Belgian* Enterprises (FEB/VBO) has published the Guidelines in both national languages in its Bulletin, which is largely circulated among Belgian companies (fourteen thousand copies). The Federation expressed clearly its support for the Guidelines in a special brochure which was drawn up from this publication. Several Trade Associations, such as Fabrimétal and Féchimie, have disseminated through their own channels the Guidelines or elements of it to their members. The Federation of Belgian Enterprises has also discussed the Guidelines in its Study Group 'Multinational Enterprises' representing major multinationals established in Belgium.

The *Canadian* Manufacturers' Association, the Canadian Chamber of Commerce and the Canadian Council of the ICC circularized some 20,000 of their members urging support for the Guidelines. In October 1977 the Chief Executive Officers of major Canadian companies and financial institutions were sent personal letters drawing their attention to the Guidelines and asking if they wished to be placed on a mailing list to receive regular reports and documentation on developments concerning guidelines or codes of behaviour. Over 40 companies responded positively and in each case a contact officer was named. The *Danish* Federation of Industries has sent copies of the Guidelines to all Danish enterprises which employ more than one hundred people and which are members of the Danish Employers' Confederation.

The *Finnish* Employers' Confederation has translated into Finnish and distributed the text to interested companies and organizations.

The Confederation of *German* Employers' Associations (BDA) and the Federation of German Industries (BDI) report that they forwarded the OECD package in July 1976, to all their member associations, as well as to the members of the BDA Working Group on Multinational Enterprises. A letter from the Federal Minister for Economics to the President of the BDA was similarly transmitted, in which the Minister stressed his conviction that the OECD Guidelines should be given due regard by enterprises. The letter of transmittal of the Confederation of German Employers' Associations supported this conviction.

The Confederation of *Italian* Industry, Confindustria, sent the June 1976 BIAC press release to the newspapers and informed all its member associations by a special communication about the contents of the Guidelines, it being the task of the member associations to transfer the information to the individual enterprises.

At the request of the *Japanese* Government, several industrial organizations sent the Declaration to their members and asked for their support. Keidanren sent the Declaration to its members; explained the main points of the Declaration to its Governing Council; held a meeting together with representatives from the Government to explain the Declaration to the members of the Japanese BIAC; and commissioned a paper explaining the Declaration and the Guidelines. Japanese BIAC regularly sends its members information on the Guidelines in order to increase their awareness of them.

The Federation of *Netherlands* Industry (VNO) and the Netherlands Christian Employers Federation (NCW) have on various occasions given publicity and support to the OECD Declaration on International Investment and Multinational Enterprises and especially to the Guidelines for MNEs.

These activities have included a public declaration supporting the OECD Declaration released by VNO and NCW on June 22, 1976; a letter addressed by VNO's and NCW's Chairmen to the Minister for Economic Affairs stating full agreement to the contents of the Declaration; and publications in the periodicals 'Onderneming' (VNO) and 'De Werkgever' (NCW). Distribution of the English text of the Declaration was undertaken in July 1976, and of the Dutch translation in February 1977 amongst the General Executives of both organizations, the affiliated employers organizations and the Dutch-based multinationals.

Information was again supplied on the OECD Guidelines, emphasizing the great importance for business and industry of observance of these rules, at a meeting in November 1977 and another in March 1978.

In *Norway* both the Norwegian Employers' Confederation and the Federation of Norwegian Industries have given their members extensive information about the OECD Guidelines for Multinational Enterprises through their information service. The Guidelines themselves have been distributed to those members more particularly involved with international activity.

The Federation of *Swedish* Industries, the Swedish Employers' Confederation and the Swedish National Committee of the ICC jointly sent letters in November, 1976, to the Chief Executive Officers of the major Swedish MNEs informing them of the background and the contents of the OECD Declaration and especially its Guidelines for MNEs. This letter suggested that enterprises should use the OECD recommendations as guiding principles for their operations. In November 1977 the organizations again wrote to the same group of enterprises reminding them, in view of the approaching elaboration of their annual reports for 1977, of the Disclosure of Information part of the Guidelines. The implementation of the Guidelines is continuously discussed in a Working Party of MNE executives and representatives of the business organizations. The information part of the Guidelines is also discussed in the Accounting Standards Working Party of the Federation of Swedish Industries.

In *Switzerland* the Federations of Swiss private industry (Vorort of the Swiss Federation of Commerce and Industry as well as the Central Federation of Swiss Employers' Organizations) and their sections have played an active role in the publication (6,000 copies sent by the Journal of Employers' Associations), explanation (by letter) and discussion (meetings, discussion groups) of the OECD Guidelines.

In the *United Kingdom* the CBI has acted both jointly with the British Government and on its own initiative to publicise and explain the OECD package. In the foreword to the Government's White Paper, it was indicated that the CBI gave its support to the Guidelines. In August 1976 the CBI gave a Seminar to about 60 representatives of companies, at which senior government officials and experts from industry explained the intent and meaning of the Guidelines. The CBI's information programme has consisted of two full reports on the Guidelines to its Council which is made up of 400 senior industrialists and directors of trade associations and employer organizations. Basic information about the Declaration has been conveyed in the CBI Bulletin to 12,000 companies and about 210 trade associations and employer organisations and a commentary on the Guidelines was sent to over 200 companies. An up-dated version was distributed in February 1978.

Major *United States* business organizations have conducted a variety of programmes to encourage support of the OECD Guidelines. The US Chamber of Commerce, the National Association of Manufacturers and the US Council of the ICC, the three sponsoring organizations of USA–BIAC have all communicated to members urging support of the OECD Declaration and Guidelines. The US business community has:
– distributed several thousand copies of a series of publications on the Declaration and Guidelines including: 'Text and General Review of OECD

Guidelines', November 1976, 'Disclosure of Information', November 1976, and 'Competition', December 1977. ('Employment and Industrial Relations' due to be published in mid-1978)
– conducted Workshops on the Guidelines in July 1976 and March 1977. The latter was attended by representatives of 57 companies, universities, and the US Government. Proceedings of the Workshop have been published by the Institute for International and Foreign Trade Law of Georgetown University.
– collected in-depth information on responses to the Guidelines from more than 50 corporations.
– prepared a paper summarising corporate responses to date, for distribution to corporations.
In addition to the associations noted above, the National Foreign Trade Council, the Emergency Committee for American Trade and other business groups have communicated to members on the desirability of supporting the Guidelines.

B. The Response of Business

The following is a summary of the responses given by companies to Member Federations of BIAC. Some Federations have been able to name companies who have publicly stated their support for the Guidelines, others have preferred to indicate the general level of awareness or acceptance by their member companies:
– An inquiry organized by the Federation of *Belgian* Industries regarding the implementation of the Guidelines indicated that companies in Belgium take a positive attitude towards the Guidelines. Some enterprises have in communications to their Board indicated their intention to conform with the principles contained in the Guidelines. Others have published the Guidelines by distributing them to members of their staff sometimes in collaboration with the unions. Some of the enterprises have indicated that their Annual Reports have for several years been meeting the requirements of the Guidelines in respect of Disclosure of Information (for example Petrofina, Agfa-Gevaert).
– 13 major corporations have reported to *Canadian* BIAC that they comply with or support the OECD Guidelines in principle. They include Alcan, IBM, Ford, INCO Ltd, Philips Electronics, Noranda, Brascan and the Royal Bank. An additional thirteen major corporations have replied that they are studying the Guidelines.
– The *Danish* Federation of Industries reported that their major members found the Guidelines to be a constructive document which should prove useful in establishing a better climate between OECD Governments and multinational enterprises. Major members have already taken the Guidelines into account in developing their policies and practices.
– The *Finnish* Employers' Confederation states 'Enterprises in general accept the principles stated in the Guidelines. Rules of behaviour between enterprise authorities and interest groups have been accepted as useful.'
– A number of *German* enterprises (e.g. Hoechst, BASF, Siemens) have made public statements that the principles of the Guidelines are in agreement with

already existing business policies. German companies have also forwarded copies of the Guidelines to their foreign subsidiaries and informed them in writing of their support of the Guidelines. On occasion efforts have been made to publicize this support of the Guidelines. On occasion efforts have been made to publicize this support of the Guidelines to their respective work forces (e.g. Siemens distributed 190,000 copies of an in-house publication). Some German enterprises (e.g. Siemens) have adjusted their 1977 Annual Reports to reflect the Disclosure of Information requirements in the Guidelines. However, there exists some uncertainty with respect to certain portions of the Disclosure of Information section, since it is impossible to foreshadow the final contents of the EEC Directive which is still in draft.

– The Confindustria has checked with major *Italian* enterprises and obtained information on their reaction to the Guidelines. These enterprises comply in a large measure with the Guidelines. They report that there are some difficulties in the field of Disclosure of Information, but several efforts are being made to adhere progressively to it. Several companies have now taken the necessary steps to inform their management on the contents of the Guidelines and on the importance to adhere to them. Some enterprises, including Fiat, have indicated their support in favour of the Guidelines.

– The *Japanese* BIAC has assisted the Ministry of International Trade and Industry, MITI, in the development of an explicit questionnaire which has been sent to both Japanese MNEs and foreign subsidiaries in Japan during December 1977. Responses to the questionnaire are presently being compiled by MITI.

– In the *Netherlands*, AKZO, Unilever, Shell and Philips made statements in support of the Guidelines in the press or annual reports, or both.

– The Federation of *Norwegian* Industries states that 'there has not been a broad tendency from the enterprises to give publicity to the Guidelines. Some have, however, referred to the main contents in their own information service, and in interviews they have all expressed their positive attitude in this connection. As far as we know, all Norwegian Multinational Enterprises are applying the Guidelines.'

– The *Swedish* Federation of Industries reports that an inquiry among the major Swedish MNEs shows that the companies generally welcome the OECD Declaration. It is pointed out that Swedish companies have a long tradition of self-regulation. Moreover, Swedish law and general business practices are, in fact, already such that the OECD Guidelines do not seem to present much difficulty for the Swedish companies. A number of Swedish MNEs (Alfa-Laval, Asea, Saab-Scania, Svenska Flaektfabriken, Swedish Match Co) have distributed the OECD Guidelines within their group. In November 1977 representatives of 9 major Swedish MNEs (Alfa-Laval, Asea, Atlas Copco, LM Ericsson, Saab-Scania, Skandinaviska Enskildabanken, Stal-Laval, Svenska Flaektfabriken, Swedish Match Co) held a special meeting for the purposes of studying and discussing the contents of the OECD Guidelines. A small group of chief executive officers of Swedish MNEs (LM Ericsson, Alfa-Laval, Electrolux, SK SKFL) and of subsidiaries in Sweden of foreign MNEs (Philips, Shell) has been set up with the aim of

following international developments concerning MNEs including the OECD Declaration.
- *Switzerland* reports: 'Swiss industry includes more than 100 enterprises of a "multinational" character, including firms of modest size. We have made an enquiry with the major ones and are able to state that these firms already apply most of the Guidelines and that progress is continuing. The enterprises concerned have taken suitable measures to distribute and explain the OECD Guidelines within their organisations, with particular attention to key managers, by means of circulars, seminars, briefings.'
- In the *UK* responses in support of the Guidelines have been made in statements by top executives, annual reports or letters to the CBI from over 40 companies including: BAT Industries, BP, British Steel, Beecham Group, Dunlop Holdings, Esso (UK), Ford(UK), ICI, IMI, Imperial Group, Lloyd's Bank, Norwich Union, Rugby Portland Cement, Shell, Stone-Platt Industries, RTZ Services and Unilever.
- To date more than 50 *US*-based corporations having world-wide sales of more than 300 billion dollars have indicated their support of the Guidelines. These US corporations have ranged in size from Exxon (number 1 on the Fortune 500 list) to Beechcraft (number 477 on the Fortune 500). Several financial institutions have also supported the Guidelines (i.e. Citicorp, Bank of America).

Responses have included:
- General statements of support (Du Pont, Philip Morris, etc.);
- Statements in Annual Reports (IBM, DOW, Kodak, Caterpillar, Exxon, Citicorp);
- Communications with employees (IBM, Caterpillar, Exxon);
- Speeches to audiences throughout the US (Exxon, GM, Bendix, DOW).

The US business community is continuing its efforts to develop further corporate support through personal communications to various members of the US corporate community.

C. Experience with the OECD Guidelines

From the above survey BIAC is pleased to note that there has developed over the past year a greater understanding and acceptance of the principles and objectives of the Guidelines in OECD countries. BIAC recognizes, however, there is still an important educational task in encouraging the small and medium-sized firms and that awareness is greater in some industries than others, and in some countries than others. It is confident that the on-going programmes of many of its Member Federations will continue to contribute to this educational process.
So far as implementing the Guidelines section on Disclosure of Information is concerned, a large number of companies already conform to the high disclosure standards required under certain national legislations which ensure their annual reports are generally in line with the Guidelines and only relatively

small adjustments have been necessary. Where there are differences in the current national disclosure requirements, or the direction of expected future developments in national legislation is uncertain, e.g. in EEC, there may be, however, some hesitation on the part of companies to embark on costly adaptations of internal systems to the specific OECD requirements at the present time.

The Netherlands Federation (VNO), for example, while reporting 'no cases of enterprises which do not intend to apply the Guidelines as such have come to our knowledge', have gone on to point out: 'However, in some cases the application of certain Guidelines on Disclosure of Information may not be possible.' Similarly the Swedish reply states: 'Swedish company law requires a relatively wide disclosure of information. This and Swedish business practice have contributed to the fact that annual reports of Swedish MNEs are of a very high international standard. For this reason the enterprises generally comply with the OECD Guidelines to a high degree. On some points, however, they comply only to a limited extent. The operating results and the sales are generally not broken down on a geographical area basis.' These are not isolated examples – the Norwegian, Italian and German Federations have made similar points on disclosure. In any event it is still difficult to assess the extent to which annual reports have already been adapted because, as Mr. Wootton acknowledged in his letter of 19th April, 1977, to BIAC, 1977 results will not be available until some time later in 1978.

BIAC therefore sees the implementation of the Disclosure Guidelines in particular as a gradual process, but is confident that with the degree of support being expressed by companies for the Guidelines as a whole, a steady improvement will be evident over the next few years. BIAC will elaborate on these and any other issues arising from the Guidelines in its oral statement on 11th April.

II. Areas for Continuing Co-operation with the OECD IIME Committee

BIAC wishes to re-affirm its desire to continue the co-operation which exists with the OECD IIME Committee and feels this is particularly important in view of the impending review period for the Declaration and Guidelines in 1979. BIAC would like already to take this opportunity to mention three specific areas: harmonization of accounting standards, restrictive business practices, and national treatment.

In the field of harmonization of accounting standards, BIAC was glad to hear that the OECD IIME Committee is considering arranging for the study of this subject. BIAC believes that an OECD effort to develop common accounting standards for major financial reporting items would be a timely undertaking. In BIAC's view, the UN efforts in this area have mistakenly focused on maximum disclosure which should not be started until comparable accounting standards have been developed. If it is intended to develop this as a subject in OECD, BIAC would very much like the opportunity to submit its views on the terms of reference and machinery for this study.

BIAC is looking forward to close co-operation between the OECD experts on

Restrictive Business Practices and BIAC experts in this field in the future. There is perhaps no other subject covered by the Guidelines which is so much dependent on technical expertise. In the past, for instance in the period before the Guidelines were promulgated, such co-operation was rather disappointing and BIAC does believe that co-operation would facilitate understanding on the part of the OECD experts of the difficulties which the business community faces in this area. It would also assist BIAC members to appreciate the objectives and needs of the OECD Governments. BIAC experts have recently discussed the whole question of co-operation with the OECD Committee of Experts and are hopeful that future meetings can be held on a regular basis to discuss the various issues being considered by that OECD Committee.

BIAC is pleased to note that a number of national governments have already begun discussions either directly or through national federations with individual corporations on the subject of exceptions to national treatment. BIAC strongly supports these continuing efforts and also remains willing to consult with the OECD on the principles involved.

In conclusion BIAC wishes to re-affirm its willingness to co-operate on the preparations for the 1979 review of the Declaration on International Investment and Multinational Enterprises. BIAC would suggest that a further consultation with the OECD IIME Committee might be helpful towards the end of this year or early 1979.

20th March, 1978»

90. January 11, 1979, BIAC forwarded to OECD a Summary of efforts by the Business Community to Propagate and Support the OECD Guidelines for Multinational Enterprises, 1976–1978:

«PART I. Resumé of Activities

A country-by-country report on business support for the Guidelines was presented as part of the background information for the BIAC consultation with the Committee on International Investment and Multinational Enterprises on April 11, 1978. Since that report is available to all members of the Committee and its Working Party on the Guidelines, there is no reason to repeat the detailed information here. For purposes of refreshing the memory, we will simply outline briefly the types of efforts made.

The business community has widely distributed copies of the Guidelines throughout the OECD area. As an indication of the extent of this distribution, in Belgium 14,000 copies and in Switzerland 6,000 copies have been provided to business executives and business organizations. To explain what the Guidelines were all about, tens of thousands of circulars and letters and publications have been sent out. In Canada alone, for example, 20,000 circulars giving general information about the Guidelines and urging support were followed by personal letters to chief executive officers of the major multinational enterprises. In Sweden similarly personal letters were sent to top executives of all major multinational enterprises, and implementation is being continuously discussed in a working party of executives of multinational enterprises and representatives of business organizations. In late 1977, when.annual reports were being considered, the Swedish Employers' Confederation wrote again to the multinational enterprises reminding them of the Disclosure Guidelines and soliciting their efforts to comply. Siemens in Germany distributed 190,000 copies of an in-house publication in an effort to publicize the firm's support of the Guidelines to the work force.

Permanent study or discussion groups have also been established in several countries, and a variety of seminars and workshops have been held to explain the intent and meaning of the Guidelines – for example, the CBI in Britain has recently held two seminars for business executives and representatives of business organizations in an effort to respond to any questions which have surfaced. In the USA, government and business representatives have participated in workshops to the same end.

Articles have been provided newspapers and other periodicals. In addition, USA–BIAC has sponsored a series of publications ['Text and General Review of OECD Guidelines' (1976), 'Disclosure of Information' (1976), 'Competition' (1977), and 'Employment and Industrial Relations' (1978)], thousands of copies of which have been distributed, not only in the USA, but in many other countries as well. A variety of additional information, including reports, studies and commentaries have been prepared and distributed by business organizations in other countries as well, including among others Switzerland, Norway and the Netherlands.

From time to time as various governments or business organizations have conducted surveys to determine degree of knowledge of or compliance with all or part of the Guidelines, the business community has co-operated in obtaining the desired data.

As a case in point, the Japanese business community has recently aided the Ministry of Industry and International Trade in the development of a questionnaire and then in obtaining the data requested therein to determine the degree of support given by Japanese enterprises to the Guidelines. Response was good, with 65 per cent of the 965 firms contacted responding to the questionnaire. Based on the returns of those firms, 80 per cent of Japanese businesses are aware of the Guidelines; 70 per cent made reference to the Guidelines in making business decisions; and three quarters of those who were previously unaware of the existence of the Guidelines have indicated that they would in the near future communicate to their officers and employees that they should comply with them.

Major efforts were made by employers' organizations to obtain and provide input for the Progress Report provided by BIAC in April, 1978; and more recently a survey has been conducted through all BIAC Member Organizations to determine the degree of compliance with the Disclosure Guidelines with a particular effort being made to define problem areas wherever disclosure was less than complete. Because this survey on the Disclosure Guidelines has been conducted since the Progress Report of Spring 1978, the results follow in detail in Part II.

In addition, several reports have been provided to the Working Party on the Guidelines, summarizing the current situation with regard to provision of information to employees under the Employment and Industrial Relations Guidelines in seven Member Countries.»

c. Disclosure of Information: Difficulties, Compliance, The Report of the IME Committee

---

Paragraph 1 of the Introduction of the Guidelines:

«In addition, the complexity of these multinational enterprises and the difficulty of clearly perceiving their diverse structures, operations and policies sometimes give rise to concern.

Chapter II of the Guidelines

Disclosure of Information

Enterprises should, having due regard to their nature and relative size in the economic context of their operations and to requirements of business confidentiality and to cost, publish in a form suited to improve public understanding a sufficient body of factual information on the structure, activities and policies of the enterprise as a whole, as a supplement, in so far as is necessary for this purpose, to information to be disclosed under the national law of the individual countries in which they operate. To this end, they should publish within reasonable time limits, on a regular basis, but at least annually, financial statements and other pertinent information relating to the enterprise as a whole, comprising in particular:

   (i) the structure of the enterprise, showing the name and location of the parent company, its main affiliates, its percentage ownership, direct and indirect, in these affiliates, including shareholdings between them;

  (ii) the geographical areas* where operations are carried out and the principal activities carried on therein by the parent company and the main affiliates;

 (iii) the operating results and sales by geographical area and the sales in the major lines of business for the enterprise as a whole;

 (iv) significant new capital investment by geographical area and, as far as practicable, by major lines of business for the enterprise as a whole;

  (v) a statement of the sources and uses of funds by the enterprise as a whole;

 (vi) the average number of employees in each geographical area;

(vii) research and development expenditure for the enterprise as a whole;

(viii) the policies followed in respect of intra-group pricing;

(ix) the accounting policies, including those on consolidation, observed in compiling the published information»

---

* For the purposes of the guideline on disclosure of information the term 'geographical area' means groups of countries or individual countries as each enterprise determines it appropriate in its particular circumstances. While no single method of grouping is appropriate for all enterprises, or for all purposes, the factors to be considered by an enterprise would include the significance of operations carried out in individual countries or areas as well as the effects on its competitiveness, geographic proximity, economic affinity, similarities in business environments and the nature, scale and degree of interrelationship of the enterprises' operations in the various countries.

---

1. Difficulties

91. During the consultations BIAC representatives indicated a number of problems in the area of information:

– *danger of comparative disadvantage*

BIAC indicated that certain types of information (e.g. operating results by geographical area) could result in competitive disadvantages, especially for firms which have customers in a particular area or region only; concern was also expressed that disclosure of intra-group pricing policies could reveal cost elements and profit margins for various products and thus conflict with the need for business confidentiality;

– *difficulties in changing established reporting systems*

Attention was drawn to cost and time factors involved in changing or supplementing existing reporting practices, in particular for smaller companies with limited experience;

– *lack of agreed definitions and diversity of national reporting*

Reference was also made to the lack of agreed definitions of the items contained in the disclosure guidelines and the diversity of national reporting;

– *Information by geographical area*

Doubts were expressed as to whether disclosure by geographical area was always the most appropriate method for disclosure of information. A preference was indicated for disclosure by lines of business in view of existing regulations and practices.

2. Compliance

92. Part II of the January 1979 communication by BIAC to the IME committee, related to the *Compliance by Enterprises with the OECD Guidelines on Disclosure of Information*:

«On July 6, 1978, BIAC initiated a survey on compliance with the Disclosure Guidelines by mailing a letter of explanation and a suggested format for obtaining the desired information from the multinational enterprises to all BIAC Member Organizations in the OECD countries. Copies of the letter and suggested format are annexed.

By the end of the year responses from organizations of employers in sixteen countries (Australia, Belgium, Canada, Denmark, France, Germany, Ireland, Italy, Japan, Luxembourg, Netherlands, Norway, Sweden, Switzerland, United Kingdom, USA) had been received, and analysis included in this report is based on the quantifiable data provided by 190 multinational enterprises. Should significant additional data be received in the near future, this will be communicated to the OECD.

As indicated in the letter to BIAC Member Organizations, there was no attempt to achieve a scientific sampling of firms, but rather an effort to solicit information from firms considered likely to respond. Additional communications by mail and by telephone and telex between July and December recalled attention to the survey and especially to the interest of the OECD in defining and understanding any reason for non-disclosure or difficulties being encountered by the enterprises.

Since the promulgation of the Guidelines, BIAC has worked through its Member Federations toward the dual goals of education and acceptance. While the education and acceptance process is still on-going, it appears from the results of the survey that significant disclosure has been achieved. In this respect, the overwhelming majority (90–99 per cent) of the enterprises responding disclosed in 1977, or in a relatively few cases intend to do so in 1978, in accordance with Guidelines on structure and ownership (i); areas of operations and principal activities engaged in (ii); sales in major lines of business (iii); new capital investment by major lines of business (iv); sources and uses of funds (v); and accounting policies observed (ix).

Recognizing that a global statement of 90–99 per cent disclosure while pleasing is perhaps somewhat less interesting to the Committee on International Investment and Multinational Enterprises at the time of the Review than an explanation of the non-disclosure by the remaining firms, a good-faith effort is made below to define where the problems lay. Wherever fewer than 97 per cent of firms disclosed on a particular item, an explanation is provided. The following analysis follows the outline and innumeration of items on the format used to collect the data (see Annex). The annual report was the means by which virtually all of the information was provided in cases of disclosure. Fewer than 5 per cent of the responding firms used an alternative method on any given item, and for this reason in the following analysis no distinction is made between reporting by means of annual report and reporting by alternative methods. Neither is any distinction made regarding whether disclosure took place in 1977 or will take place in the next year or two, since on any given item fewer than 7 per cent of responding firms indicated that disclosure would be postponed for some period of time. With this in mind, 'disclosure' as used below means, for the most part, in 1977 by means of annual reports.

Any discrepancies noted between the sum of 'disclosure' and 'non-disclosure' may be explained by a variety of factors, including an occasional failure to respond to a particular item, but for the most part by some degree of partial rather than full disclosure.

1.(a) the structure of the enterprise, showing name and location of the parent company:
99 per cent of the responding firms disclose.
1.(b) name and location of its main affiliates:
98 per cent of the firms disclose.
1.(c) its percentage ownership, direct and indirect, in these affiliates, including shareholding between them:
90 per cent of the firms disclose. Several additional firms show direct ownership only. Swiss firms were the only national group indicating rather general non-disclosure of percentage ownership in and between affiliates. It was said that the problem is being studied and it looks as though improvement can be anticipated in the near future. Apparently local enterprises, rather than the parent companies are hesitant to divulge this data.
2.(a) the geographical areas where operations are carried out:
98 per cent of responding firms disclose.
2.(b) the principal activities carried on therein by the parent company and the main affiliates:
97 per cent of the firms disclose.
3.(a) the operating results and sales by geographical area:
73 per cent of responding firms report fully and an additional 14 per cent report sales, but not operating results, while 11 per cent report neither of these by geographical area – mainly for competitive reasons. A few indicated that the accounting burden was considered too great relative to any potential use of such data.
3.(b) the sales in the major lines of business for the enterprise as a whole:
91 per cent of responding firms disclose. Among the 8 per cent not disclosing, competition was the most frequent reason offered; although a few firms felt that their production is too diversified to permit a meaning-ful determination or definition of lines.
4.(a) significant new capital investment – by geographical area:
More than three quarters of the responding firms disclose. 21 per cent of responding firms did not disclose. (40 per cent of French firms reporting, 30 per cent of the USA firms and 22 per cent of the Dutch firms account for most of this.) The reasons given for not disclosing by geographical area by US firms was simply the lack of legal requirement and the resulting fact that no conscious decision had yet been taken. There appeared to be little concern with effects on competition. In France and Holland, however, the effect on competitive position and business strategy were mentioned as reasons for not wishing to disclose. Several

91

firms indicated that this breakdown by geographical area is considered of minor importance from a business standpoint, while a breakdown by sector or product line offers more interesting information.

4.(b) by major lines of business for the enterprise as a whole:
90 per cent of the firms disclose, while 8 per cent of responding firms do not. Reasons given included insignificant size of investments and competitive considerations.

5. sources and uses of fund by the enterprise as a whole:
99 per cent of the firms disclose.

6. average number of employees in each geographical area:
More than two-thirds of the firms disclose, while slightly more than a quarter of the responding enterprises indicated no intention to disclose (50 per cent of USA firms responding account for most of this). Most non-disclosing firms indicated that they have no internal reasons for compiling this data and consider it rather meaningless for annual reporting purposes and somewhat onerous. It was apparently not considered of a confidential or sensitive nature. In several cases mention was made of the technical difficulty of classifying employees by geographical area due to overlap in responsibilities and the fact that significant numbers of employees are continually being assigned to different areas. A few firms provide such data as of the end of each year, rather than 'average' for the year; a few provide it occasionally, but not annually.

7. research and development expenditure for enterprise as a whole:
71 per cent of the firms disclose, while 20 per cent of the responding firms do not intend to report on R & D expenditure (80 per cent of the firms responding from Switzerland, 57 per cent of the ones from Holland, 30 per cent from Sweden and 29 per cent from France accounted for virtually all of the non-disclosure on this item). Most firms do not report because of the insignificance or non-existence of this type of expenditures by the enterprises or because of competitive disadvantages in disclosing such data. A few of the non-disclosing firms signalled difficulty due to imprecise definitions of 'research' and more significantly of 'development', since development is perceived as a continuing process, virtually impossible to delimit. Any disclosures made would certainly be noncomparable among firms.

8. policies followed in respect of intra-group pricing:
Over half of the responding firms disclose while an additional 5 per cent of responders reportedly have no intra-group exchange. 43 per cent of the respondents reported no current intention to disclose the information cited. (70–100 per cent of the firms having responded from Holland, Switzerland, Belgium, and Germany; 35–50 per cent of those having responded from France, Australia and Sweden and 20 per cent of the USA firms indicated incomplete disclosure. It seems that US law as of 1977 requires some disclosure, but there is not yet a clear understanding of whether what is required and what is disclosed meet the OECD Guidelines requirement.) Reasons offered for not disclosing included the fact that there is no unique method of establishing transfer prices, but

rather a great variety, not only from enterprise to enteprise, but even from product to product. This renders it technically difficult to disclose meaningfully, especially for firms with a large number of products which sometimes establish prices by a combination of different methods. Many firms also withhold such information for competitive reason. A few felt that there was no good reason to bother, since it is neither useful nor required by law. And others indicated the irrelevance of such data due to the insignificant size of any intra-group exchange.

9.   the accounting policies including those on consolidation, observed in compiling the published information:

99 per cent of the firms disclose.

As can be easily seen from the results summarized above, wherever Disclosure under the Guidelines is less than complete, the reasons for not disclosing lie in the overwhelming majority of instances with relative size of the firm, business confidentiality, or cost, all of which are recognized and accepted in the preamble to the Guidelines on Disclosure. Non-disclosure for such reasons cannot realistically be interpreted as non-compliance with the Guidelines.

Two questions relating to Disclosure were raised in OECD document 78.14 (Summary of Discussions on BIAC Materials on Disclosure of Information) to which BIAC Member Organizations have been asked to respond.

The first had to do with whether precise definitions in the Guidelines on Disclosure would assist multinational enterprises in applying those Guidelines or whether they would render conformity more difficult by reducing an element of flexibility.

All of the direct responses to this question indicated that precise definitions would in general tend to make compliance more difficult in light of the many different countries, companies and customs involved. Concern was expressed that prescription of detailed guidance satisfactory to many governments would not only be most difficult to achieve but would likely be counter-productive to the increasing recognition by multinationals of the OECD objective embraced by the Disclosure Guidelines. It was also felt probable that additional details would tend to create conflict and inconsistency with existing national requirements among OECD members in the absence of a successful harmonization effort in the near future.

The second question had to do with possible conflicts between the disclosure standards and national laws and regulations.

No conflicts have been identified.

At the beginning of 1979 the Committee on International Investment and Multinational Enterprises begins to consider the Review of the Declaration and Decisions taken by the OECD Ministers in late June 1976. In the two and a half years since the time of that Declaration, the business community has supported the implementation of the Guidelines for multinational enterprises though such means as are outlined above and these efforts are continuing. Given the time available to date, and the fact that the process is largely one of education, we feel that significant progress has been made and we pledge our continuing efforts in this direction.

January 1979

93. ANNEX

Dear Sir,

BIAC Committee on International Investment
and Multinational Enterprises

With our telex of June 19, 1978, the BIAC Secretariat informed you of the commitment to provide the OECD Committee on MNE's with an update on the implementation of the Guidelines on Disclosure of Information. You may recall that the OECD is to review the Guidelines on MNE's during 1979.
After much consideration of this matter the BIAC Committee on MNE's decided to begin work on this project immediately. The Committee recognized potential advantages to business and industry in stressing the merits of voluntary compliance and thereby minimizing the risk of mandatory regulations. It was also recognized that business interests can be well served by illuminating areas of compliance where industry has little or no difficulty in complying and highlighting areas of conceptual difficulties and/or restraints.
It must be stressed that the OECD Committee has evidenced a strong interest in and attaches great importance to discovering the reasons for non-compliance, whether this is merely a matter of time, or whether significant conceptual barriers exist. The BIAC Committee feels that it is in our interest to obtain the information requested.
As to the implementation of the project, that is, the actual gathering of the information, the BIAC Committee on MNE's wishes to provide some suggestions for expediting the effort, but, of course, leaves it to the discretion of each Member Federation as to the method to be used.

Our suggestions are five in number:
(1) In the interest of timely responses, it is suggested that the Member Federations use discretion in selecting companies from which a speedy response can be expected. I suggest that you should choose enterprises of various sizes, keeping in mind that if the responses are to be of assistance to the OECD Committee, we must provide them by early December. Since the BIAC Committee is meeting on September 15, we would appreciate your efforts to get your responses to us by that date. If that proves impractical, please return them at your earliest convenience.
(2) To make your task easier and to facilitate collation and compilation of the information, we are enclosing a suggested format for use in requesting the desired information from companies. This format (or your own) could be reproduced and distributed to the selected companies with your covering letter encouraging co-operation.
(3) If you should choose to develop your own format, please remember that emphasis should be placed in determining *why* companies do not comply. Please ask for a full explanation for non-compliance on each item.
(4) It is suggested that all individual company responses be sent to the BIAC Secretariat. You may, of course, prefer to summarize the responses; but if

you do so, again we urge that you provide us with all reasons or causes stated for non-compliance.

(5) Please assure companies that no company names will be divulged to OECD without advance approval.

The Committee on MNE's and I personally will appreciate your efforts in implementing this project.

Sincerely,

G. A. Wagner
Chairman of the BIAC Committee on MNE's»

To: – Presidents and Directors General of BIAC Member Federations

Suggested format for collecting information
from industry members of the BIAC National Organizations

*Update on Compliance by Enterprises with the OECD Guidelines on Disclosure
of Information*

The information indicated below is requested by the BIAC Committee on
MNE's in order to provide the OECD with a promised update on this subject
during 1978
The following statement is taken from the OECD *Guidelines for Multinational
Enterprises*: 'Disclosure of Information'. Please indicate your enterprise's
degree of compliance by checking the appropriate blocks, providing explanation
where requested or where you feel it may make your position more clearly
understood.

Name of enterprise _____
may ☐   may not ☐ be divulged in discussion with the OECD.

'Disclosure of Information:
Enterprises should, having due regard to their nature and relative size in the
economic context of their operations and to requirements of business confidentiality and to cost, publish in a form suited to improve public understanding a sufficient body of factual information on the structure, activities and
policies of the enterprise as a whole, as a supplement, in so far as is necessary
for this purpose, to information to be disclosed under the national law of the
individual countries in which they operate. To this end, they should publish
within reasonable time limits, on a regular basis, but at least annually, financial
statements and other pertinent information relating to the enterprise as a
whole, comprising in particular: '*

---

* Whenever the response to an item is 'no intention to respond', OECD is very interested in
understanding where the difficulty lies. We urge you to provide a full explanation in these cases.

Items taken from the Guidelines on Disclosure	Company Reported for 1977		Company intends to report in due course (state time period)	Company does not intend to report (please provide specific reasons)
	by means of the annual report	by other means (please identify)		
1.(a) the structure of the enterprise, showing name and location of the parent company				
(b) name and location of its main affiliates				
(c) its percentage ownership, direct and indirect, in these affiliates including shareholding between them				
2.(a) the geographical areas where operations are carried out				
(b) the principal activities carried on therein by the parent company and the main affiliates				
3.(a) the operating results and sales by geographical area				
(b) the sales in the major lines of business for the enterprise as a whole				
4.(a) significant new capital investment by geographical area				
(b) by major lines of business for the enterprise as a whole				
5. sources and uses of fund by the enterprise as a whole				
6. average number of employees in each geographical area				
7. research and development expenditure for enterprise as a whole				
8. policies followed in respect of intra-group pricing				
9. the accounting policies including those on consolidation, observed in compiling the published information				

97

3. The Report of the IME Committee

«Disclosure of Information
94. 'The complexity of these multinational enterprises and the difficulty of clearly perceiving their diverse structures, operations and policies sometimes give rise to concern' (paragraph 1 of Introduction to the Guidelines). The purpose of the chapter on Disclosure of Information was to give greater transparency to the activities of MNEs through the publication of a greater volume of information, 'presented in a form suited to improve public under- standing'. In the opinion of the business community also, as conveyed to the Committee notably by BIAC, this is an area where management should make best efforts to show results. Here again, however, it must be recognized that the time which has elapsed since the summer of 1976 when the Guidelines were made public is fairly short – in fact, two accounting years – for implementing any changes needed to bring the practice of companies into line with the chapter on disclosure (paragraph 46).

95. On the basis of information available to the Committee, it can be seen that progress has been achieved by a number of large companies whose annual or other published reports reflect all or most of the disclosure standards of the Guidelines. However, the observance of these disclosure standards to date appears to be considerably less widespread among the medium and smaller sized MNEs, which may be due to their relative size in the economic context of their operations and to cost. Even among the larger firms there are consider- able differences according to the home country of the parent, reflecting histori- cal differences in prevailing practices. Thus, the Committee believes that significant further efforts will be needed to encourage wide observance of the recommended standards (paragraph 47).

96. In its discussions with BIAC and through the reports it received from Member governments, the Committee noted a number of concerns some enterprises expressed with respect to this chapter, some of which reflect diffi- culties of adjustments while others reveal problems of a more conceptual nature. The following comments refer to the problem areas that have been identified:
a. Some enterprises considered that the disclosure of certain types of informa- tion (cf. operating results by geographical area) may result in competitive disadvantages, especially for firms which have only one or a few customers in a particular country or region. In this regard, the Guidelines on disclosure contain a certain number of qualifications which make allowances for the specific situations of companies in the context of their operations. These qualifications, however, are not intended, other than in very exceptional circumstances, as complete or permanent exemptions from certain dis- closure standards and should be invoked only for valid reasons.
b. Reference was also made by enterprises to cost and time factors involved in changing or supplementing existing reporting practices, in particular, for smaller companies with limited international experience. As cost and the

relative size of the company are specifically mentioned as qualifications in the Chapter on Disclosure of Information, the Guidelines provide the necessary degree of flexibility for the adjustment of reporting practices over a reasonable period of time.

c. Certain enterprises also referred to the diversity of national reporting and accounting requirements with respect to the items contained in the disclosure guidelines. The recommendations in the chapter, as explicitly stated in the text, were intended to supplement, where necessary, the disclosure and reporting requirements laid down by national law to increase public understanding 'on the structure, activities and the policies of the enterprises as a whole'. National requirements which are less comprehensive should not prevent MNEs from taking action under the Guidelines. Given the present absence of internationally-agreed accounting standards, such reports concerning the enterprises as a whole will usually follow the accounting principles generally accepted in the country in which the parent company or a controlling entity at the intermediary level is domiciled. For the use of such information it is important, according to item (ix) of the chapter on Disclosure of Information, that companies state the accounting principles which have been used.

d. Problems were also raised with respect to segmentation of information. In particular, a number of firms expressed doubts as to whether disclosure by 'geographical area' was always the most appropriate method of segmentation. These problems of geographical breakdown should, however, not be exaggerated. As explained in the footnote to the text, the Guidelines leave some degree of flexibility for companies to determine the most appropriate geographical breakdown. This may be an issue where the interests of some users of the published data differ in some cases from those of the enterprises, which may find a line of business approach more useful for internal purposes. It has to be emphasized, however, that the Guidelines reflect the value Member governments place on geographical segmentation of information (paragraph 48).

97. The Committee is presently exploring the ways and means of improving comparability or achieving harmonization of the accounting concepts referred to in the Disclosure of Information Guidelines. For this purpose, inter alia, an ad hoc technical Working Group on Accounting Standards has been set up and is conducting a survey on the accounting requirements, standards and practices in Member countries which are of particular relevance to the Guidelines so as to be in a position to advise the Committee, by the autumn of 1979, on the feasibility of OECD undertaking further work in this area (paragraph 49).

98. Meanwhile, the Committee is aware that the standards laid down by the OECD for disclosure go beyond actual practice in most Member countries and that adjustment to these standards in some cases presents difficulties and costs. Nevertheless, the Committee believes these standards are reasonable and are sufficiently flexible. It confirms the importance which Member countries attach to the objectives of this chapter of the Guidelines and reiterates its view that

companies which have not yet taken steps to observe the disclosure Guidelines, making due allowances for adjustment difficulties, should make every effort to reflect in their next annual published accounts the Disclosure of Information Guidelines. It invites governments and the business community to undertake further promotional and educational efforts so as to enhance the effectiveness of the Guidelines in this area and, in recognition of the fundamental importance of this chapter of the Guidelines, intends to pay continuing attention to this matter (paragraph 50).»

d. BIAC's General Attitude Regarding the Discussion of Cases and the Role of the IME Committee

99. BIAC's general attitude is shown clearly from a letter of June 16, 1978 which was sent to OECD concerning this issue:
«. . . There seem to be three general principles involved when considering the conduct of specific enterprises in relation to the Guidelines. The first is that in order to minimise unnecessary strain on international relations, and paying due regard to the territorial jurisdiction of member states and indeed also as a practical matter, consultation machinery at a multilateral level should normally only become a possibility when national or bilateral procedures have been exhausted. The second principle is that the CIME should not assume the role of a tribunal nor indeed appear to have such a role. I understand that this consideration was much in the mind of the negotiators when the Inter-Governmental Consultation Procedures were negotiated. Thirdly, the CIME 'shall not reach conclusions on the conduct of individual enterprises'. On this the Decision of OECD's Council is specific.
The reason for reiterating these principles is because BIAC does have concerns regarding the Consultation Procedures with the advisory bodies where so-called 'cases' – naming specific companies – are cited as violations or as illustrations of a particular point of issue. Unfortunately you will be aware that, in the press, assertions are often treated as if they are established facts, and as if CIME were a quasi-judicial tribunal. This can be unhelpful for the settlement of differences of opinion, as well as harmful for Multinational Enterprises in general.
In order, therefore, to be consistent with the three principles referred to earlier, I would urge that every effort should be made to settle specific situations in the country which has jurisdiction over the matter, or if two jurisdictions are involved, the matter could be pursued bilaterally through mutually acceptable arrangements. It is when these procedures have been exhausted without satisfactory resolution that the principles and issues in debate might be submitted by the member government (or governments) concerned to CIME in an effort to promote consensus on the interpretation of the relevant Guidelines. CIME in turn may wish to seek the views of BIAC and/or TUAC on the issues of interpretation raised relating to the OECD Guidelines. Under the terms of the Declaration, of course, CIME may also invite the enterprise itself to express its views if it so wishes, and, if an enterprise decided to do so, it should

have the choice of appearing before CIME or communicating in writing. Separate and distinct from situations in which the conduct of an individual enterprise is involved, there could be situations where the issue is one of interpretation which is raised without involving an individually named enterprise or enterprises. In such a general context involving the interpretation of the Guidelines, BIAC and TUAC might each be given the opportunity to raise with the CIME questions of interpretation, but it would be for the CIME to decide whether the matter on which interpretation is sought justifies further consideration. This procedure is, of course, already embodied in the Consultation mechanism with BIAC and TUAC.»
BIAC's specific attitude concerning particular issues, involved in the different cases, will be discussed further, in PART II, where an evaluation of the impact of the Guidelines is made.

e. The Composition of the BIAC Delegation

100. The BIAC delegation to the IME Committee and to the Levy group, was representative from the point of view of the number and importance of the countries present, as well as from the point of view of the caliber of personalities involved, as the following example (delegation to the February (26) meeting, 1979) shows:

Chairman	Mr. G. A. Wagner
	Chairman of the Supervisory Board
	Royal Dutch Petroleum Company Ltd.
Belgium	Mr. Y. van der Mensbrugghe
	Director, Public Affairs
	S. A. Bekaert
	Mr. P. Chaumont
	Director, Governmental Affairs
	Ford of Europe, Inc.
Canada	Mr. K. H. J. Clarke (Vice-Chairman of BIAC)
	Consultant, Corporate Affairs
	Inco Limited
France	Mr. V. Carbonel
	Chef du Service des Affaires Européennes
	CNPF
Germany	Dr. G. Tacke
	Senior Executive Consultant to the Managing Board
	Siemens AG
	Dr. F. Dribbusch
	Former Member of the Executive Board
	BASF AG
Italy	Dr. V. Sallier de la Tour
	Direction des Problèmes Communautaires et Rapports
	avec les Organisations Internationales

101

	Relations Internationales, Société FIAT
Japan	Mr. K. Sonoda
	Former Member of the Executive Board, Bank of Tokyo
	Vice-Chairman, Japanese BIAC Committee,
	Keidanren
Netherlands	Dr. M. Weisglas
	Economic Adviser
	Unilever NV
Portugal	Dr. O. Morbey Rodriguez
	Administrateur Délégué
	Philips Portugal, SARL
Sweden	Mr. B. Lundvall
	Chairman of the Board
	L. M. Ericsson Telephone Company
	Mr. H. Lindgren
	Senior Vice-President
	Skandinaviska Enskildabanken
Switzerland	Dr. H. Glättli
	Head of Economic Affairs Department
	Sandoz Ltd.
United Kingdom	Mr. P. Macadam
	Chairman
	BAT Industries
	Mr. C. H. A. F. Castle
	Manager Group Industrial Relations
	The British Petroleum Co. Ltd.
United States	Mr. R. Lockwood
	Chairman
	General Motors – European Advisory Council
	Mr. R. D. Fitzgerald
	Director
	Price Waterhouse & Co.
	Mr. Holling
	Manager of Governmental Affairs
	Caterpillar
	Mr. R. W. Markley
	National Commissioner
	US Council of the International Chamber of Commerce
	Mr. R. Copp
	International Labor Affairs Manager
	Labor Relations Staff
	Ford
	Mr. D. L. Guertin
	Senior Planning Adviser – Public Affairs
	Exxon Corporation

101. Also attending   Mr. C. K. Preston

102

Economic Affairs Department
Sandoz Ltd.
Mr. John Blair
International Law Consultant
Shell International Petroleum Company Ltd.
Miss J. Turner
Public Affairs
Shell International Petroleum Company Ltd.

BIAC Secretariat   Mlle Yolande Michaud
Secretary General
Mrs. Gerri M. Casse
Deputy Secretary General

B. TUAC's Point of View

1. TUAC's Qualified Welcome of the Guidelines

102. There is no doubt that TUAC's welcome of the Guidelines, was only a qualified one.[8] This attitude did not change.

'By giving support to the OECD Guidelines', a TUAC statement to the OECD committee on 11th April 1978 reads:

«TUAC has stressed the point that it considered the work undertaken by OECD as a first step which should lead to further international arrangements and agreements, as announced by the Ministers. TUAC has not been informed so far of any endeavours within the OECD which may lead to extend co-operation among Members in the area of international investment and multi-national enterprises and to new operational instruments.

Secondly, TUAC has never omitted to express its belief that only firm governmental action and binding rules can curb abuses of concentrations of economic power and solve the conflicts with national policy objectives which stem from the uncontrolled activities of multinational enterprises. However, TUAC repeats its willingness to make the voluntary Guidelines operational which, in its views and after an experience of already two years can only be effectuated by applying effective consultation procedures.»

103. In his oral statement to the IME Committee, TUAC's President, Mr. Svend Backe Vognbjerg (L.O.–Denmark) declared:

«The support we gave in 1976 to the Guidelines was based on the strong hope that they would be useful at home for our members working in multinational enterprises. In 1978, the situation in many countries is that nothing has much changed, but to the worse with continued malpractices, decisions taken without consultation or sufficient notification, continued anti-trade-unions campaigns, etc. The few examples where the Guidelines were helpful to some limited extent are still mere exceptions and do not constitute a trend.

We have never been hiding our belief that more binding rules than the

8. See above no. 50.

Guidelines and firm governmental action might succeed to curb abuses of concentrations of economic power and solve the conflicts with national policy objectives which stem from the uncontrolled activities of multinational enterprises. However, we had engaged our responsibility behind the Guidelines as one potentially useful instrument in the hope that positive and effective action would follow, not only from enterprises, but also from governments. TUAC itself was fully aware that the OECD IIME Committee 'would not reach conclusions on the conduct of individual enterprises'. During the past 2 years, TUAC refrained itself from pinpointing publicly bad behaviour of multinational enterprises under the provisions of the Guidelines, as well as from conducting any campaign aimed at its members and the public opinion. We hoped that positive action by the governments under the Guidelines, actual changes in the behaviour of the enterprises and our efforts of explanation and information on the basis of successful cases, detailed interpretation and clarification from the IIME Committee would produce results in the right direction. Little of that has come to date. Workers, in many of our countries, are still not aware of the Guidelines themselves because no clear and positive trend of reform and action has been created during the past 2 years or, if they are aware, they are sceptical and disenchanted about the usefulness of the instrument.»

104. The same attitude, and somewhat disappointed feelings, were expressed in a written statement by TUAC on the occasion of the 1979 review of the Guidelines:

«I. General

1. Both through the Trade Union Advisory Committee and at the national level, the trade unions participated actively in the preparation of the OECD Guidelines for Multinational Enterprises and the related Decisions of the OECD Guidelines for Multinational Enterprises and the related Decisions of the OECD Council in June, 1976. TUAC has been involved in consultations with the Committee for International Investments and Multinational Enterprises and, lately, its Working Group on the Guidelines. The trade unions have had a major and in some cases decisive role in bringing cases related to the Guidelines to the attention of the Governments and the OECD. They will continue their active involvement in the follow-up of the Guidelines. A basic demand of TUAC is that the methods for doing this and carrying out the necessary consultations be improved both at the company, national and international levels.
2. The trade unions judge the Guidelines from the point of view of their impact on the real world. Their existence created expectations among the unions who hoped that the climate for their relations with multinational enterprises would change for the better. Evidence of this, after almost three years of experience, still is not forthcoming. There is very little to show that the world of the multinational enterprise has been changed. Furthermore, there is very little evidence that the present voluntary set of Guidelines is being vigorously

pursued or that there is effective action to create a framework within which their implementation could be ensured.

3. TUAC underlines that even if its involvement in the follow-up of the Guidelines so far has been active and will continue to be so, it is not primarily for the trade union movement to see to the functioning of the Guidelines. They were agreed upon by Governments, who took upon themselves the responsibility to address them to the multinational enterprises. Consequently, they should also ensure their implementation.

4. Unless the Guidelines are really implemented, the trade union movement will have to seriously consider their usefulness and also any further support to them. As a compromise, TUAC accepted the Guidelines in 1976 as a first step. At that time, the trade unions clearly envisaged not only their implementation but also further development. If no change to the better has taken place in the real world due to the Guidelines, what was the use of the whole exercise? And if this remains the verdict, all parties will be confronted with a loss of credibility due to a collapse of the discussions. In 1979, OECD must thus be prepared to take the next step.

5. In the context of the present review process, and also looking beyond it, TUAC attaches importance to the implementation, the interpretation and a revision of the Guidelines. Implementation will have to take place both at the company, national and international levels. Interpretation of the provisions of the Guidelines is a *sine qua non* for any meaningful implementation. And a revision of the text itself is necessary in order to make it conform to general developments in other international organizations as well as to respond to cases that have demonstrated lacunae in the present text itself.»

2. Role of the IME Committee

105. Since the very first formal consultation in 1977 between the IME Committee and TUAC, the latter insisted upon the IME Committee's role in the *interpretation of the Guidelines*, through the introduction of cases as can be read in the following abstract of the
«*Note from the Secretary-General of the TUAC to the Chairman and Members of the Committee of International Investment and Multinational Enterprises giving details of the cases to be discussed during the exchange of views on 30th March, 1977 between the Committee and the TUAC.*

– Transmitted to the Secretary-General of the OECD on 24th March, 1977.

1. In our Note of 11th February, 1977 we said that we would bring to the Committee's attention about fifteen cases of problems experienced by the trade unions in local entities of multinational enterprises or with such enterprises generally, these being problems relating to the application of one or other of the Guidelines and to their interpretation. We also said that these cases would be submitted to Members of the Committee for information and in order to illustrate the types of problem which, in the experience of the trade unions,

the implementation of the Guidelines involves. We are now forwarding these cases for preliminary study by the Members of the Committee, together with *the following observations regarding the issues they raise and how they should be dealt with during the joint Review on 30th March.*

For purpose of information and illustration

2. The following cases are submitted at this stage for purposes of information and illustration when the Committee discusses the scope of the Guidelines and more particularly of the General Policies, the policies for achieving the economic and social objectives of Member Countries, and the Policies for Employment and Industrial Relations. They comprise the cases raised by the International Metalworkers' Federation (IMF): MOTOR IBERICA, MASSEY FERGUSON, BLACK and DECKER LTD, PHILIPS, POCLAIN, BENDIX, SIEMENS, WARNER-LAMBERT, LITTON INDUSTRIES, and INTERNATIONAL TELEPHONE AND TELEGRAPH CORPORATION (ITT), together with the following case raised by the International Federation of Employees and Technicians (FIET): CITYCORP.

It is hoped that the IME Committee will take note of the problems illustrated by these cases and that an exchange of views will be held on whether the Committee could give special attention to such questions as trade union recognition, the supply of information when consultations are held regarding decisions of importance to employees, and the need for meeting with enterprises at decision-making level.

3. It should be added that two or three of the above-mentioned cases may lead to developments as a result of which the Committee, together with the Member Governments directly concerned, may be faced with problems regarding how to interpret the Guidelines.»

The Badger Case, involving the problem of the responsibility of headquarters for the debts of its affiliates, on which I will expand later in detail[9] was introduced as a test case for the effectiveness of the Guidelines.

106. At the occasion of the first meeting of the Levy group the General Secretary of TUAC, Henri Bernard, insisted again on this role of interpretation. In a letter of October 12, 1977 to the Chairman of the Ad-Hoc Working Group, he wrote:
«At the occasion of the meeting, on 13th and 14th October, of the Ad-Hoc Group of the Committee on International Investment and Multinational Enterprises, we wish to reaffirm the abiding interest of our affiliated organizations that the Committee should reach conclusions concerning the implementation of the principle of the social responsibility of a mother company in case of a closure of an affiliated entity, on the basis of the request of the Belgian

9. See Part II, I.

Government and our own request in relation to the interpretation to be given to article 6 of the section on employment and industrial relations of the guidelines for multinational enterprises.

We have enclosed a copy of the agreement which was reached on 25th April in the case of the closure of the Belgian subsidiary of Badger Inc. All parties involved in the satisfactory solution reached (international management, local trade unions, host government) in that case will agree that they duly respected the OECD Guidelines.[10]

However, questions remain to be answered as to the limits and scope of implementation of the Principle, as well as to the significance as a precedent of the case of implementation referred to above.

Our organizations attach a vital importance to the Committee giving a considered reply to the above questions.

We wish finally to state that our organizations would be ready to examine jointly with the IIME Committee the working of the consultation procedures and we anticipate to make our views known on this issue to the Chairman of the IIME Committee.»

107. The following letter of 7 December 1977 was forwarded by the OECD Secretariat to the Secretary General of TUAC:

«Dear Sir,

I have been requested by the Committee on International Investment and Multinational Enteprises to invite your Organization to a second exchange of views with the Committee on matters arising under the OECD Guidelines for Multinational Enterprises. If you agree, this meeting could take place in the morning on Tuesday, 11th April 1978, beginning at 10.00 hours.

As you know, the Committee has been studying the material which was submitted by the TUAC on 30th March 1977 when the first exchange of views took place. At its subsequent meeting on 7th–8th July 1977, the IME Committee again discussed these matters and set up an Ad Hoc Working Group to examine this material further which met on 13th–14th October 1977 so that the plenary Committee, at its meeting on 5th–6th December, had before it a report from the Working Group. The comments which follow are designed to give your members as complete an account as possible of the Committee's discussions in the hope that they will prove useful in your preparations for the next exchange of views.

A number of points of procedure arising in connection with the meetings with TUAC and their follow-up by the Committee were mentioned in the letter which was addressed to you on 19th April 1977 by Mr. C. G. Wootton, Deputy Secretary-General of the OECD. The subsequent deliberations of the Committee have confirmed its members in their opinion that it is important for a proper functioning of the Guidelines, as one of the three elements of the Ministerial Declaration and the Council Decisions of June 1976, that all parties

10. See further no. 125.

should understand and follow the procedures that were laid down at that time.

Of particular relevance in this connection are paragraph 3 of the Council's 1976 Decision which lays down that: 'The Committee shall not reach conclusions on the conduct of individual enterprises'; paragraph 2 'the Committee shall periodically invite the BIAC and the TUAC to express their views on matters related to the Guidelines and shall take account of such views in its report to the Council'; paragraph 4 'Member countries may request that consultations be held in the Committee on any problem arising from the fact that multinational enterprises are made subject to conflicting requirements.'

In conformity with the above procedures, the Committee has used the material presented by TUAC with a view to gaining experience of the practical problems that arise in connection with the Guidelines and this in view of the preparation of the report the Committee has to submit to the OECD Council after three years of application of the 1976 Ministerial Declaration and the related Council Decisions. In this connection, the Committee sought to discern what issues of a more general application were raised in the material on cases submitted by TUAC which would help the Committee to determine any areas where the intent of a particular Guideline, or the coverage of the Guidelines as a whole, seemed to call for further discussion.

It was noted that most of the cases submitted by TUAC in their presentation did not seem to call for further discussion of either the intent or coverage of the Guidelines and would seem to be best dealt with under national legislation and procedures, as appropriate. Some cases seemed to fall outside the intended scope of the Guidelines. It can be said already at this stage, and although some of the matters raised by the TUAC submission still remain to be discussed, that the remaining cases have proved to be extremely useful to the Committee in the framework of the review process and the report to the Council noted earlier. The issues thus raised refer to a number of paragraphs of the Employment and Industrial Relations Guideline, notably paragraph 1 (activities of trade union and other bona fide organizations of employees), paragraph 2 (facilitating collective bargaining), paragraph 3 (dealing with the provision of information to employees), paragraph 4 (standards of employment and industrial relations), paragraph 6 (provision of reasonable notice to employees of changes in their operations and mitigation to the maximum extent practicable of adverse effects), paragraph 8 (influence on negotiations), paragraph 9 (negotiations on collective bargaining) and to the Guidelines on 'General Policies', 'Science and Technology', 'Disclosure of Information', as well as to the general issue of the responsibility of a parent company in the application of the Guidelines.

Thus, the material provided by TUAC in its first exchange of views with the IME Committee on experience under the Guidelines has proved to be very useful to the Committee in raising issues meriting further consideration and in stimulating discussion. As noted above, and as was no doubt inevitable in the very early stages of a new undertaking for all parties, the Committee did find itself faced with some problems in dealing with the material submitted by TUAC, notably in extracting from some of the cases the matters that were relevant to clarification of the intent or coverage of the Guidelines and as regards a possible wish by TUAC to secure the opinion of the Committee on specific cases. The Committee would like to suggest that submission of any written material some time in advance of the next exchange of views would permit better preparation of the meeting as would as clear an indication as possible of the general point at issue in any submission of material relating to a specific case.

The Belgian Government presented its understanding of the application of the Guidelines in the light of a specific case which the Committee dealt with under its responsibility to hold an exchange of views on matters related to the Guidelines at the request of a Member Government, as noted above, the same case having been submitted also by TUAC. The Committee has since been informed by the Belgian Government that, in this particular affair, a solution judged satisfactory by all parties involved has been reached. The Committee has further noted statements by the Belgian Government and TUAC expressing satisfaction with the settlement. The Committee was also informed by the Danish authorities – as well as by TUAC – of an issue relating to the coverage of the Guidelines with respect to an industrial dispute. The Committee and the Ad Hoc Working Group mentioned above have not yet discussed this issue in detail. The Committee will be taking account of the issues raised by the Belgian and Danish Governments in its future work.»

108. In his opening statement at the occasion of the consultation with the IME Committee on April 11, 1978, TUAC's President remarked:
«I am bound to put to you questions and issues, some of which were already submitted by TUAC last year. Indeed, we have no choice than to seek clarifications and answers from your Committee which is the most authorised and competent body to clarify matters related to the OECD Guidelines for Multinational Enterprises.»

In its statement, at the occasion of the same meeting TUAC underlined that «it is fully aware that OECD 'shall not reach conclusions on the conduct of individual enterprises' as the Council's Decision states, but it strongly resents the absence of any effort to explain and specify to TUAC affiliated organizations the often vague and ambiguous text of the Guidelines. It resents the refusal of the IME Committee to interpret the Guidelines at the hand of numerous concrete examples of their interpretation in practice which TUAC submitted to the Committee over a year ago.
To quote some issues which need clarification:
  (i) what responsibility do parent companies have under the Guidelines for the actions of their subsidiaries? Do such responsibilities, when existing, depend on the degree of ownership or on the nature of the control held by the parent and what its control means in this context?
 (ii) what does 'the right of employees to be represented by trade-unions' imply, specifically in terms of encouragement to use such right, and what are the limits of intervention of international headquarters in relation to local management in this field?
(iii) Does the IIME Committee recognize that the transfer of workers, pro-

109

duction, facilities and products from foreign affiliates 'in the context of bona fide negotiations with representatives of employees on conditions of employment, or while employees are exercising a right to organise is incompatible with the spirit of the Guidelines'. If so, does it recognize that not mentioning this practice is a loophole in the Guidelines?

(iv) To what extent is the transfer abroad of profitable production compatible with paragraph 5 of the Guidelines' General Policies?

(v) Does the IIME Committee consider that the concept of 'reasonable notice' in paragraph 6 of the Guideline on Employment and Industrial Relations is applicable to notice given to employees before and not after a firm decision on changes in operations has already been made and begun to be implemented?

(vi) Does not paragraph 9 of the Guideline on Employment and Industrial Relations apply in the case of the closure of a subsidiary by a mother company? Specifically, should not the mother company management itself create consultations with representatives of the employees?

(vii) Are groupings of the kind such as the European airline groupings within the coverage and intent of the Guidelines?

In addition to the submission made by TUAC last year, further illustrations of these issues are given by cases raised by ITF, CNV (Holland), and USS (Switzerland).»

. . . .

«Individual cases submitted to the IIME Committee by governments, BIAC or TUAC, should be used not only 'with a view to gaining experience of the practical problems that arise in connection with the Guidelines, in view of the preparation of the report the Committee has to submit to the OECD Council after three years of application' (as stated in the letter of December 7, 1977), but also with a view to clarifying for the members of TUAC and BIAC the relevant provisions of the Guidelines and to gradually promoting agreed international custom and practice.»

. . . .

«If the Committee should remain silent on these matters and appear unable to explain the meaning of the Guidelines on a current basis, to indicate its short-comings or eliminate contradictions, to give interpretations without of course taking sides in individual conflicts, trade-unions will not be able to refer to the Guidelines as a source of authority in their day-to-day dealings with multinational enterprises and solve problems on their bases.

The result must be that the OECD texts lose their credibility, interest and support needed to make them function.»

109. TUAC's President concluded his opening remarks at the April 11, 1978 meeting as follows:

«Colleagues, who will speak after me, will qualify some of these questions with additional facts and circumstances related to cases which are actually going on. Before they speak up, I would like however to underline the main reasons why we attach such a decisive importance to your answers.

Indeed, we insist to get answers to these questions because, behind them, there are situations where workers, hundreds and thousands, are in danger of loosing their jobs. Because there are situations where workers cannot effectively be represented by trade-unions, or where employees representatives cannot negotiate because this right is effectively denied by anti-trade-union man-oeuvres or by the distance and obstacles put between them and the levels of effective decision makers. Because there are situations where vital decisions affecting the livelihood of the workers concerned are taken without appro-priate notification and consultation, without the necessary information being passed and discussed. . . .

Increasingly, questions are being put whether trade-union support to the Guidelines is still justified. The urge for more and more binding rules will no doubt increase if the OECD Guidelines by their non-binding nature should appear to be an inefficient instrument to control the activities of multinational enterprises.

The non-binding nature of the Guidelines make the consultation procedures between governments, enterprises and trade-unions a key to their effective implementation. We regret to note that the governments were not able, until now, after a full year of meetings and discussions on our cases, to come answering to the questions we had been putting to them. We know, indeed, that this failure reflects various national complex situations, home and host coun-tries difficult reconciliation of interests. We experience this too. But, should the Committee remain silent on these matters and appear unable to explain the meaning of the Guidelines on a current basis, to indicate its short-comings or eliminate contradictions, to give interpretations without of course taking sides in individual conflicts, trade-unions will not be able to refer to the Guidelines as a source of authority in their day-to-day dealings with multinational enterprises and solve problems on their bases.

The result must be that the OECD texts lose their credibility, interest and support.

We would find this a step backward and a blow to international co-operation aimed at problem solving. We do not want this to happen. TUAC repeats its willingness to make OECD Guidelines operational but, for that, it needs answers from the Member Governments to the questions and issues we are putting to you. We would like you to inform appropriately the OECD Council of TUAC attitude and we refer to our written statement for further suggestions on how to improve the consultation procedures both at OECD and national levels.»

. . .

«In conclusion, TUAC would like to make Member governments conscious of the long and difficult process involved in disseminating information about the

Guidelines and their implementation, to the key level of shop stewards and local trade-unions officers directly confronted with the problems created by the growing activities of multinational enterprises.
- At this stage, what is vital is to provide the workers representatives at the rank and file level with the clarifications and concrete examples which will prove that the Guidelines are useful for trade-unionists.
- At this stage, what is also needed is that national governments individually spell out before the public opinion and specially before trade-unions representing workers directly experiencing difficulties and problems with multinational enterprises, the concrete governmental and/or legislative commitments to see to it that the provisions of the OECD Guidelines be given effect.»

110. TUAC insisted again on the interpretation of the Guidelines by the IME Committee at the occasion of the informal consultation between the Working Group and TUAC held on 29th January 1979.
«Unless there is a clear interpretation of the meaning of the Guidelines» the TUAC statement read, «the responsibility for observing and implementing them can be evaded. TUAC regrets that despite the discussions on a number of cases by the Committee for International Investments and Multinational Enterprises and its Working Group on the Guidelines, no interpretation of in particular questions of paramount trade union interest have been given. Unless the Governments agree on the meaning and general purpose of what they have collectively adopted, and say so to all parties concerned, the implementation of the Guidelines is seriously impaired. It is the view of TUAC that, as part of the review process, the report to the OECD Council in June 1979 should give a clear interpretation of the Guidelines. Furthermore, arrangements should be made for the further development of the interpretation process. It is only against this background that TUAC has been prepared to participate in the informal discussions with the Committee's Working Group on the Guidelines.
Regarding the interpretation of the Guidelines in their present form, there are a number of questions that have to be dealt with urgently. To the extent they are already discussed by the Working Group on the Guidelines, together with TUAC and BIAC, such discussions will have to serve an interpretation by the Summer of 1979. There are important questions, such as the responsibility of the parent company, which have not yet been discussed, and they will have to be taken up in the review process as well, in consultation with TUAC and BIAC.
TUAC does not wish to present an exhaustive list of questions where interpretation is asked for. The cases brought forth by the trade unions hitherto illustrate concerns, and difficulties, that have come up during the first years of experience of the Guidelines. In stressing the need for interpretation, the trade unions are above all concerned about the usefulness of the Guidelines to their own members. Both the Governments and the OECD have recently increasingly solicited the views of the unions and have recognized that the trade unions have a role in following up the Guidelines, both nationally and, through

TUAC, internationally. But in the absence of clearer rules and interpretations, the unions, just as Governments, will have to make interpretations nationally themselves. Differences from one country to another in such interpretations only serve confusion and render the Guidelines inefficient.

The interest of TUAC at this stage focusses itself above all on the following questions:

a. *Parent company responsibilities* (paragraphs 6 and 8 of the Guidelines). It must be recognized that the parent company has a responsibility for all areas covered by the Guidelines, and a responsibility to inform the local entity of decisions and strategies affecting it.

b. *Local law and regulations* (introduction to the section on employment and industrial relations). The words 'within the framework of law' etc. should not be interpreted so as to enable the enterprises to take a minimalistic line and abstain from their obligations under the Guidelines merely by referring to the absence of specific national legal obligations. The interpretation should at least correspond to the meaning of 'taking into account national circumstances' in the ILO.

c. *Recognition of trade unions* (paragraph 1 of the employment and industrial relations section). An unequivocal pronouncement on this is a precondition for the Guidelines being a useful instrument for the trade unions. It should be classified that this concerns non-manual workers as well, and especially bank employees. The words 'and other bona fide organisations of employees' should be interpreted in a way to cover the International Trade Secretariats.

d. *Right to trade union consultation within multinational enterprises* (paragraph 2 of the employment and industrial relations section). Necessary facilities must be interpreted in a way to cover facilities for contacts with employees in other parts of the same multinational enterprise. Information, to be meaningful, must include enterprise. Information, to be meaningful, must include information on the enterprise as a whole. The provisions of the Guidelines must also be interpreted in a way that will not hinder representatives of the International Trade Secretariats to participate in negotiations when necessary.

e. *Information to employees* (paragraph 3 of the employment and industrial relations section). This information will have to include future plans, in order to give a true and fair view of the entity or the enterprise.

f. *Obligation to negotiate future plans* (paragraph 6 of the employment and industrial relations section). Such negotiations should be seen as mandatory, and they should be introduced immediately when such changes in operations can be anticipated as would have major effects upon the livelihood of the employees. This paragraph, in the view of TUAC, contains both the obligation to give reasonable notice, i.e. notice as soon as the management becomes aware of an impending situation, and also the obligation to mitigate adverse effects through negotiations. Such negotiations should take place before any final decisions are made, and, whenever necessary, they should enable to alter any decision made without the participation of the representatives of the employees.

113

g. The Guidelines should also be recognized to cover such groupings as those of airline companies which regardless of their legal structure or the presence or absence of direct investment by the participating companies function as multinational enterprises.

TUAC notes that there cannot be conflicting interpretations between those of the OECD Guidelines and other relevant instruments, in particular the Tripartite Declaration on Multinational Enterprises and Social Policy, adopted by the ILO Governing Body. As the ILO instrument will also have its own follow-up procedure, it is imperative that OECD Governments, when interpreting the Guidelines, ensure that there are no conflicts with other relevant international instruments.

IV. Conclusions

For the trade union movement, the OECD Guidelines were a first step towards more specific, functioning rules of the game. There has been little progress in making them work, and the follow-up has largely been a theoretical exercise on the level of the Committee for International Investment and Multinational Enterprises. The key question now is their implementation on the everyday working level, in the enterprises themselves. Within this implementation process, the crucial element is the creation of a system of information and consultation at both the company, national and international levels.»

111. TUAC presented also at the occasion of the April 11, 1978 meeting with IME a number of *suggestions for effective consultations procedures*. These read as follows:
«On the 21st of June, 1976, the governments of the OECD Member countries opened a new field for co-operation in the area of international investment and multinational enterprises. At the same time, they introduced a new procedure as they addressed themselves to non-governmental bodies.
By addressing guidelines for behaviour to multinational enterprises operating in their territories, the governments made the effectiveness of their initiative dependent on the co-operation of these enterprises and all those who are directly involved in their activities. In full recognition of the major role trade unions play in this domain, the governments set up consultation procedures providing discussions with TUAC on matters related to these Guidelines. This, of course, should not preclude OECD and Members governments from taking into account TUAC's views on all matters covered by the Declaration including the effectiveness of the consultation procedures themselves and the follow-up which the IIME Committee has been giving to the work which was concluded by the OECD some two years ago.

. . . .

Satisfactory answers related to specific cases cannot be found in a restricted monologue between governments. The consultation procedures, therefore, should consist of continued consultations and exchange of views with the TUAC. Such a discussion should include the participation of individual enterprises as intended in article 3 of the consultation procedures. TUAC expresses the hope that Member countries will make proposals to that effect to the Committee, and that the other Members will not object to such proposals. TUAC noted with satisfaction the positive attitude towards the invitation of individual enterprises expressed by Sir Michael Clapham, BIAC representative, during the March consultation last year.

In meetings of this nature, matters such as fact-finding, the settlement of disputes at a national level, the requirement for uniformity of interpretation, the inter-action between national, bilateral and multilateral actions, should be equally discussed. A fact-finding procedure should be established. The IIME Committee should also help to establish ad hoc co-operation, bilateral or multilateral, between the home and host countries, involving governments, employers' organizations and trade-unions and the enterprises concerned in order to further the settlement of conflicts arising in respect to matters within the scope of the Guidelines.»

112. In its statement of April 11, 1978 TUAC expanded also on:
«Possible further TUAC contributions to the work of the IIME Committee. Should a dialogue be established at last on the above requirements for making the Guidelines more effective TUAC will endeavour to contribute further to the work of the IIME Committee. The governments of OECD Member countries have decided to review the Guidelines for multinational enterprises including the consultation procedures within three years from the adoption of the Declaration on International Investment and Multinational Enterprises. TUAC attaches the greatest importance to the revision and suggests that the TUAC should be closely associated to the work in all its stages.

Information on activities, results and plans of multinational enterprises as a whole and of their different entities is one of the crucial issues on which the effectiveness of the Guidelines depends. TUAC has noted the work pursued in this field by the UN as well as the efforts of BIAC. The situation is, however, still unsatisfactory and very important problems remain unsolved. This hampers collective bargaining and consultation for the sake of eliminating or reducing adverse effects of changes in operations. The IIME Committee is requested to undertake, in co-operation with BIAC and TUAC, a survey of national laws, rules and practices and their applicability to multinational enterprises both in the home and the host countries in order to formulate adequate general principles. These efforts should not be limited to harmonization of accounting standards. TUAC reflects the problems experienced in this field in the Scandinavian context in a paper[11] and submits it to the Committee as a proposed starting point.

The applicability of the Guidelines to international banking requires careful examination by the IIME Committee. While the problem of recognition of trade unions in the spirit of point 1 of the chapter, Employment and Industrial

11. See no. 177.

Relations, confronts the trade unions concerned with considerable difficulties in this sector – the refusal to recognize trade unions being often a matter of policy defined by international headquarters – this is merely the tip of the iceberg. TUAC requests the IIME Committee to proceed with this examination. More specifically, the Committee is requested first to identify those provisions of the Guidelines that apply to transnational banks, then to identify those aspects of international banking which, though they cause concern, are beyond the scope of the Guidelines. TUAC considers that to deal satisfactorily with international banking, OECD should complement the Guidelines by a spearate instrument of a mandatory nature – see the presentation by TCO and FIET in Appendix 4 hereafter.

The IIME Committee is requested to proceed with the consultations and surveys mentioned in the Decisions of the Council on National Treatment and on International Investment Incentives and Disincentives, and to inform TUAC on its findings.

However, before considering new efforts and plans for further co-operation, TUAC has to answer questions from its members who represent workers directly confronted with problems created by multinational enterprises, namely whether TUAC support to the Guidelines is still justified.

The answer depends a great deal on the outcome of today's consultation.»

3. TUAC and the 'legal' nature of the Guidelines

113. Karl Nandrup Dahl from LO – Norway presented a paper on the legal nature of the Guidelines to the TUAC Working Group on Multinational Enterprises (Paris, 19–20 February 1979). It was decided that the Group should discuss the paper at its meeting after the review process has been complemented, after which a document could possibly be forwarded to the OECD for discussion. The Dahl's proposal reads as follows:

«*Revision of the OECD Guidelines for Multinational Companies:*

The memberstates should be committed by international law to implement in their national legislation in the guidelines respecting multinational companies.

I. Background and procedure for the decisions taken by the OEEC Council that are binding by international law.

When the OEEC was established in 1948 the members agreed that the OEEC should be given the power to take decisions that could commit the memberstates by international law. It was recognized that so far no intergovernmental organization had been given the power by member states to take decisions that were legally binding. The coming economic problems of co-operation, however, were considered to be so important and difficult that it would not be possible to solve them without making the OEEC competent to take binding decisions. According to the OEEC Convention of 1948 the Council could take such decisions, as follows:

1. Adopt internationally legally binding decisions which the member states were committed to implement in their national legislation.
2. Adopt recommendations which the member states, other governments and international organizations would be called upon to implement in their national legislation.
3. Adopt resolutions on how to apply the OEEC decisions and tasks.

II. When the OEEC was reorganized on 14 December 1960 with a new title: 'Organization for Economic Co-operation and Development' the power vested in the OEEC Council to adopt internationally legally binding decisions was essentially maintained.

III. To-day the OECD Council may take internationally binding decisions in accordance with Article 5 and Article 6 of the Convention. Article 5 reads as follows:

'In order to achieve its aims, the Organisation may:
a. take decisions which, except as otherwise provided, shall be binding on all the Members;
b. make recommendations to Members, and
c. enter into agreements with Members, non-member States and international organisations.'

Article 6 reads as follows:
'1. Unless the Organisation otherwise agrees unanimously for special cases, decisions shall be taken and recommendations shall be made by mutual agreement of all the Members.
2. Each Member shall have one vote. If a Member abstains from voting on a decision or recommendation, such abstention shall not invalidate the decision or recommendation which shall be applicable to the other Members but not to the abstaining Member.
3. No decision shall be binding on any Member until it has complied with the requirements of its own constitutional procedures. The other Members may agree that such a decision shall apply provisionally to them.'

IV. The OECD Council decisions under the below A, B, and C have been taken according to Article 5 of the Convention reading as follows:
'In order to achieve its aims the Organisation may:
a. take decisions which, except as otherwise provided, shall be binding on all the members.'
A. The OECD Council decision on intergovernmental consultation procedure, concerning the implementation of the guidelines for multinational enterprises.
B. The OECD Council decision on national treatment of foreign investments and companies.

C. The OECD Council decision concerning measures to promote or limit international investments.

V. The OECD Council decisions under the below A and B have been taken in accordance with Article 5 of the Convention, reading as follows:
'In order to achieve its aims the Organisation may:
b. make recommendations to Members.'
A. The Declaration concerning international investments and multinational companies.
B. The appendix to the Declaration concerning international investments and multinational companies under the title: *'Guidelines for Multinational Enterprises'*.

VI. The OECD recommendations according to Article 5, p.b) of the Convention on guidelines for multinational companies (above B) may be replaced fully or partly an international legally binding decision with the same contents as the Guidelines for multinational companies. If so, this internationally legally binding decision must be taken by the OECD Council by virtue of Article 5, p. a) of the Convention.

VII. The OECD recommendation according to Article 5 p. b) of the Convention concerning Guidelines for multinational companies (above B) may be maintained. The OECD Council may take internationally legally binding decisions which may cover certain or all of the guidelines for multinational companies, which in such a case would supplement the OECD recommendation on guidelines for multinational companies. The Member states who wish to be bound by such an internationally legally binding decision would vote for the decision, while the member states who do not wish to be internationally legally committed to apply the guidelines for multinational companies in their national legislation may abstain from voting during the voting by the OECD Council on the proposal for legally binding decisions.

VIII. A draft internationally binding decision by the OECD Council on the application of the Guidelines for multinational companies by the Member states might read as follows:

Decision of the OECD Council

Adoption of Guidelines for Multinational Companies

———— 1979

The Council

Having regard to Articles 2 a) and 5 a) of the Convention on the Organization for Economic Co-operation and Development of 14th December 1960;
having regard to the Declaration on International Investment and Multi-

national Enterprises of 21st and 22nd June 1976 by the governments of OECD Member countries;

having regard to the Decision of the Council of 21st–22nd June 1976 concerning

Inter-governmental Consultation Procedures on the Application of the Guidelines for Multinational Enterprises;

having regard to the Decision of the Council on National Treatment of Multinational Enterprises of 21st–22nd June 1976;

having regard to the Decision of the Council on Measures to Promote and Limit International Investments of 21st–22nd June 1976;

having regard to the Tripartite Declaration of Principles of the International Labour Organization on Multinational Enterprises and Social Policy, adopted by the ILO Governing Body on 16th November 1977;

On the proposal by the Committee on International Investments and Multinational Enterprises have take the following:

Decision:

I. The authorities concerned in each Member country shall instruct the multinational enterprises to submit each year the following information on the enterprises and their activities:

1. The structure of the enterprise indicating the name and location of the parent company, affiliates and its percentage ownership.
2. The geographical area where the activities are carried out by the parent company and its affiliates.
3. The account of results and gross sales per geographical area for the main groups of products and for the enterprise as a whole.
4. Significant capital investments per geographical area and investments in important groups of products for the enterprise as a whole.
5. An analysis of financing for the enterprise as a whole.
6. The average number of employees in each geographical area.
7. Research and development expenditure for the enterprise as a whole.
8. Principles followed in respect of intra-group pricing.
9. The control systems established to secure the correctness of the information supplied by the enterprise to the authorities.

II. The authorities concerned in each member country shall prohibit the multinational enterprises to take measures leading to:

a. Purchase limiting competition in the relevant marked area.
b. Use of questionable business methods.
c. Unreasonable refusal of business.
d. Abuse of patents, trade marks or other rights in order to limit competition in the relevant market area.
e. Discriminatory pricing and . . . using such pricing between affiliated enterprises as a means tax of affecting competition for competing companies.
f. Restrictions on the freedom of purchasers, distributors and licensees to resell, export, purchase and develop their operations consistent with the need for specialization and sound commercial practice.

119

g. Participation in or otherwise contributing towards strengthening international or national cartels limiting competition, or agreements limiting competition which are in contravention with international law and practice.

III. The authorities concerned in each Member country shall instruct the enterprise to:
a. provide the information on all activities on its territory and abroad which is necessary for the correct taxation of the enterprise.
b. refrain from pricing (transfer pricing) which is contrary to the market prices in order to avoid national taxation of the profit of the enterprise.

IV. The authorities concerned in each Member country shall secure that:
a. The enterprise respects the freedom of association and the free right of collective bargaining.
b. The organizations representing the employees in the enterprises should be given the necessary conditions to participate in the development of collective agreements.
c. The employees should be given information on the budgets and accounts of result of the parent company and its affiliates.

V. The authorities concerned shall consult with the most representative organizations of employees and employers in the Member country on the application and implementation of this Council decision.

VI. The Member country shall report each year to the Committee on Investments and multinational companies on the application of the Council decision by its national legislation and practice.

VII. This Council decision shall take effect on. . . . 19 . .

VIII. The OEEC until 1960 and the OECD since 1960 previously by its Council has taken internationally legally binding decisions in virtue of the Convention Article 5. Below are examples on such decisions taken by the OEEC Council and the OECD Council:
1. The OEEC Council Decision of 30th October 1953, as amended later, governing the Employment of Nationals of other Member countries.
2. The OECD Council Decision of 12th December 1961 on 'Code of Liberalisation of Current Invisible Operations'.
3. The OECD Council Decision – Resolution of 12th October 1967 on the Draft Convention on the Protection of Foreign Property.»

4. Composition of the TUAC delegation

114.   TUAC's delegation consisted mostly of representatives from different affiliates of TUAC. With rare exceptions, these representatives are members of the Study departments of their respective organizations. On October 23, 1978, the

following delegation participated in the consultations with the Levy Group:
Mr. Paul Barton, AFL–CIO – United States
Mr. John Harker, CLC – Canada
Mr. Kai Aagaard, LO – Norway
Mr. Lennart Nyström, LO – Sweden
Mr. Peer Carlsen, LO – Denmark
Mr. Tom Etty, FNV – Netherlands
Mr. Bartho Pronk, CNV – Netherlands
Mr. Carl Wilms-Wright, ICFTU (Brussels)
Mr. Emile Vervliet, WCL (Brussels)
Mr. Sten Lindahl, Nordic Council of Trade Unions (Stockholm)
Mr. Karl Casserini, IMF (Geneva)
Mr. K. A. Golding, ITF (London)
Mr Charles Ford, ITLGWF (Brussels)
Mr. Kari Tapiola, General Secretary, TUAC

Part II. The Impact of the Guidelines. Cases – Issues and Clarification

115. All the cases and ensuing issues, which were discussed in the IME Committee, were introduced by TUAC. Three cases were also introduced by Governments, one by the Belgian Government, namely the Badger Case, one by the Danish Government, the Hertz Case and one by the Dutch Government, the Batco Case.[1] These individual cases and the general issues they involved were examined by Governments, in the IME Committee and in the Levy Working Group as well as with BIAC and TUAC during the formal and informal discussions they had with the IME Committee and the Levy Working Group respectively.

116. In fact, these discussions served two purposes: firstly, as an input for the review of the Guidelines in 1979, and secondly, in order to obtain clarification of certain Guidelines. The review led to one amendment of the Guidelines, changes in the follow-up procedure, whilst the IME report also contains an important number of clarifications.

117. The cases and the issues they involved are as follows:

Introduced March, 30th, 1977:

– The co-responsibility of the parent company and subsidiaries. *The Badger Case*
Trade union rights: *MOTOR IBERICA*, Spanish subsidiary of *MASSEY FERGUSON*
Trade union recognition by the multinational subsidiary of *BLACK AND DECKER LIMITED* in Great Britain
PHILIPS: permission for leave of absence for participation at an international trade union seminar on developments within PHILIPS, and meetings with trade unions at world level
Information by *POCLAIN* in a situation of economic difficulties, mass dismissals and possibility of takeover

---

1. The difference is important. The advisory bodies can *express* their point of views under point 2 of the Decision of the Council on Intergovernmental Consultation Procedures; point 1 foresees that on request of a Government *an exchange of views* shall be held. This means that when a Government raises a problem, exchange of views, a discussion thus, will be held, while when TUAC or BIAC raise a problem, the Committee may or may not discuss the problem at his own discretion.

International structural reorganization within *BENDIX* and the loss of employment; job guarantees based on state subsidies
Closure of *SIEMENS* plant in Belgium and employment commitments between the Government and SIEMENS in Belgium
Policy of *WARNER-LAMBERT* to close down its operations in Sweden
Production transfer with plant closure in Sweden by *LITTON INDUSTRIES*
PHILIPS Company: information of the trade unions and co-operation with them on plant closures in the Federal Republic of Germany
Changes in company structure by *INTERNATIONAL TELEPHONE AND TELEGRAPH CORPORATION (ITT)* in the Federal Republic of Germany, representation, direct information and participation by trade unions
World-wide union policy by *CITIBANK-CITICORP*
The transfer of staff across borders during a labour dispute (*Hertz*)

Introduced April 11th, 1978:

- Are European airline groupings, such as *KSSU or ATLAS*, Multinational Enterprises in the sense of par. 8 of the Introduction to the Guidelines?
- Transfer of a profit-making subsidiary to another country: *BRITISH AMERICAN TOBACCO COMPANY (BATCO)*
- Closing down of subsidiary by *FIRESTONE*. Access to the real decision makers
- Illustrative example: disclosure of information;
  International Credit Market and the *Multinational Bank.*

118. In the pages which follow, I will only deal with those cases and the issues involved which I consider relevant in relation to the Guidelines.[2] Where documents are available I shall relate the position of the concerned Government, of TUAC and of the Multinational, Enterprise or BIAC; and will then refer to the position taken by the IME Committee in its report to the Council and eventually give some personal comments. A short summary of the issue(s) with respect to the relevant Guideline, will be given for each of the involved cases and/or issues previously published.

2. One of the cases or issues, which TUAC introduced, was not relevant in relation to the Guidelines, and consequently was not further discussed in the IME report to the Council. It is published in annex IV.

I. The Co-Responsibility of the Parent Company and Subsidiaries. The Badger Case.[3]

«A precise legal definition of multinational enterprises is not required for the purposes of the guidelines. These usually comprise companies or other entities whose ownership is private, state or mixed, established in different countries and so linked that one or more of them may be able to exercise a significant influence over the activities of others and, in particular, to share knowledge and resources with the others. The degree of autonomy of each entity in relation to the others varies widely from one multinational enterprise to another, depending on the nature of the links between such entities and the fields of activity concerned. *For these reasons, the guidelines are addressed to the various entities within the multinational enterprise (parent companies and/or local entities) according to the actual distribution of responsibilities among them on the understanding that they will co-operate and provide assistance to one another as necessary to facilitate observance of the guidelines.* The word 'enterprise' as used in these guidelines refers to these various entities in accordance with their responsibilities.»

1. THE ISSUE

119. The question which was put to the IME Committee reads as follows: Is it consistent with the Guidelines that a 100 per cent owned and fully-controlled subsidiary of a foreign company ceases operations:
– without having given to its employees the legally required notice, which must allow the employees time to look for new jobs;
– without the affiliate disposing of the financial means necessary to pay the severance indemnities which are legally due if no term of notice is given, and without the assets to pay the indemnification which are legally due in the case of the closing down of an enterprise?

Has the parent company to assist the local entity in complying with its legal obligations? Badger C° headquarters, claimed it did not have such a responsibility on the basis of the principle of the limited responsibility of corporations.

3. See Blanpain R., *The Badger Case and the OECD Guidelines for Multinational Enterprises*, Kluwer, Deventer, 1977, 210 p.

2. NOTE BY THE BELGIAN DELEGATION

120. The Belgian delegation, headed by Mr. M. Eyskens, Secretary of Regional Economy, introduced following note:

«1. In the Declaration on International Investment and Multinational Enterprises, adopted by our Governments on 21st June, 1976, Member countries agreed that OECD countries should strengthen their co-operation and consultation procedures with respect to issues relating to international investment and multinational enterprises.
At that time OECD Member countries declared their readiness to consult one another on the above matters in conformity with the Decision of the Council relating to Inter-Governmental Consultation Procedures on the Guidelines for Multinational Enterprises. By its decision of 22nd December, 1976, the Council gave to the Committee on International Investment and Multinational Enterprises a mandate to the effect that it should periodically undertake exchanges of views on issues relating to the Guidelines and on experience acquired in their application. The Committee was to report periodically to the Council on these matters.

2. Experience of the application of the Guidelines by multinational enterprises can only be acquired by asking the Committee to give its opinion on behaviour or action by an individual enterprise deemed to be contrary to the Guidelines.
It is fully understood that, in accordance with the Decision of the Council, the Committee cannot reach any conclusions as to the behaviour of the enterprise in question. However, it is essential that members of the Committee should be able to express their views on the extent to which such behaviour is compatible with the spirit or letter of certain rules of good conduct contained in the Guidelines.

3. The Belgian Government is herewith submitting a memorandum on a specific case for the attention of members of the Committee on International Investment and Multinational Enterprises. This memorandum consists of two parts.
In the first part, the Belgian Government defines its interpretation of paragraphs 7 and 8 of the Introduction to the Guidelines and of paragraphs 6 and 9 of the section on 'Employment and Industrial Relations'.
The second part briefly describes the facts which have led the Belgian Government to submit this interpretation for the Committee's opinion.

4. The Belgian Government would like a constructive exchange of views on this interpretation to be held in the Committee, thus enabling it to define its own position more clearly and providing valuable information for the Governments of other Member countries which might be confronted with a similar situation.

126

5. It is by no means the intention of the Belgian Government to get the Committee on International Investment and Multinational Enterprises to pass judgement on the enterprise referred to in the Annex.

However, we draw the Committee's attention to the fact that the press, public opinion, employers' associations, trade unions and the Belgian Parliament all attach great importance to this matter and will be closely following the developments in terms of practical effects on the conduct of multinational enterprises.

6. Belgium's attitude towards international investment has always been inspired by confidence and fairness. Moreover, the activities of multinational enterprises have made a major contribution to the economic expansion of our country which, owing to its size, is extremely open to international trade. Our Government intends to pursue this action which aims at increasing co-operation among OECD Member countries.

7. In the absence of energetic action by our Governments, through the Committee on International Investment and Multinational Enterprises, other bodies – whether appropriate or not – will very quickly manifest their willingness to draw up another code of conduct that would be more effective and credible. The text prepared by the Committee for the meeting in June 1976 cannot be regarded as an end in itself and its application must be seen to give rise to tangible results.

8. The next meeting of the Committee is to be preceded by consultations with the Business and Industry Advisory Committee to the OECD and the Trade Union Advisory Committee to the OECD. The Belgian Government would like the views of these two organizations on the Guidelines in question to be made known, with a view to obtaining a diversified basis of opinion on which to establish the position to be adopted in similar cases. It is for this reason that the Belgian Government has requested the Secretary-General of the OECD to send this memorandum to the two advisory bodies in question.

9. As provided in the Decision of 21st June, 1976, we propose to members of the Committee that the enterprise in question should be given a hearing with a view to expressing its views on the application of the Guidelines.[4]

10. In accordance with the same Decision, the Belgian Government would like the Committee to set out Member countries' views on the matter in a report to the Council.»

«Annex I

The Belgian Government's interpretation regarding paras. 7 and 8 of the

4. Considering the successful outcome of negotiations between the Badger Company Inc. and the trade unions, the Belgian government dropped its request concerning the invitation of Badger to express its views on the case before the IME Committee.

120 — II. Impact of the Guidelines

Introduction to the Guidelines and paras. 6 and 9 of the section 'Employment and Industrial Relations'.

1. The subsidiary of a multinational enterprise is subject to the laws of the host country in the case of the cessation of its activities and in the case of the closure of this entity involving collective lay-offs or dismissals. This is in conformity with para. 7 of the Introduction which states that 'the entities of a multinational enterprise located in various countries are subject to the laws of these countries'.

The Guidelines also lay down that enterprises should take into account the general policy objectives of the Member countries in which they operate (General Policies, para. 1).

In the section 'Employment and Industrial Relations' it is specified that 'enterprises should within the framework of law, regulations and prevailing labour relations and employment practices, in each of the countries in which they operate, in considering changes in their operations which would have major effects upon the livelihood of their employees, in particular in the case of the closure of an entity involving collective lay-offs or dismissals, provide reasonable notice of such changes to representatives of their employees, and where appropriate to the relevant governmental authorities, and co-operate with the employee representatives and appropriate governmental authorities so as to mitigate to the maximum extent practicable adverse effects'.

2. A parent company is obliged to help its subsidiaries to fulfil their obligations. Para. 8 of the introduction to the Guidelines lays down that 'the guidelines are addressed to the various entities within the multinational enterprise (parent companies and/or local entities) according to the actual distribution of responsibilities among them on the understanding that they will co-operate and provide assistance to one another as necessary to facilitate observance of the guidelines. The word "enterprise" as used in these guidelines refers to these various entities in accordance with their responsibilities.'

The Guidelines thus recognize that the distribution of responsibilities as between the parent company and the local entities is of great importance. In the case of a multinational enterprise whose parent company has all the decision-making powers, the parent company must provide assistance to the local subsidiary to enable it to fulfil its obligations towards its employees. This means that in the case of the closure of a subsidiary the parent company must make a contribution towards financing the subsidiary's debts so as to 'minimize and resolve difficulties which may arise from its various operations' (para. 3 of the preamble to the Declaration).

3. Although observance of the Guidelines is voluntary (para. 6 of the Introduction), these Guidelines are nonetheless recommendations of our Governments to multinational enterprises and rules of conduct for them.

In accordance with the consideration that 'co-operation by Member countries can imporve the foreign investment climate, encourage the positive contribution which multinational enterprises can make to economic and social progress,

128

and minimize and resolve difficulties which may arise from their various operations', the Belgian Government takes the view that it is necessary within the framework of such co-operation to devise the means to compel a parent company to fulfil its obligations.

Annex II

The facts

1. The Belgian joint stock company BADGER (Belgium) NV is a 100 per cent subsidiary of the company Badger Co. Inc. The latter is wholly owned by Raytheon, and its head office is in Cambridge, Massachusetts, USA.

2. The Badger Group's operations in Europe are handled by a subsidiary in London – which also controls Badger France – and by the Hague Group of Companies which comprises Badger BV at the Hague, Badger Belgium NV in Antwerp, Badger GmbH in Wiesbaden and Badger Italiana Spa in Milan.
The Group as a whole has some 2,700 employees throughout the world. Its activities are devoted to design and construction services for petroleum and chemical works.

3. All the important decisions, e.g. contracts, selling prices, financial transactions, the establishment of pay scales and staff policy, are taken by the parent company in the United States.
The fact that Badger (Belgium) was completely 'integrated' and had no decision-making powers was recognized by the Tribunal de Commerce (Commercial Court) in Antwerp in its judgement of 14th February, 1977. Approval of a Composition with its creditors was refused by the Court. This is a joint agreement under the terms of which the enterprise which has suspended payment, but which is not guilty of fraud or a serious offence, avoids bankruptcy by obtaining from its creditors partial remission of its debts or time for payment, or even both these concessions.
Badger (Belgium) accepted the judgement and did not appeal.

4. The Badger (Belgium) NV company was formed in 1965. At the time of its closure in January 1977, 250 highly skilled employees were working for the enterprise. On 13th October, 1976 the staff was informed that orders were not forthcoming and that the enterprise was experiencing difficulties in continuing to operate. An attempt would be made to find valid solutions, in consultation with the Government.
On 23rd December, 1976 the staff was informed of the fact that efforts to find a new owner for the firm had failed and that the firm would shortly be closed down.

5. On 12th January, 1977 the staff was informed that the shareholders had decided to close down the enterprise. The members of the management of the parent company recognized the fact that this decision was taken by them.

On 14th January, 1977 the employees received letters terminating their individual contracts. The January salaries were paid.

6. Compulsory winding-up of Badger (Belgium) has been ordered and it has not paid its creditors. The compensation owed to members of staff in the case of the closure of an enterprise amounts, according to Belgian law, which makes no distinction here between national and foreign enterprises, to BF 250 million ($6,500,000) (compensation for dismissal + additional compensation for workers in the case of the closure of an enterprise). The parent company has refused to intervene to settle the liabilities of its subsidiary not covered by the available assets.»

3. TUAC's NOTE OF MARCH 24, 1977

121. TUAC's submission to the IME Committee reads as follows:

«*Test case of the effectiveness of the Guidelines*

5. The BADGER case raised by the Confédération des Syndicats Chrétiens de Belgique (CSC), the Fédération Générale du Travail de Belgique (FGTB), the International Federation of Employees and Technicians (FIET) and the World Federation of Non-Manual Workers (FMTNM), is dealt in a Note from the Belgian Delegation which the IME Committee will consider at its meeting on 31st March.

6. *In view of the Belgian Government's Note* and of the procedure which the IME Committee is adopting as a result, the TUAC will do no more than provide the joint review with factual information submitted by the Belgian employees and trade unions directly involved.
  (i) This factual information shows the absolute dependence of the local Belgian entity on the parent company and the full responsibility borne by the latter for the business done by its puppet company,
  (ii) It also shows that the sole function of the local entity was to supply the Group's other entities with technical services connected with the engineering, design and construction of chemical and petrochemical plant, these services being provided by the Belgian entity's employees. The local Belgian entity, apart from their technical execution, had no hand in the contracts which were negotiated and concluded with its customers by the companies in the Badger Group's companies higher up the scale (Badger BV in the Netherlands, the Group's leader in Europe, and Badger Inc., the parent company). The local Belgian entity did the technical work under these contracts for the most part in complete ignorance of their financial and commercial terms and were paid for it on inter-company pay conditions for technical work which were fixed entirely by the parent company. The workload on the local Belgian entity was decided entirely at other levels in the Group, as also were many other

matters (including the engagement of staff and renting office space; indeed, two months before the decision to close down, the local Belgian entity had been instructed to double its office space to cope with a planned extension!). The only freedom left to the local Belgian entity was to optimise its technical organization so as to produce construction plans and render related services in accordance with the standards fixed by the Group, but at minimum cost in terms of hours of work.

(iii) The facts show that actually the local Belgian entity did not possess the attributes of a normal commercial enterprise, i.e. profits or commercial and technical risks, the latter being borne at other levels in the Group. In particular, although the profits generated by the local entity's technical work were large, only a small part of them appeared in its accounts and it is the Group's leader for Europe, Badger BV Holland, which takes most of the profits from the work done by the dependent entities, pays dividends to the parent company in the United States (when there is not a mere direct channel).

(iv) The facts also show that the decision to close down the local Belgian entity was taken entirely by the international management, solely on account of factors within the Group, but quite regardless of Belgian economic and social objectives and, what is more serious, with the deliberate intention of violating Belgian social legislation and current labour relations practice by evading them.

(v) For this purpose the parent company took advantage of the legal status (joint-stock company) of the local Belgian entity to make it bankrupt, i.e. literally doing the vanishing trick as employer and putting itself completely outside the reach of Belgian jurisdiction and social legislation.

7. Such behaviour would be inconceivable on the part of Belgian domestic enterprises, which neither wish nor can escape from Belgian jurisdiction and social legislation in order to evade their social responsibilities. Moreover, foreign enterprises which have disinvested in Belgium have so far met their social responsibilities.

8. On 21st February, 1977 when the FIET and the FMTNM representing the local trade unions directly concerned met the firm's international management, the latter's representatives stated that their Group and parent company accepted and applied the OECD's Guidelines and that the bankruptcy of the local Belgian entity, being legally a Belgian joint-stock company, absolved them from any obligation towards their employees *under these Guidelines*. According to this interpretation, the obligation to observe the legislation and current practice with regard to employment and relations with enterprises (introductory paragraph to the section on industrial relations) and the obligations stated in Article 6 from Declaration to mitigate to the maximum extent practicable adverse effects in the case of the closure of an enterprise applied *only to the local entity*.

9. The BADGER case has in fact *immediate and grave* implications for the

131

credibility of the Guidelines, i.e. of the policy decision taken by Member Governments on 22nd June, 1976, and of the support given at the time by the trade union organizations belonging to the TUAC on condition that the effectiveness of these initial measures should first be tested.

10. As a result of developments in the Badger case, the Belgian trade unions and political authorities, as well as the employers' organizations and foreign enterprises in Belgium, are confronted with a situation which directly challenges the authority of the OECD and its Member Governments.

  (i) A direct blow has been dealt at the system of industrial relations and current practice as regards employment and labour relations, with the serious consequence that there is now an element of uncertainty in the behaviour of foreign enterprises in Belgium which gravely impairs the climate for industrial relations, economic development and foreign investment in Belgium.

 (ii) Public opinion, the press and the media are following the case with close attention and are particularly interested in the fact that OECD Governments have *direct responsibility for seeing that the Guidelines are applied effectively by enterprises, both at the international level of the IME Committee so as to ensure that the Guidelines are correctly interpreted, and at the level of individual Governments in order to ensure that the Guidelines are applied effectively by enterprises in their territories, including through bilateral and multilateral co-operation.*

(iii) The ex-employees of Badger-Belgium, the trade unions who represent them and public opinion in general expect tangible results from the consultation with the TUAC on 30th March, from subsequent consultations between Member Governments and from renewed efforts by those Member Governments which are directly concerned by the case.

(iv) The absence of tangible results would be taken by Belgian public opinion, rightly or wrongly, as an attack on the legislation and current practice regarding employment and labour relations in Belgium, to the extent that the Guidelines and operation of the OECD's consultation procedures would be seen, rightly or wrongly, as a loophole found by an enterprise for evading current Belgian legislation and practice.

11. In view of the developments briefly described above in the Badger case and of the interpretation which Belgian public opinion puts on the political decision taken by the Ministers of the OECD countries when they published the Declaration on the Guidelines, the Belgian Trade Union Confederations which are members of the TUAC are obliged:

– *to regard the Badger case as a test of the effects of the Guidelines on multinational enterprises*

12. As regards the consequences of the situation thus created in connection with the position taken up by the TUAC's member organizations in its communiqué of 21st June, 1976, it is still too soon to assess them, since they depend

on how the case develops and on the effectiveness of the intergovernmental consultation procedures. Nevertheless it is quite clear that neither the Governments nor indeed the TUAC's member trade union organizations could for long tolerate a situation in which 'the Guidelines would appear to be unnecessary for those enterprises which behave well anyway and normally apply the standards specified in them, *and without effect on those enterprises which violate the said standards'.*»

Annex: Judgment of the Commercial Court of Antwerp, declaring Badger NV Belgium bankrupt

122. «Judgment given and passed in the Court-House in Antwerp, on Monday the fourteenth of February 1900 seventy-seven.

---

in the open session of the eleventh chamber of the Commercial Court of the Antwerp district, in which sat:

K. Van den Bossche	President
Gh. Lamiroy	Judge in commercial cases
A. Van Put	Judge in commercial cases
L. Huybrechts	Public Prosecutor
H. Van Damme	Clerk of the Court

IN THE CASE OF: Bankruptcy ex officio
N. V. BADGER (Belgium)
A. R. 2974/77 – F 59II

Considering the petition for statutory composition, in accordance with the co-ordinated laws of September 25th 1946, brought in at this Court, on January 12th 1977;
Considering the judgment of January 12th 1977, with which M. Gh. Lamiroy, judge in commercial cases, was appointed judge-commissary;
Considering the judgment of January 27th 1977, with which pursuant to section 6 of the said law, the petition was admitted;
After hearing at the session, in council-chamber of February 3rd 1977, the judge-commissary in his report; the petitioning company through its counsellor, Dr. Grolich of the Brussels bar, in his means and conclusions; M. C. De Hondt, deputy-Crown Prosecutor, in his verbally given report.
Considering it rests with the Court to examine whether petitioner complies with the terms of section 8 of the co-ordinated laws of September 25th 1946, in order to carry on the proceedings of the statutory composition; the statutory composition being a favour which can only be granted to the trader who is

133

unfortunate and in good faith; both conditions 'unfortunate' and 'good faith' being required together;

Considering M. H. Dhondt has been appointed by the judge-commissary as accountant, with as duty: to inform the Court about the circumstances which led the company to file the petition for statutory composition and to supply the necessary information in order to enable the court to adjudicate upon the soundness of the petition filed;

Considering it appears from the report that petitioner belongs to a 'Multinational', of which the head office 'The Badger Cy' is established in Cambridge, USA; that petitioner has acted from the start as a 'satellite company' and that the company has to be considered simply as an executive entity of the head office;

Considering the accountant during his examination did not find a single element pointing out that petitioner's situation was critical and that the carrying on of the business was impossible;

Considering petitioning company, at the moment when it proceeded to the close-down of the business, was not in a state of suspension of payments; that the closedown of the business, which has serious consequences for the employees, is the sole cause of this situation; that, precisely, because of the close-down the notice-indemnifications for the staff have become due and have passed into the liabilities of the company, for an amount of about 200 millions of francs.

Considering that, as it is certain that from 1966 until 1975 included, petitioner has been able to build up reserves for an amount of 153.789.000 fr., with a reduction of 5.202.000 fr., in 1972; it seems strange to the Court that suddenly, in 1976, a reduction of 40.903.000 fr is to be noted; that the point made by petitioner that the collapse of the reserves has started during the summer of 1971, can hardly be accepted; that the period from 1972 until 1975 included, has in fact given reserves amounting to 52.551.000 fr. or 34.17 per cent of the total reserves constituted from the company's formation in 1957 until 1975 included;

Considering that the reduction of orders, which occurred from 1972 on, is chiefly due to the rationalization policy conducted by the head office in the USA and to which petitioner, as part of the 'Multinational' was subjected;

Considering that the decision to close the business in Antwerp was taken by the general meeting of the shareholders, on the instruction of the Dutch associated company, the BV 'Badger' – The Hague, who on its side had received instruction from the head office in the USA;

Considering that from the foregoing, the conclusion can be taken that the situation which petitioning company has arrived at is not the result of events which occurred outside its control, condition necessary to be considered as 'unfortunate'; that the head office in the USA, for the determination whether petitioner is unfortunate or not, in the frame of a 'Multinational', to which petitioner belongs, cannot be considered as third party; that the instructions given by the head office cannot be considered as external events;

Considering therefore that petitioning company is not unfortunate; that it does not comply with one of the conditions of the statutory composition;

134

Considering therefore that the continuation of the proceedings for the obtention of the statutory composition cannot be conceded;

Considering that the petition for the statutory composition implies that petitioning company has avowed that it complies with the conditions for the bankruptcy; that petitioning company is in a state of suspension of payments and that its credit is damaged;

FOR THESE REASONS

The Court of Justice, considering the sections 2, 34, 35, 36, 37 and 41 of the law of June 15th 1935, governing the use of languages in lawsuits;

dismisses the petition for statutory composition brought in by the limited company BADGER BELGIUM on January 12th 1977,

declares to be EX OFFICIO IN STATE OF BANKRUPTCY:

the limited company BADGER BELGIUM, established in Antwerp, Tavernierskaai 2, entered in the trade-register of Antwerp, under Nr. 183740;

1. fixes provisionally the date on which payment has ceased, on January 12th 1977;

2. appoints M. Ghislain Lamiroy, judge in commercial cases, to be judge-commissary and Dr. Lode Van de Vyver, lawyer in Antwerp, as trustee;

3. directs that shall be proceeded to the taking of the inventory, without affixing of the seals, in presence of the judge-commissary;

4. declares that the debt-claims must be lodged before March 4th 1977;

5. declares that the official report of examination of the debt-claims shall be closed on March 22nd 1977;

6. refers to the session of Wednesday April 6th 1977, 8th chamber, room 19, at 9.30 a.m.: the verbal discussions of the disputations which gave rise to this examination;

7. directs the judge-commissary to exercise the powers granted to the justice of the peace, by virtue of the stipulations of the bankruptcy Act;

8. orders the publication of this judgment in the Belgian Government Gazette published in Brussels and in the daily papers De Financieel Economische Tijd, Gazet van Antwerpen, Volksgazet, published in Antwerp.

Makes costs chargeable to the bankrupt estate.

February 14th 1977
eleventh chamber
Nr. 159»

4. Position of BIAC

123. Mr. Wagner, Chairman of BIAC's Committee on International Investment and Multinational Enterprises, meeting with the IME Committee on April 11, 1978, stated the following:

135

«The general issue of any responsibility of a parent company in the application of the Guidelines raises two separate points. The first, concerns the question of whether the parent company has any responsibility to ensure the compliance of the various entities within the Multinational Enterprises with the Guidelines. This question is affected by the degree of autonomy of each entity in relation to the others. This, as paragraph 8 of the introductory part of the Guidelines rightly states, varies widely from one multinational enterprise to another. The parent's role will in this connection be to emphasize the need for reasonable, honest and sound policies on the part of its subsidiaries and affiliates. The management of each subsidiary and affiliate will have to adapt these policies within the framework of local legislation and practice.

The second point concerns the question of whether the parent has any responsibility for the debts of its subsidiaries. In the absence of specific legal provisions no such liability can exist in any legal sense. However, there have been parent companies which have assumed liability in given situations on an ad hoc basis and without prejudice on an ex gratia basis for claims of employees. These cases are exceptional because of the risk of suits brought by shareholders for alleged dissipation of shareholders' funds by the making of payments for which there is no legal obligation. Depending on the laws and courts decisions which vary from country to country, in some jurisdictions, notably that of the USA, this risk can be substantial.»

5. POSITION OF BADGER C[o5]

124. «The Company's Side of the Story.

The following comments on the recently closed case of Badger (Belgium) NV were sent to the Chamber President by the Chairman of the Board of the Badger Company, Inc.

The Closure of Badger (Belgium) NV in January 1977 has now been ended in June 1978 by the judgment of the commercial court at Antwerp, approving the settlement agreed upon by the creditors of Badger (Belgium) NV.

The Badger Company, Inc. ('Badger') ranks among the major international engineers and constructors of processing plants for the chemical, petrochemical, petroleum and fertilizer industries. Worldwide, the company has a staff of 2,500 including 800 professional engineers. Each of Badger's integrated, fully staffed offices in Europe and North America is capable of handling projects from conception to initial operation with complete responsibility for all work functions.

The decision taken by Badger to close Badger (Belgium) NV was necessary because of continuing poor prospects for orders in Belgium and in other areas served by Badger (Belgium) NV. Although Badger (Belgium) NV had all the capabilities to generate its own workload, on some occasions in the past it had been necessary for it to perform work for other Badger companies in a subcon-

---

5. *Commerce in Belgium, The Monthly Review of the American Chamber of Commerce in Belgium*, nr. 316, October 1978, pp. 17–18. We add this document, published in 1978, in order to give a full picture of the facts. It was never introduced before the IME Committee.

tracting capacity. Because of rapidly increasing costs of personnel services in Belgium in comparison with other countries and because of client and government restrictions, it became increasingly difficult as a subcontractor to other Badger companies.

In the fall of 1976 negotiations were opened with Belgian and US companies in an effort to sell Badger (Belgium) NV. The Belgian government authorities were notified and were requested to assist in the sale of the company or by other means to preserve the employment of its personnel and to mitigate the adverse effects of closing. The 250 employees and the unions were kept advised of these efforts. All employees were kept on the payroll and paid in full during an extensive low workload period up to the closing date. It was not until all prospects for the sale of the company were exhausted that the decision was made to close. The employees were all given individual notice as of 14 January 1977.

Severance settlement formulas in Belgium are the most extensive in Europe and are fixed by negotiations or by the courts. In recognition of that fact, the entire assets of Badger (Belgium) NV approximately 100 million Belgian francs ($2.8 million), were left in Badger (Belgium) NV, which represented an average termination salary of 8 months per employee on the closing date. Since operations started in 1965, all earnings and profits of Badger (Belgium) NV have remained in Badger (Belgium) NV. No dividends were ever paid.

The Belgian unions demanded from Badger a supplemental payment of over 100 million Belgian francs. The unions demanded full payment for all employees, irrespective of when the employees succeeded in finding new employment. Although the unions subsequently relaxed their excessive financial demands somewhat, their high demands resulted in a complete impasse in December 1976, when the last potential buyer declined interest. The Belgian unions were adamant that the employees should not receive payment out of the Belgian government fund designed to indemnify employees in the event of the insolvency of their employer.

The commercial court of Antwerp did not question the good faith of Badger (Belgium) NV, in declining the request for a settlement by Concordat filed by Badger (Belgium) NV at the time of the closing and declaring the company bankrupt on 14 February 1977.

Despite Badger's efforts to comply with the voluntary guidelines of the Organization for Economic Cooperation and Development (OECD) formulated in June 1976, attempts were made by the unions and the Belgian governments to bring the Badger (Belgium) NV situation before the OECD as a test case to impose on multinationals extensive obligations far beyond those applicable to national companies.

Since Badger and the Belgian unions were willing to come to a reasonable solution, negotiations were reopened after the Belgian government decided to act as mediator. This occurred prior to the meeting in Paris on 31 March 1977, of the committee on International Investment and Multinational Enterprises (IME) established by the OECD Council. The tripartite discussions with the Belgian government and the unions were satisfactorily concluded. To meet its social obligations in full, Badger agreed in April 1977 to increase the assets of Badger (Belgium) NV from 100 to 120 million Belgian francs.

The ongoing bankruptcy proceedings resulted in a significant delay in payment for the employees and the other creditors. Despite strong efforts by all interested parties to accelerate the execution of the tripartite agreement, it took until May 1978 before the employees were paid. During this period all assets of Badger (Belgium) NV and the interest accruing thereon were under the control of a receiver appointed by the court.

In May 1978, Badger (Belgium) NV, supported by Badger, proposed a settlement. After acceptance of this settlement by all remaining preferred and non-preferred creditors, it was approved by the commercial court in Antwerp, in June, 1978.»

6. AGREEMENT BADGER — BELGIAN TRADE UNIONS

125.

BOND DER BEDIENDEN,	LANDELIJKE BEDIENDE
TECHNICI EN KADERS	CENTRALE
(B.B.T.K./SETCA A.B.V.V.)	(L.B.C.)
17 VAN ARTEVELDESTRAAT	KIPDORP 45
B–2000 ANTWERPEN	B–2000 ANTWERPEN
BELGIUM	BELGIUM
Tel/031.32.59.60	Tel/031.31.38.70

Antwerpen, May 3rd 1977.

TUAC
Mr Henri Bernard, General Secretary
26 Avenue de la Grande Armée
F.75017 Paris (17e)

Dear Friend,   FRANCE

Re: *BADGER BELGIUM LTD.*

We give you now the last information about the happy end of the Badger case.

On April 21st 1977, the International Management of Badger Inc. (U.S.A.) and the Belgian Unions (B.B.T.K. & L.B.C.) reached an agreement providing with satisfactory, settlement of the claims of the Employees of Badger Belgium.

On April 27th, all 198 staff members present in the assemblee of the personnel of Badger Belgium accepted as unanimously the agreement.

Badger Inc. (U.S.A.) agreed with the principle of indemnification for the closure of enterprises, with a maximum of 120 million Belgian Franks.

Moreover, employees taken back an employment by Badger Holland, have received guarantees about job security and a maintenance of the level of their pay.

Under art. 4 of the agreement, the Belgians Unions agreed to declare that the satisfactory settlement reached, means that Badger Inc (U.S.A.) has met all its obligations under the belgian law and the OECD Guidelines for Multinational Enterprises.

This is ending the dispute and the Belgian Unions agreed to inform TUAC and through your mediation the OECD Governments.

Pray accept our best thanks, for the trouble you have taken and of course we wish to express officially our sincere thanks for the contribution, that the OECD Governments have been making to fulfill their responsibilities and observing the OECD Guidelines.

We sincerely beg to thank you Henri, for the support you have favoured us in the course of this difficult situation.

Yours faithfully,

Louis VAN ALPHEN   Vic NAVEAU
Secretary (B.B.T.K./Setca/A.B.V.V.)   Secretary (L.B.C./C.S.C.)

STREEKECONOMIE
RUIMTELIJKE ORDENING
EN HUISVESTING

1000 BRUSSEL
Anspachloan 1 (Bus 8)
Tel. 02/219.49.90

DE STAATSSECRETARIS

April 21, 1977

PROTOCOL
AGREEMENT

I.   1.   The BADGER Co Inc. agrees with the principle of indemnification of the dismissed employees of BADGER (BELGIUM) in accordance to the formula CLAEYS, as agreed between parties on April 5th, 1977, as well of the indemnification for the closure of enterprises, and as laid down in the attached document drawn up by Mr. GROLIG O., with a maximum of 120 million Belgian Fr. provided correction for material mistakes for an amount of 500.000 Belgian fr.
2.   The BADGER Co Inc. will arrange for the payment to the receiver of a sum of 20 million B.F. as a contribution to capital of BADGER (BELGIUM) for the purpose of the settlements of the law suit concerning the employees' claims.

If the assets are less than one hundred million B.F., The BADGER Co Inc. will make an additional payment to bring the assets up to one hundred million B.F. up to a maximum of 5 million B.F.

If the assets are more than one hundred million B.F. but less than 120 million B.F. the BADGER Co Inc. will pay the difference between 120 million B.F. and the amount of the actual assets. Parties agree, in consideration of the above payments, that all claims of the employees under Belgian law will be fulfilled.

If the assets are less than 95 million B.F., parties agree to meet again under the presidency of the Secretary of State of Flemish Regional Economy.

II.   It is understood that concerning the employees engaged by BADGER B.V. no indemnification for lack of notice and premium for closing down of enterprises is due provided that the salaries and other terms of employment under their employment contract with BADGER B.V. (or any other BADGER subsidiary) are substantially similar to the conditions enjoyed during their employment by BADGER BELGIUM. In regard to job security BADGER undertakes that such personnel will be employed for a minimum period of not less than the notice period stated in the attached calculations.

III.   The trade unions engaged themselves to defend this agreement before their members and to do their utmost to obtain from them a waiver of

140

their claims against BADGER and in accordance with the text of the waiver attached hereto.

They engage themselves to obtain such a waiver from at least 90% of their members, which total 229, with the exception of the employees in service of BADGER B.V. as indicated before. It is expressly agreed that delivery to BADGER of such minimum number of waivers shall be a condition for the making of the payments referred to above.

IV. The unions agree that they shall inform the international unions about the satisfactory settlement reached meaning that BADGER has met its obligations under Belgian law and this will end the dispute.

V. The parties hereto shall exert their best efforts to obtain a court approved settlement with the creditors of the bankruptcy along the line of this agreement.

In witness whereof the parties have signed this protocol in five copies in Brussels. This 21st day of April 1977 and each party acknowledges having received a duly signed copy.

FOR BADGER

P.H. SEAVER,
Executive Vice President
The Badger Company Inc.

G.F. WUNDER,
Vice President
The Badger Company Inc.

NAMENS L.B.C.
Namens B.B.T.K.

Vic NAVEAU

Louis VAN ALPHEN

G. DE BROECK,
Adjunct-Kabinetschef
Ministry of Employment and Labor

Roger BLANPAIN,
Professor – Adviser to
the Secretary of State

Mark EYSKENS,
Secretary of State
Flemish Regional Economy

7. The Report of the IME Committee

126. Paragraphs 39, 41 and 42 of the IME report deal with the responsibility of the parent companies. They read as follows:

«Second, paragraph 8 notes that the various entities, which include parent companies, local subsidiaries, as well as intermediary levels of the organizations, are expected to co-operate and to provide assistance to one another as necessary to facilitate the observance of the Guidelines, taking into account the degree of autonomy or of dependence of each entity in practice. To the extent that parent companies actually exercise control over the activities of their subsidiaries they have a responsibility for the observance of the Guidelines by those subsidiaries. (paragraph 39)
While arising out of the text of *paragraph 8*, the question as to what extent observance of the Guidelines implies responsibilities for the parent companies and/or for the subsidiaries, respectively, is important to the Guidelines as a whole. Considering, first, non-financial responsibilities, the Committee noted that one area in the Guidelines where the parent company clearly is being addressed directly concerns the chapter on Disclosure of Information, which refers to the publication of 'a sufficient body of factual information on the structure, activities and policies of the enterprises as a whole' that is, information which must be gathered and prepared by the parent company. In other areas such as competition and taxation, where it may be important for the specific purposes of the relevant chapters of the Guidelines to obtain a full picture of the operations of the enterprise as a whole, enterprises, including parent companies, should co-operate with national authorities, inter alia, by providing information. The chapter on Employment and Industrial Relations, particularly in its paragraphs 3, 6 and 9, also raises matters germane to the criteria for assessing the respective degrees of responsibility of parents and subsidiaries for facilitating observance of the Guidelines, which are considered at more length in relation to that particular chapter. (paragraph 41)
The Committee also considered the question whether good practice in conformity with observance of the Guidelines should, in some instances, lead parent companies to assume certain financial obligations of their subsidiaries. The Committee has found that this question raises difficult and complex problems in view of the principle embodied in national laws of all Member countries of limited legal liability of companies. The Committee wishes to underline that the Guidelines, according to their nature described in paragraph 38 above, introduce, where relevant, supplementary standards of non-legal character and thus do not set standards which could be seen as superseding or substituting for national laws governing corporate liability, which are part of the legal basis on which companies operate. For this reason, in the view of the Committee, the behaviour recommended by the Guidelines in this context cannot be seen in a legal framework and does not imply an unqualified principle of parent company responsibility. Nonetheless, the Committee has noted that parent companies on a voluntary basis have assumed in certain cases such financial responsibility for a subsidiary. The Committee considers generalization in this

area difficult, but the question of such responsibility as a matter of good management practice – in light of such factors as e.g. aspects of the relationship between the parent company and the subsidiary and the conduct of the parent company – consistent with observance of the Guidelines, could arise in special circumstances. The question of assumption of responsibility, for example, could be of particular relevance in the circumstances set out in paragraph 6 of Guidelines on Employment and Industrial Relations relating to important changes in the operations of a firm and the co-operation as to the mitigation of resulting adverse effects. (paragraph 42)»

8. SOME COMMENTS

127. The problem of the co-responsibility of the parent company for the obligations of its subsidiaries goes to the heart of the multinational matter since it involves the central decision making structure of the multinational enterprise, which constitutes, as earlier indicated, the essence of a multinational enterprise. Indeed the question arises, what is the responsibility of headquarters, for the consequences of decisions, concerning a subsidiary in relation to the local (minority) shareholders, creditors and employees? Can one, in such a case, still invoke the principle of limited responsibility, which means that each legal entity is only liable to the extent of its assets?

128. The problem is due to a discrepancy between the legal and the economic realities; to the legal structure of the enterprise on the one hand and the economic behaviour of the enterprise on the other hand. Legal reality is such, that headquarters and affiliates are constituted as separate legal entities. Being separate means that each one has a separate responsibility and that each entity is, as already indicated, only liable to the extent of its assets. Economically, however, headquarters and subsidiaries are part of the same group, which acts as a unit, controlled and managed by headquarters, which means that headquarters are, in fact, responsible for a number of decisions . . . this raises the question whether this economic responsibility should also be legal . . . which conflicts with the legal principle of limited responsibility, meaning that headquarters are not legally responsible for the consequences of its decisions versus the affiliates . . .

129. The principle of limited responsibility is a well established one in the laws of OECD's member countries. There are, however, a number of exceptions to this rule aiming at the protection of the interests of creditors, among which are employees and shareholders.
To give a few examples.
German law provides for direct company responsibility in two instances:
– Creditors of a subsidiary can request the parent to offer security or to guarantee their claims when a contract involving the transfer of profits is terminated.[6]

6. Section 303 Stock Corporation Act. In the course of such a contract, creditors are protected by the parent company's obligation to assume the losses of the subsidiary.

– In the case of the closest form of connection between enterprises, the integration of one company into another, the parent company is liable jointly and severally together with the subsidiary for the obligations of the latter.[7] According to Article 101 of the *French* Bankruptcy Act which confirms an earlier judicial practice, courts may extend the subsidiary's bankruptcy to the parent company if the latter has abused the bankrupt enterprise as a cloak or façade for conducting its own operations or abusively disposed of the subsidiary's assets. In *Belgium* and *Italy* case law provides for a similar approach. *Belgian* courts have extended bankruptcy to 'the real master' where separate corporations were only used to organize the activities of a single enterprise. The concept of the unity of the group is also reflected in legal systems governing *collective labour relations.* Law and practices in several Member countries (*Germany, Belgium, Sweden*) require companies to disclose information to employees on the economic situation of the group as a whole. Under *German* law, management in case of plant closures has to negotiate with employee representatives a social plan for the mitigation of adverse effects. In determining the amount of severance payments or other measures contained in this plan not only the situation of the subsidiary but of the Group as a whole will be taken into consideration.

The systems of workers' participation established in *Germany* and the *Netherlands* provide for the establishment of central works councils at the level of national groups. These councils are competent for matters concerning the group as a whole but upon delegation by the respective individual councils can also deal with problems arising at the level of the component enterprises.

More examples of exceptions to the principle of limited responsibility could be given in the areas of company law, bankruptcy law, labour law, tax law, and law against restrictive business practices, but the examples given are sufficient to illustrate our point.

130. In considering the issues related to the Badger Case, the IME Committee has also accepted certain exceptions to the principle of limited responsibility. In fact, the IME Committee does distinguish between two kinds of responsibilities: the non-financial and the financial responsibility.

131. In the *non-financial area* the parent company should see to it that the local affiliate is in a position to live up to local law and practices and to the Guidelines,[8] especially the paragraphs 3, 6 and 9 of the Employment and Industrial Relations Chapter.[9]

Following paragraph 3 of that Chapter, representatives of employees should obtain, where this accords with local law and practice, *information* which enables them to obtain a *true and fair view* of the performance of the entity or, where appropriate, the enterprise as a whole. Headquarters should provide local management with the necessary information in reasonable time, so as to enable the local managers to comply with Guideline 3.

Guideline 6 foresees that multinational enterprises 'in considering changes in their operations, which would have major effects upon the livelihood of their employees; in particular in the case of the closure of an entity involving collective lay-offs of dismissals, provide *reasonable notice* of such changes to representatives of their employees, and where appropriate to the relevant Governmental authorities. They should co-operate with the employee representatives and appropriate Governmental authorities so as to mitigate, to the maximum extent, practicable adverse effects.' It is self-evident that here, also, headquarters must inform local management in due time so that they can provide the 'reasonable notice of such changes' as required by Guideline 6.

Finally, Guideline 9, which sets the *principle of access to real decision-makers* provides that multinational enterprises should enable authorized representatives of their employees, to conduct negotiations on collective bargaining on labour-management relations issues with representatives of management, who are authorized to take decisions on the matters under negotiation. Guideline 9 is clear:

the multinational must delegate sufficient authority to local level or else negotiate at international level, by sending headquarters managers down to the local level.

132. As important, if not more so, directly confronting the principle of limited legal liability, is the problem of the *financial* responsibility of headquarters for the debts of its subsidiaries. The IME Committee has stated, in line with the arguments developed by the Belgian Government, that *the Guidelines do not imply an unqualified principle of parent-company responsibility*; this means, however, that there is a 'qualified' principle of parent company responsibility; this responsibility is, in the IME report, further *qualified in the light of such factors as aspects of the relationship between the parent company and the subsidiary* (e.g. 100 per cent ownership as in the Badger Case, the extent to which decisions are taken by headquarters and the like) *and the conduct of the parent company*. Again, in the light of the Badger Case, the IME Committee states that this responsibility of the parent company could be of particular relevance in the circumstances set out in Guideline 6 of the Chapter on Employment and Industrial Relations relating to important changes in the operation of a firm, and the co-operation concerning the mitigation of resulting adverse effects.

133. The IME Committee's conclusion on the co-responsibility of the parent for the affiliate is of the utmost importance, in establishing standards of behaviour and responsibilities going beyond national law, which constitute the very 'raison d'être' of the Guidelines. This step by the Committee, although important, is undoubtedly, but a first step! More experience under the Guidelines is needed with more cases and issues to see how the principle of co-responsibility, still an exception to the general rule, can evolve further in the direction of a more far-reaching responsibility of the parent for the daughter, thus bridging the gap between the law of the Guidelines and economic reality.

II. Access to the real decisionmakers. The Firestone Case

> **Guideline 9 of the Employment and Industrial Relations Chapter:**
> «enable authorised representatives of their employees to conduct negotiations on collective bargaining or labour management relations issues with representatives of management who are authorized to take decisions on the matters under negotiation.»

1. The Issue

134. The FIRESTONE Case[10] introduced through TUAC by the Swiss Trade Union Centre, refers not only to the closedown of an allegedly profitable subsidiary[11] but above all raises issues with respect to the access of employee representatives to the real decision makers within the company.

2. Submission by the Swiss Trade-Union Centre

135. «Request for interpretation of paragraphs 5 of General Policies, 6 and 9 of the Section on Employment and industrial relations of the OECD Guidelines for Multinational Enterprises, concerning the case of the subsidiary, at Pratteln Switzerland, of Firestone.

ISSUES

The following interpretation of the OECD Guidelines for multinational enterprises is brought to attention of the IIME Committee:

Paragraph 5 of the General Policies:
'Allow their component entities freedom to develop their activities and to exploit their competitive advantage in domestic and foreign markets, consistent with the need for specialisation and sound commercial practice.'
1. Article 5, in our opinion, is inconsistent with the practice of closing a profitable subsidiary, which continuity is guaranteed, in order to maximise profits elsewhere.

---

10. Oaklander H., "The Swiss call it 'the Firestone Affair' (roneo), 1978, 21 p. intended for publication by The Interstate Case Clearing House, Boston.
11. See for the discussion of that problem: The BATCO case, Part II, III.

2. This paragraph allows neither to curtail the freedom of a subsidiary less profitable in order to make another more profitable.
3. Neither does this paragraph allow the curtailment of the freedom of a subsidiary in order to close it down, in spite of its competitive advantages in domestic and foreign markets.

Paragraph 6 of the Section about Employment and industrial relations
In considering changes in their operations which would have major effects upon the livelihood of their employees, in particular in the case of the closure of an entity involving collective lay-offs or dismissals, provide reasonable notice of such changes to representatives of their employees, and where appropriate to the relevant governmental authorities, and co-operate with the employee representatives and appropriate governmental authorities so as to mitigate to the maximum extent practicable adverse effects;
1. In our opinion this paragraph asks for a maximum of co-operation between management and workers representatives in cases involving major changes upon the livelihood of employees. This maximum of co-operation is not met when the collective lay-off was totally unnecessary.
2. This paragraph involves an open consultation between management and representatives of employees. It is not in agreement with this paragraph that decisions are made by the management but this decision is held back from the employees. Long term decisions involving lay-offs etc. should be told to the employees as soon as possible as soon as the decision at central level is made.

Paragraph 9 of the Section about Employment and industrial relations
'Enable authorised representatives of their employees to conduct negotiations on collective bargaining or labour management relations issues with representatives of management who are authorised to take decisions on the matters under negotiation.'
When the (local) management of a subsidiary is not in a position to take decisions, for example about a closure, it should not mislead the workers, their representatives as well as the local and national public authorities, but the level of (for example from the international headquarters) management authorised to take such a decision of closure or decisions involving collective lay offs and dismissal should be ready to pass the necessary information, discuss it, negotiate on conditions of employment and/or closure, before the final decision is made.

FACTS

The local management of Firestone at Pratteln had been giving misleading information which appears so now that the facts are known. For example, it was stated to Mr. Rickenbacker, Mayor of the local authority, that a closure was out of question and that the activities of the subsidiary were 'more or less normalised'.
In relation with the preliminary debate following the question of the Member

147

of Parliament, Mr. Wagner, the enterprise published, in December 1976, a press communiqué indicating that, in no event, the subsidiary of Pratteln would be closed. This statement was repeated to the workers by the director, Mr. Thompson, in September 1977.

After the decision to close was announced, the State Counsellor, Mr. P. Jenni, Member of the Parliament of the Canton of Bâle campagne, publicly stated the following:

'Representatives of the Government of Bâle campagne have negotiated with the local management of Firestone, at Pratteln, for already a year. At that time, the management had promised us to keep us informed of any new development. This was not done.'

Finally, into the collective agreement concluded between the enterprise and the trade-union, under article 2, paragraph 2.8, it was agreed that 'collective lay-offs of dismissals following a lack of orders . . . as well as closure of enterprises should be discussed with the trade-unions and the workers committee prior to any move'.

In order to emphasize the unilateral and sudden character of the decision of closure, it is necessary to underline that the enterprise had recruited 4 persons on the 1st of April and that on the 21st March advertisements continued to be published into the local press for the recruitment of staff.

After the measures of restructuration introduced by Firestone at Pratteln 3 years ago, the local trade-union and the representatives of the workers had requested a negotiation with the authorised representative of the management of the Firestone Group (international). The local management of the subsidiary, at Pratteln, stated that they were not authorized to answer to all the questions and demands of the workers and of the trade-unions. It is only after a decision of closure was announced suddenly and unilaterally that Firestone international management declared itself ready to receive a Swiss delegation at Akron (USA).

Firestone also refused negotiations with the International Chemical and Energy Workers Federation.»

3. POSITION OF BIAC

136. At the occasion of the consultations with the IME committee on April 11, 1978, BIAC declared as follows:

«In regard to the last Employment and Industrial Relations Guideline (9) BIAC would just reiterate that collective bargaining procedures and labour relations issues are matters to be settled between the management of the affiliate and the authorized representatives of its employees in the country concerned in accordance with national law and practice.»

4. THE REPORT OF THE IME COMMITTEE

137. The report reads as follows:

148

«*Access to decision makers* (paragraph 9)

When negotiations or collective bargaining are proceeding in the context of any parent subsidiary relationship, there is clearly a possibility that the subsidiary may not be fully empowered to negotiate and to conclude an agreement. There may be special problems in the case of a subsidiary which is situated in one country whilst the parent company is situated in another. The purpose of the text of paragraph 9 was to lay stress on the access of employee representatives to management representatives 'who are authorised to take decisions on the matters under negotiation'. This is the key consideration and the management of an MNE should see that it is observed in the circumstances of each case. (paragraph 71).
There is also paragraph 8 of the Introduction to the Guidelines which is germane to the matter discussed under paragraph 9 of the Employment and Industrial Relations Guidelines. This text recalls that 'the Guidelines are addressed to the various entities within the multinational enterprise (parent companies and/or local entities) according to the actual distribution of responsibilities among them on the understanding that they will co-operate and provide assistance to one another as necessary to facilitate observance of the Guidelines.' Parent companies, therefore, are expected to take the necessary organisational steps to enable their subsidiaries to observe the Guidelines, inter alia, by providing them with adequate and timely information and ensuring that their representatives who carry out negotiations at the national or local level have sufficient authority to take decisions on the matters under negotiation.» (paragraph 72).

5. SOME COMMENTS

138. The problem of 'access to the real decision makers' is another one, which goes to the heart of the multinational matter, given the centralized decision making structure of the multinatonal enterprise. This decision-making structure may indeed have, as a consequence, that strategic decisions affecting the livelihood of the employees are taken in far away headquarters, with the possibility that even local managers are only informed about decisions which affect the subsidiary they manage after such decisions are taken.
The Guidelines are clear: there must be timely information and access to the real decision makers. Timely information, also prescribed by Guideline 6 of the Employment and Industrial Relations Chapter,[12] will be discussed in depth later, but it is self-evident that headquarters must provide local management, with appropriate information so that they can inform the employees, unless top management itself prefers to inform the employees directly. Guideline 9 is also very explicit concerning access to the real decision-makers and has, as a consequence, that the multinational will eventually have to adapt its decision-making structure. Guideline 9 gives two possibilities: the multina-

12. See further Part II, VB.

tional enterprise must delegate to the local managers authority to conduct negotiations or send duly authorized representatives from headquarters for negotiations with the employees. What is meant by 'to conduct negotiations on collective bargaining or labour management relations issues' is to be determined by national law, regulations and practice, which is prevalent in the entity, affected by the decisions. This is self-evidently different from country to country and includes investment and disinvestment decisions in Sweden, to take one side of the spectrum and at the other side the social consequences of economic decisions taken within the framework of management perogatives in the United States.

III. The Closedown of an Allegedly Profitable Subsidiary. The Batco Case

---

Guidelines 1, 2, 4 and 5 of the General policies:

«Enterprises should
(1) take fully into account established general policy objectives of the Member countries in which they operate;
(2) in particular, give due consideration to those countries' aims and priorities with regard to economic and social progress, including industrial and regional development, the protection of the environment, the creation of employment opportunities, the promotion of innovation and the transfer of technology,
. . . .
(4) favour close co-operation with the local community and business interests;
(5) allow their component entities freedom to develop their activities and to exploit their competitive advantage in domestic and foreign markets, consistent with the need for specialization and sound commercial practice;»

---

1. The Issue

139. The Batco Case refers to the Dutch subsidiary of British American Tobacco Company. The principle issue raised by that case was the application of the Guidelines to the closedown of an allegedly profitable subsidiary. The questions arising are whether the Guidelines can be seen to impose limits or qualifications on the rights of companies to make disinvestment decisions and whether the profitability of a given entity is a relevant factor in this regard.

2. «CNV – Holland. Submission to TUAC and to the OECD IME Committee:

140. Request for Interpretation of the Paragraphs 5 and 6 of The OECD Guidelines on Multinational Enterprises, Concerning British American Tobacco Company

ISSUE

The following interpretation of the OECD Guidelines for Multinational Enterprises are brought to the attention of the IME Committee.
Request for interpretation of Paragraph 5 of the General policies: 'Allow their component entities freedom to develop their activities and to exploit their competitive advantage in domestic and foreign markets, consistent with the need for specialisation and sound commercial practice.'
1. Art. 5 in our opinion is inconsistent with the practice of closing a profitable subsidiary which continuity is guaranteed in order to maximize profits elsewhere.
2. This paragraph allows neither to curtail the freedom of a subsidiary less profitable in order to make another more profitable.
3. Neither does this paragraph allow the curtailment of the freedom of a subsidiary in order to close it down, in spite of its competitive advantages in domestic and foreign markets.

Interpretation of paragraph 6 of the section about employment and industrial relations.

'In considering changes in their operations which would have major effects upon the livelihood of their employees, in particular in the case of the closure of an entity involving collective lay-offs or dismissals, provide reasonable notice of such changes to representatives of their employees, and where appropriate to the relevant governmental authorities, and co-operate with the employee representatives and appropriate governmental authorities so as to mitigate to the maximum extent practicable adverse effects.'

1. In our opinion this paragraph asks for a maximum of co-operation between management and workers representatives in cases involving major changes upon the livelihood of the employees. This maximum of co-operation is not met when the collective lay-off was totally unnecessary.
2. This paragraph involves an open consultation between management and representatives of employees. It is not in agreement with this paragraph that decisions are made by the management but this decision is held back from the employees. Long term decisions involving lay-offs etc. should be told to the employees as soon as possible as soon as the decision at central level is made.

151

FACTS

The case concerns the transfer of production of cigarettes from Amsterdam to Brussels, involving the lay-off of personel presently working in Amsterdam. The jobs of 230 workers are endangered by this procedure.
The production in Amsterdam takes place under the responsibility of the British American Tobacco Company BV (the Netherlands) a 100 per cent subsidiary of the British Tobacco (BAT). Industries Limited which has its office in London on Westminster House 7, Millbank, London.
The Belgium company of BAT Ltd., is a 100 per cent subsidiary of BAT BV (the Netherlands).

Since 1971 the production capacity in Brussels has been expanded and the production in Amsterdam has been diminished.

The reasons for these developments cannot be found in the development of the sale figures nor in the profits of the separate subsidiaries. This can be deduced from the figures given by the management of BAT-Netherlands.

Table 1

Mln cigarettes a day	Development of the production capacity		Development of the sales	
	Brussels	Amsterdam	Estimated	Real
1973/1974	22.5	27.5	41.3	39.7
1974/1975	32.0	13.4	44.4	41.6
1975/1976	33.0	13.4	43.0	38.1
1976/1977	35.8	13.4	42.6	38.5

Note: From 1973/1974 till 1974/1975 Amsterdam changed from a shiftwork to dayservice.

The figures show that the capacity in Brussels has been extended in spite of the development of the sales which stayed behind expectation. The reason has been the attempt to concentrate production in Brussels.

The remarks of the Works-Council of BAT BV (the Netherlands) show that this development has been announced already in 1971. However, in 1974 the management stated that the production in Amsterdam would remain on 14 million cigarettes a day.

In spite of that promise the production capacity in Brussels has been extended with 1 million in 1975/1976 and with 2.8 million in 1976/1977.
If there is overproduction now, as management of BAT suggests it is caused by the policy of the management aimed at an extension of capacity in Brussels.
It has nothing to do with the profits of the subsidiary in Amsterdam.
This is shown by the figures given by the management:

152

Table 2

Turnover in mln tons	Turnover		Profits	
	Brussels	Amsterdam	Brussels	Amsterdam
1974/1975	5.172	6.138	3.2	3.4
1975/1976	5.072	5.672	3.6	4.5
1976/1977	5.064	6.096	3.6	5.8

Note: Amsterdam pays yearly a big compensation for the product manufactured in Brussels.

At present the management has made a proposal to concentrate the production in Belgium. It is said that the trade-union organizations will be consulted.

However:
The management has already made the following decisions:
– the option on ground for a new factory in Amsterdam has been cancelled.
– packing materials for the cigarettes which are fabricated in Amsterdam are brought to Belgium,
– bands for the Dutch Market are brought to Belgium,
– new production capacity is realized in Brussels.

Those steps can only be explained by the fact that the decision about transfer of production has been made by the management and that the consultations promised to the trade-unions are only pro-forma. That no real consultations take place. On 09-03-1978 the predient of the court of Amsterdam ordered BAT BV to stop the replacement to Brussels awaiting further consultations with the unions (see Judgement).
Those are the facts of the concrete case of BAT Ltd. We would like to take them into consideration interpretating the paragraphs of the guidelines as mentioned here after.

ANNEX
Judgement 9.3.'78

The President of the Arrondissementsrechtbank in Amsterdam

Immediate judgment in the case:

No. KG 78/112 of:
C.V.A.T., in Utrecht
contra
BATCO (Nederland) B.V., Amsterdam

Hearing the parties concerned and after reading the documents:

Considerations with regard to the facts:

During the session of 1st March '78 plaintiff has made demands in conformity

153

with the summons attached as photocopy to this judgement thereby submitting 17 items;

Defendant has answered to this with the conclusion to refuse the provision asked for. Defendant has submitted 6 items.

After further debate parties have submitted their documents and pleadings of which parts of the contents have to be seen as being inserted in this judgment.

Taking into consideration LAW:
Between parties the following are facts:

1. Plaintiff is a trade union having statutory as purpose to defend the interests of their members, working in the establishment of defendant.

Between plaintiff on the one hand and defendant on the other hand a collective labour agreement is valid, running from 1.1.1977 to 31.3.1978, called hereafter: the CAO.

Part of defendant's establishment in Amsterdam, among others producing cigarettes, is a Works Council as meant in the Act on Works Councils, which Act is applicable to defendant's enterprise.

Defendant, part of a multinational concern, produces together with a subsidiary Batco Benelux S.A. in Brussels, cigarettes for the Dutch market, by which each of both factories takes the half of their combined market share for its account. Both factories are considered as an economic unity. Three directors of defendant are members of the board of the Brussels establishment.

Defendant's factory has a production capacity of 13.4 million cigarettes per day.

In accordance with the provisional profit- and loss-account of defendant with regard to the financial year 1976/77 they made on the turnover in Holland of that year a profit after tax of D.f 3.1 million, whereas that profit in the preceding financial years 1975/76 and 1974/75 was f 3.0 mln. and f 1.5 mln. respectively.

2. From 1972 onwards repeatedly the employment opportunity in and the future of Defendant's establishment in Amsterdam have been points of discussion in the Works Council.

From the relevant minutes, attached to the documents used in this case, the following appears:

In a meeting of 10th March 1972 defendant has – in first instance after having announced his intention to close the Amsterdam factory – (see his letter of 3rd March 1972) – informed the Works Council and also on the same day all his employees, that the making and packing departments of the establishment permanently will be maintained on a level of 12 million cigarettes per day.

In a meeting of 4th April 1973 defendant informs that the position of his employees in Amsterdam is ensured, if the factory in Amsterdam is an efficient and competitive part of the establishment, which has been elucidated by defendant in the meeting of 20th June 1973 in so far that this is the case when the standard of approx. 11,000 cigarettes per manhour is achieved, or a

154

machinery-use of 65 per cent. This should be the highest figure of all factories of the Holding company.

In the meeting of 9th November 1973 defendant states that he has come to the conclusion that the primary dept. in Amsterdam should not be closed, that this department remains necessary and 12 ton leaf per day will be handled, which means that the establishment remains in full production and this will be also the case for the future.

In a meeting on 16th January 1974 defendant announces that at that moment investments will be made in the factory in order to make a production of approx. 14 mln. cigarettes per day, which should not have been done by him if he has the intention to close the factory within a short term. Furthermore defendant informs that a slight decline of his sales will be no reason for him to decrease the production in Amsterdam, not to speak about stopping it, but that this latter could happen in case an emergency should arise and viz. by a strong decrease of the sales both the Amsterdam and Brussel factories should become insolvent.

On 8th December 1975 defendant informed the members of the Works Council that he is not considering to stop the production in Amsterdam at this moment, neither wholly nor partly.

Finally in the meeting of 2nd June 1976 defendant states that in the study in preparation by Mr. Rombaut with regard to the position of both factories in the Benelux, the full employment in Amsterdam is an issue, of fact.

3. The study of Mr. Rombaut, mentioned before, has resulted in a report dated 30th November 1977, which has been presented on 14th December 1977 by defendant to the Works Council. In this report it is stated that stagnation and deterioration have occurred and that also in the future this is to be expected in the cigarette consumption in Holland and Belgium. As causes are mentioned the intensifying of anti-smoking campaigns during the last 2 years and the excise increase especially in Belgium.

Consequently, according to the report, the sales of defendant and the Brussels enterprise have not met the expectations on which the planning of both factories have been based.

The expected growth has not become a reality.

The report concludes that the existing overcapacity of both factories together can only be reduced and that the expected losses can be decreased by closure of the Amsterdam factory and concentration of whole the production for the Benelux territory in Brussels.

Closure of defendant's factory means the dismissal of 206 (originally 230) employees at present still in service of defendant, to whom defendant cannot offer replacement.

After study of the report the trade unions concerned, amongst whom plaintiff, have sent written comments to defendant on 24th January 1978. In this comment they set out their objections against the contents of the report and inform that they are of the opinion that the contents of the report do not offer a basis for a discussion with defendant. Furthermore they formulate a number of questions – according to them left open in the report – and also a number of

155

demands which boil down that defendant should abandon his intention to stop the production in Amsterdam and transfer it to Brussels as planned in the report, and that defendant will maintain the employment on the existing level. On 20th February 1978 defendant gives his reaction on these comments to the unions, after in the meantime between them it was agreed that the question under consideration should be discussed between unions and defendant on 2nd March 1978.

In this reaction defendant announces to proceed with his intended measures to close the Amsterdam factory and not to postpone them pending the negotiations with the unions.

Accordingly defendant reports in his letter of 22nd February 1978 to the director of the Districts Labour Office his intended collective dismissal of approx. 230 employees. At the same time defendant requests the director his agreement to this dismissal, which – as he further writes – he wishes to realize in the course of the first half of 1978.

4. In the course of 1977 Batco Benelux SA, who had already created during the years before a considerable overcapacity, ordered new machinery on behalf of the production in the Brussels factory, by which machinery the production capacity is extended with 11 million cigarettes per day, bringing the total production capacity in Brussels on the level of both, Brussels and Amsterdam factories, together at the moment. Of this extension of the machinery in Brussels defendant has made no mention to plaintiff or the other unions nor to his Works Council.

5. Articles 2 of the Collective Labour Agreement concluded between parties concerned reads, as far as of interest in this case:

Par. 1:
Parties commit themselves to fulfil this agreement in good faith and not to perform or promote any action whatever which envisages to amend this agreement in another way than that defined in the 2nd paragraph of art. 25.

Par. 5:
The unions commit themselves not to call a strike during the time that this CSO is in force, envisaging a change in this agreement by another way than defined in art. 25 *and furthermore to give the employer their strong support to an undisturbed continuance of the factory.*

Par. 7:
a. within the framework of the obligations resulting from the SER. Rules for Amalgamations and the Works Council Rules respectively, the employer who *considers* to amalgamate, to close a business or part of a business and/or to drastically regroup the manning, has the obligation to include in his decision the social consequences. By doing so, the employer will as soon as the necessary secrecy makes it possible – inform the unions, works council and employees involved about the measures *under consideration*.
   Further to this the employer will discuss with the unions and the works

council the measures and, if any, the social consequences resulting thereof for the relevant employees.

b. the employer commits himself to inform the unions in normal consultation about investment plans which will lead to a marked change in the employment situation.
When giving this information the task and the position of the Works Council has at the same time to be taken into account.

Art. 5 of the Work Council Rules is verbally equal to art. 25 of the Act on Works Councils, reading:

1. Unless important interests of the company or interested parties directly involved come into conflict with it, the employer gives the Works Council the opportunity to give him advice about a decision to be taken by him or by another person related to the company, with regard to:
a. transfer of the control of affairs or part thereof to another company;
b. termination of the activities of the company or of part of same.
c. important reduction, extension or other changes in the activities of the company.
d. important changes in the organization of the company.
e. change in the place where the company carried on its business.
f. to enter into or to stop permanent co-operation of the company with other companies.
2. the employer gives to the Works Council a survey of the reasons behind the decision, and also of the consequences which to his opinion will result from this decision with regard to the employees working in the establishment and of the measures which to his opinion have to be taken in this respect.
3. The employer is always obliged to inform the Works Council as soon as possible about a decision as meant in the 1st par. and to seek the advice of this council with regard to the fulfilment of that decision, notably with a view to the consequences it will have for the people working in the establishment.
The 2nd paragraph is of equal application.
If the employer does not apply to the first paragraph with regard to the decision under review, he informs the works council about the ponderous interests which came in conflict with the application of that paragraph.
4. When a decision will have as a consequence the dismissal of a considerable part of the personnel, the employer determines after consultation with the unions at which point of time the works council has to be consulted about this decision, or has to be informed about it and consulted about the execution thereof.

6. Plaintiff states that defendant by acting as prescribed sub. 2 to sub. 4 is in default and acts contrary to his obligations laid down in the CAO and therefore in any case acts wrongful against plaintiff, by which plaintiff is restricted in his possibilities to stand up for the interests of the employees, members of plaintiff, in a way as laid down in the law and the CAO, at least obviously meant therein and demand that we in order to ensure that plaintiff will as yet be

157

able to realize this protection of interests forbid defendant to anticipate further the intended closure and further to undo certain already taken measures to this extent, all this as formulated in the petitum of the summons.

7. In support of this claim plaintiff mentions amongst other the right to request in accordance with Art. 344 etc. Civil Code for an inquiry into the conduct of affairs of defendant by the Chamber of Enterprises of the Court of Amsterdam, which right in fact should be made illusory in case the business should be ended in the first half of 1978 in conformity with the intention's of defendant and furthermore that taking this consideration into account serious deliberations about the question of the necessity of a closure is really existing, could no longer take place.

8. In order to defend this action, defendant points out from the very start that the report of 30.11.'77 mentioned above was handed to the Works Council and unions, including plaintiff, on 14.12.1977 by this fully complying with the obligations mentioned in the CAO to inform parties concerned as soon as possible about their measures under consideration and to offer them the opportunity to give comments, whereas according to defendant there is no question of default as stated by plaintiff, as defendant has never explicitly guaranteed that the establishment in Amsterdam should never be closed.

9. As regards this latter mentioned guarantee. We share the opinion of defendant that in this case no reference can be made to a legally enforceable undertaking, which, however, does not alter the fact that the statements of defendant as quoted in sub. 2 in another context are indeed relevant by right, hereafter to be dealt with.
Taking into account defendant's reply of 20.2.1978 to plaintiff cum suis and his reasons in his letter of 22.2.'78 to the District Labour Office in Amsterdam, requesting a permit to collective dismissal of all employees concerned in the production sector in Amsterdam in the first half of 1978.
We are of the opinion that it cannot reasonably be made good that defendant has complied with his obligations resulting from the stipulations quoted sub 5.
Taking into account the interdependent context and conjunction, defendant is obliged in a case as under review to inform plaintiff as early as possible about his intentions and to give him the opportunity to give in advance advice, unless ponderous reasons stand against this, which has not been stated or appeared in this matter.
This is still more cogent now it appears from quotations from reports, mentioned under sub. 2, that defendant has repeatedly given – be it no legally enforceable undertakings – very reassuring guarantees with regard to the question of the employment in Amsterdam.
By acting as afore said and this in a period of strong declining employment in Holland, defendant has not taken into account the due care towards plaintiff, which care defendant behoves in society and thus acting wrongful against plaintiff.
It is immaterial that plaintiff has stated amongst others; in his written com-

ments of 24.1.'78 with regard to the litigious report of defendant, that the unions are not prepared to negotiate about the contents of the report and the measures laid down therein, now this refusal has been reasoned by the unions by adding to this that they are only prepared to consult with the board of management on the basis of reality, whereas apart from the foregoing, in confesso, both parties as yet the matter under review will be discussed on 2nd March 1978.

10. With regard to the question whether plaintiff under the present circumstances has sufficient interest in the provisions asked for. We are together with plaintiff of the opinion, that the guarantees given to plaintiff in the CAO and, if any, also in art. 344 etc. of the Civil Code, should become totally illusoir, when under the present circumstances defendant should have the liberty to execute without more his obvious intention to closure at very short notice.

11. Finally we have to weigh against each other the interests of both parties. Taking into account that the Amsterdam establishment, as also that establishment in Brussels, up to now as appears from quoted figures, is reasonably profitable and further that the unfavourable prognoses of defendant in connection with the excise increase are not shared by the Minister of Social Affairs, as appears from a letter dated 25.11.'77 from this Minister, whereas also the unfavourable effect of the anti-smoking campaigns is still to be considered speculative, a more or less serious development appears certainly not to be real at short notice for defendant, against which may be set however that the execution of the closure in Amsterdam will mean in any case the dismissal at short notice of more than 200 employees with under the present circumstances a very little chance to replacement of employment.
In principle therefore the claim will be considered proper to judgement against defendant.

12. Proceeding on the proposition that for a serious study and connected deliberations of defendant's proposal on the one hand sufficient and on the other hand a limited term has to be fixed, we will give the prohibition as asked for in sub 1 of the petitum for the time of at least one year and in a form to be described hereafter, by which we take into account, that – also in conformaty with defendant's intention as appears from a statement of the pleadings – the division of production will be maintained, which means that 50 per cent of the Dutch market requirements will be produced in Amsterdam.
Further. We presume that within the mentioned term plaintiff can have addressed its request, if any, to the Chamber of Enterprises and will possibly have obtained the decision whether or not its request will be granted as meant in art. 350 Civil Code.
With regard to the petitum sub. 2 we are of the opinion, – as considered before – that the maintenance of the division of the production has been contained in the prohibition sub. 1, so that no conditions exist for a separate provision to this end.
With regard to the requested order to apply anew for the option on a plot of

industrial ground for the extension or new building in Amsterdam, we are of the opinion that plaintiff has not established prima facie the necessity thereto within the framework of the aim envisaged by him at short notice such as considered above.

However, contrary to this is the necessity that the manning will be brought within 2 months on the usual level and maintained.

Uncontradicted Plaintiff has stated that the manning of 231 in the meantime has been reduced by natural waste to 207 and that by this problems will arise when in the near future as usual an increased production will be required for the build-up of a holiday stock.

Therefore this part of the claim is allowed and in its total the following will be decided:

JUDGEMENT IS GIVEN AS FOLLOWS:

1. The defendant is ordered to abstain from any action or omission of which it must reasonably be presumed that it has the tendency to anticipate or to effect that the production of the company in Amsterdam will be changed radically or ended, pending the necessary study of and the following consultation between the parties as considered before and also pending the decision on a possible request as considered before, addressed by plaintiff to the Chamber of Enterprises of the Court in Amsterdam, however at the most for the term of one year after this judgement.

2. The defendant is ordered to bring the manning of the company in Amsterdam, within sixty days after the legal notice of this judgment, again up to the level, necessary for the usual production of the Amsterdam company and to maintain the same since then on the usual level during the term as mentioned in sub. 1.

3. It is stated that defendant will fall into a penal sum of Dfl. 1,000,000 – (one million guilders) for any offence against the orders of sub 1 and 2 and for each day that defendant will possibly default on the subject.

4. This judgment will so far be enforceable by anticipation.

5. What was claimed further or in another way by plaintiff will be refused.

6. The defendant is condemned to pay the costs of his passing, beneficial to plaintiff, amounting to Dfl. 88.75 (eighty eight guilders and seventy five cents) for outlays and Dfl. 650. — (six hundred and fifty guilders) for salary of the solicitor.

Pronounced by Mr. W. J. PORGERHOFF MULDER, President of the District Court in Amsterdam and passed during the public sitting of the Court on Thursday, 9th March 1978 in the presence of Mr. P. BRIL as a registrar.»

3. «MEMORANDUM BY THE DUTCH GOVERNMENT ON THE FACTS AND ISSUES IN THE CASE OF BATCO (NEDERLAND) BV

141. I. Introduction

II. Factual information

III. The view of the National Federation of Protestant Trade Unions (CNV)

IV. The view of the management of BATCO (Nederland) BV

V. Submission by the Dutch Government

I. INTRODUCTION

During the consultations of 11 April 1978 the TUAC reported on the difficulties surrounding the Dutch subsidiary of the British American Tobacco Company. The Dutch Government's view is that the BATCO case should be dealt with by the Committee on International Investment and Multinational Enterprises, in accordance with the Guidelines for Multinational Enterprises and it wishes to report on the BATCO case in terms of the procedure laid down in paragraph 1 of the Decision of the Council on Inter-Governmental Consultation Procedures on the Guidelines for Multinational Enterprises which states: 'The Committee shall periodically or at the request of a Member country hold an exchange of views on matters related to the guidelines and the experience gained in their application . . .'

Moreover, in so doing the Government is responding to the point of view adopted by BIAC during the consultations of 11 April 1978, that BIAC should give serious consideration to studying and clarifying matters raised by a national government. Since the Dutch Government considers that both sides of the matter should be heard, it has felt obliged to report the views of the employees' organizations and of the management.

The Government does not wish at present to adopt a standpoint because the facts of the matter have not yet been clearly established. Besides, as far as any contravention of Dutch law is concerned, the matter is sub judice. Its wish at this stage is simply to stress the importance it attaches to the case, and the issues which it considers to be involved, being dealt with.

II. FACTUAL INFORMATION

The facts, as far as the Dutch Government has been able to ascertain them, are as follows:

The British American Tobacco Company (Nederland) BV is a 100 per cent subsidiary of the British American (BAT) Industries Limited, a multinational tobacco-processing enterprise, whose headquarters are established in London. The enterprise has a staff of some 250,000 spread throughout the world and an annual turnover of approximately 26 billion guilders, with a net profit for 1976–1977 after correction for inflation of 672 million guilders.

161

The firm (BATCO Benelux SA) which was established in Brussels, was originally a full subsidiary of BAT London but later became a 100 per cent subsidiary of BATCO (Nederland) BV. Over the years BATCO Benelux has expanded considerably through finance borrowed from BATCO Nederland. These borrowings were discharged by issuing new shares which were acquired by BATCO Nederland.

The case in question involves the plan of the management of BATCO (Nederland) BV to transfer cigarette production from the factory in Amsterdam to the one in Brussels. There are 361 people employed in the Amsterdam factory and the management's plan puts 231 jobs at risk. According to the management, the transfer is necessary because the two Benelux establishments produce at a loss and production can be made profitable only by a concentration of activities. The employees' organizations contest this view since it is their opinion that the Amsterdam factory operates at a profit.

The Benelux establishments' share of the Dutch cigarette market together amounts to 25 per cent. This has remained constant over a long period. The Amsterdam and Brussels establishments each cover 50 per cent of this share of the market with their production. In addition the Brussels factory produces cigarettes for the Belgian market and for export.

The production capacity of the enterprise in Brussels is larger than that of the Amsterdam factory and it is increasing while the Amsterdam factory's capacity remains at the same level. This is apparent from the figures provided by the BATCO management:

	Cigarettes per day (millions)	
	Brussels	Amsterdam
1973–74	22.5	27.5
1974–75	32.0	13.4
1975–76	33.0	13.4
1976–77	35.8	13.4

Note: The sharp decline in the Amsterdam production after 1973–74 was caused by a change from a partly double shift to day duty.

The Brussels enterprise is established in modern premises which have sufficient space for further expansion, while the Amsterdam enterprise occupies old buildings which are too small for expansion.

To enable it to consider the possibility of expanding the Amsterdam enterprise, the management took an option on a plot of land on which new premises could be constructed next door to the existing distribution centre. However, after studying the situation it came to the conclusion that this would not provide a profitable alternative. Since it is the management's view that concentration is necessary, in particular to keep overheads down, this must take place in

Brussels. In addition there is a social argument in support of this: concentration in Brussels puts 230 jobs at risk in Amsterdam, while concentration in Amsterdam would put 596 jobs at risk in Brussels.

The study undertaken by the management is the reason for the present case for it was established that sales forecasts and profit expectations were unfavourable. It gives two reasons for this: firstly, the intensification of the anti-smoking campaign, and secondly increased prices – both in Holland and Belgium – which are the largest in the history of cigarette production. In order to maintain the return on production in Amsterdam the management examined a number of alternatives in the study. As none of these met their requirements, it concluded that concentration in Brussels and thus closure of the Amsterdam establishment was the only remaining possibility of raising production in the Benelux to a profitable level.

The CNV (National Federation of Protestant Trade Unions) applied to the Amsterdam District Court for an interlocutory injunction against BATCO (Nederland) BV restraining the BATCO management from defaulting on its obligations and thereby creating an irreversible situation and from committing unlawful acts that would cause damage that could scarcely be rectified, if at all.

During the hearing the Court established that BATCO Amsterdam had repeatedly given certain assurances in recent years to employees, to the Works Council and to trade unions about maintaining employment in the Amsterdam factory. It was established further that various actions and events involving BATCO Amsterdam indicate that the decision to close and transfer activities had already been taken before the end of the first half of 1977 and that a start had also been made then on implementing the decision.

The Court found that BATCO was in default of its obligations and had committed a tort against the Food Industry Union of the CNV; the Court therefore ordered that BATCO Amsterdam should maintain the division of production between BATCO Amsterdam and BATCO Brussels at the level which applied prior to 1 January 1978 and that the staff should be increased within two months to the level necessary for normal production. BATCO has to comply with this ruling until the situation has been thoroughly studied and serious consultations have taken place with the employees and the trade unions. The President of the Amsterdam District Court thus found in favour of the CNV. The management of BATCO has appealed against this judgment. It was evident during the hearing that BATCO and the CNV differed on the establishment and interpretation of the profit figures.

III. THE VIEW OF THE NATIONAL FEDERATION OF PROTESTANT TRADE UNIONS (CNV)

For the facts as presented by the CNV reference may be made to the TUAC's submission made during the consultations of 11 April 1978.

Since 1971 production capacity in Brussels has expanded and in Amsterdam it has decreased. From the details provided by the management of BATCO Nederland the reasons for these developments cannot be found either in the sales figures or in the profits of the two establishments taken separately:

| | Cigarettes per day (millions) | | | |
| | Production Capacity | | Sales | |
	Brussels	Amsterdam	Estimated	Actual
1973–74	22.5	27.5	41.3	39.7
1974–75	32.0	13.4	44.4	41.6
1975–76	33.0	13.4	43.0	38.1
1976–77	35.8	13.4	42.6	38.5

The above figures show that capacity in Brussels was expanded in spite of the fact that sales did not come up to expectations. The reason was the attempt to concentrate production in Brussels.

The minutes of the Works Council of BATCO Nederland show that this development had been announced as early as 1971. Nevertheless, in 1974, the directors stated that production in Amsterdam would be maintained at the level of 14 million cigarettes a day. Notwithstanding this promise production capacity in Brussels was expanded by one million in 1975–76 and by 2.8 million in 1976–77.

If, then, it is a matter of over-capacity, as suggested by the BATCO management, this was caused by its policy which after all had been aimed at expanding capacity in Brussels. The over-capacity had been intentionally created. Moreover, the management ordered additional machines in mid-1977 for BATCO Benelux in Brussels with a capacity of 10 million cigarettes a day.

The management's policy cannot be ascribed to the development in the yield of the Amsterdam establishment. The management's figures provide further information on this:

| | Turnover (millions of tonnes) | | Profit | |
	Brussels	Amsterdam	Brussels	Amsterdam
1974–75	5.172	6.138	3.2	3.4
1975–76	5.072	5.672	3.6	4.5
1976–77	5.064	6.096	3.6	5.8

(Profit is before tax)

As appears from its report the management proposed to concentrate production in Brussels. Moreover, consultation was to take place with the trade unions. In spite of the undertaking to have consultations the management has meanwhile taken the following steps:

a. the option on building-land for a new factory in Amsterdam has been terminated;
b. sufficient packing material has been assembled in Brussels – by way of channels not normally used – for the production of cigarettes which up till now have been produced in the Netherlands;
c. by way of channels not normally used the management has acquired a quantity of tax stamps for cigarette packets intended for the Dutch market, sufficient for about one month's production;
d. additional machinery has been or is being acquired in the short-term without any justification being offered in the normal capacity summary.

No other conclusion can be drawn from this than that the management has already taken a decision and in the CNV's view there can be no question of open and meaningful consultation taking place with the trade unions. The transfer of production capacity from Amsterdam to Brussels has now been decided upon by the management. The only objective which the management can have in mind in regard to the transfer is to increase profits: in brief, the maximization of profits.

To understand the internal relations of the organization it is important to realize that the Chairman of the Brussels enterprise is also Chairman of the Amsterdam company. In the eyes of BAT (London), Brussels is the parent company of the Benelux branch and not Amsterdam, while Brussels is in reality a full subsidiary of BATCO (Nederland) in Amsterdam. Because of this the formal legal structure of the company does not accord with the position in practice. These facts lead the CNV to consider the OECD Guidelines. It wishes these facts and the court's judgement to be examined against the interpretation of the paragraphs of the Guidelines set out below.

1. As regards the question whether it is possible, under the Guidelines, to close a profitable enterprise and transfer it elsewhere in order to increase profits, the CNV would refer to paragraph 5 of General Policies which reads:
   '(Enterprises should) allow their component entities freedom to develop their activities and to exploit their competitive advantage in domestic and foreign markets, consistent with the need for specialization and sound commercial practice.'
   In addition the organization makes the following points:
   a. Paragraph 5 is not compatible with the practice whereby a profitable establishment whose continued existence has been guaranteed is closed so as to maximize profits elsewhere.
   b. This paragraph does not permit the freedom of a less profitable establishment to be restricted in order to render another establishment more profitable.
   c. Neither does this paragraph permit the freedom of an establishment to be restricted with a view to closing it down despite its competitive advantages on the domestic and foreign markets.
2. As regards the question whether it is permissible to exclude the employees' organizations and present them with a fait accompli, as in the present case, the CNV would refer to paragraph 6 of the section on Employment and Industrial Relations which reads:

'(Enterprises should) in considering changes in their operations which would have major effects upon the livelihood of their employees, in particular in the case of the closure of an entity involving collective lay-offs or dismissals, provide reasonable notice of such changes to representatives of their employees, and where appropriate to the relevant governmental authorities, and co-operate with the employee representatives and appropriate governmental authorities so as to mitigate to the maximum extent practicable adverse effects.'

In this connection the CNV states:

    a. This paragraph seeks the maximum co-operation between management and employees' representatives in cases which have important consequences for the employees' livelihoods. This maximum of co-operation has not been achieved.

    b. This paragraph implies open consultations between management and employees' representatives. This paragraph does not provide for the management to take decisions without informing the employees of them. When long-term decisions relating to lay-offs etc. have been taken at management level they must be communicated as quickly as possible to employees.

The CNV submits these interpretations for the attention of the IIME Committee. It requests clarification of the paragraphs of the Guidelines for Multinational Enterprises referred to above, with specific reference to the BATCO case.

IV. VIEW OF THE MANAGEMENT OF BATCO (NEDERLAND) BV

In the view of the management there is no question of intentionally created over-capacity. The expansion of the factory building in Brussels took place for the main part as early as 1972–73. In this connection and on the basis of anticipated increases in sales for 1972–73 and 1973–74, production capacity was increased from 22.5 million to 32.0 million cigarettes a day by the acquisition of additional machinery. Since then the expansion of machine capacity has been proportionally small. In any case, the management states that too large a capacity in machines is no real problem as surplus machinery can always be sold.

The problem is rather that there are at present two production units, while only one in fact is necessary. If production is concentrated, on the one hand there is the possibility of optimum use of the machines, while on the other a large number of jobs and activities which reflect duplication of effort are dispensed with. It has been calculated that, with concentrated production, 193 less staff are required while production can be maintained at the same level. Of the 231 jobs and activities which would be lost in Amsterdam, 38 are necessary for production in Brussels. The over-capacity has arisen because the sale of cigarettes has not been as high as was anticipated in the planning. This is the result of a number of factors which have led to stagnation and even a decrease in the consumption of cigarettes. These factors are firstly the intensified anti-smoking campaign and secondly the higher prices consequent upon increased taxes.

These adverse developments influence the yields of the enterprises. If the Amsterdam factory continues to operate, according to the management the figures for Brussels and Amsterdam will be:

	Brussels	Amsterdam	Total
	(millions of guilders)		
Losses in			
1977–78	2.5	0.9	3.4
1978–79	2.0	1.5	3.5
1979–80	4.4	6.1	10.5

It should be noted that the above figures have not been corrected to allow for the adverse effects of inflation which are estimated at approximately 5 per cent of about 50 million guilders or an additional loss of 2.5 million guilders a year.

The management wants the effects of inflation to be taken into account. However, since there is no uniform method in the Netherlands of allowing for correction for inflation, the figures are based on historic costs. BATCO, therefore, is not a profitable enterprise: its losses are even increasing.

Because the only profitable alternative for the Amsterdam production is concentration and as the Brussels factory could, if only a small number of machines were transferred, fulfil the total future requirements for the two factories, the management has been forced to conclude that the Amsterdam factory must be closed.

It was not a hasty or ill-considered decision to close the Amsterdam factory and concentrate production in Brussels. The management incurred the expense of having a detailed study carried out concerning the construction of a new factory in Amsterdam. The present premises are after all too old and too small. The management also went to the expense of retaining an option on land where a new factory could have been built. This option was terminated on 1 January 1978. The management would not have incurred this expenditure had they taken a decision at an earlier stage to close down and transfer production. It was only after a comprehensive study of the possibilities of raising the production in Amsterdam to a profitable level that the management came to the conclusion that the Amsterdam factory would have to be closed.

This conclusion was referred to the trade unions together with a request that the report, which included the above study, be studied and discussed with the management. The fact that the trade unions were not prepared to have a discussion of this kind does not point to a lack of willingness to co-operate on the part of the management, but rather to the trade unions' lack of willingness to co-operate.

It was the unco-operative attitude of the trade unions which led to the management ordering additional machines at an earlier stage.

These machines were not intended to increase capacity but to enable precautionary measures to be taken in the case of the Amsterdam factory being occupied by the employees. Without such precautionary measures a sit-in would bring production to a standstill and the company's share of the market would be lost.

For the above reasons the management did not agree with the judgment of the President of the Amsterdam District Court and therefore lodged an appeal. It has opted for a normal, non-expedited procedure in the case so that judgement can be expected towards the end of this year at the earliest.

On these grounds the management has concluded that the case submitted by the CNV and the issues raised are not relevant. Firstly, the enterprise does not run at a profit and so there is no basis to the argument founded on paragraph 5 of the General Policies. Secondly, paragraph 6 of the section on Employment and Industrial Relations is not relevant here because the trade unions themselves were not willing to have consultations.

V. SUBMISSION BY THE DUTCH GOVERNMENT

The Dutch Government does not wish at this stage to adopt a standpoint on the BATCO case as it is sub judice as regards co-operation and consultation with the employees' representatives and as the facts concerning ascertainment of profits have not been clearly established.

It reserves the right to refer to these aspects of the matter at a later stage. However, the Dutch Government now desires to submit to the IIME Committee the following issue which is based on the facts that have so far emerged from this case, with a request that it receive attention and study. It is after all important that the meaning of the Guidelines be clarified. Moreover, it is important to examine the extent to which the Guidelines need to be adapted or supplemented. It need hardly be stated that the Dutch Government is concerned about the matter of employment which is at stake in this case.

The Dutch Government therefore wishes to raise the issue of the closure and transfer of a profitable enterprise in order to obtain more profit elsewhere. The question that may be asked is: 'To what extent is the transfer abroad of profitable production compatible with paragraph 5 of the section on General Policies.'

Paragraph 5 reads as follows:
'(Enterprises should) allow their component entities freedom to develop their activities and to exploit their competitive advantage in domestic and foreign markets, consistant with the need for specialization and sound commercial practice.'

The Netherlands is especially interested in the interpretation of the terms 'component entities' and 'sound commercial practice'.

Reference may also be made, as regards this issue, to paragraphs 1 and 2 of the section on 'General Policies' which read:
'Enterprises should

1. take fully into account established general policy objectives of the Member countries in which they operate;
2. in particular, give due consideration to those countries' aims and priorities with regard to economic and social progress, including industrial and regional development, the protection of the environment, the creation of employment opportunities, the promotion of innovation and the transfer of technology.'

It must be stated here that this issue is relevant if it is established that BATCO (Nederland) is in fact a profitable enterprise. This underlines the need to establish precisely the facts of this case.

The CNV has raised a second issue, namely: Co-operation and consultation with the employees' representatives.

As this matter is sub judice in the Netherlands, the Dutch Government wishes only to refer to it and to reserve its position while awaiting the court's decision on the appeal lodged by the management of BATCO.

It will be easier to study and deal with this issue after the court has established the facts upon which judgement will be given.

There are various questions linked to this issue and reference may be made to those raised by the TUAC under paragraph 6 of its statement of 11 April 1978.

In any case reference may be made to paragraph 6 of the section on Employment and Industrial Relations which reads:

'(Enterprises should) in considering changes in their operations which would have major effects upon the livelihood of their employees, in particular in the case of the closure of an entity involving collective lay-offs or dismissals, provide reasonable notice of such changes to representatives of their employees, and where appropriate to the relevant governmental authorities, and co-operate with the employees' representatives and appropriate governmental authorities so as to mitigate to the maximum extent practicable adverse effects'.

The Netherlands is especially interested in the interpretation of 'reasonable notice' and 'cooperate . . . so as to mitigate to the maximum extent practicable adverse effects'.»

4. QUESTIONS AND ANSWERS IN THE DUTCH PARLIAMENT[13]

142. Two members of the Second Chamber, Mr. Beumer and Gerritse (Christian Democratic Party) on June 19, 1978 put the following written *questions* to the Ministers of Economic Affairs and of Social Affairs:
1. Is it, for the Ministers, acceptable that a reasonably profitable subsidiary of an international concern, established in the Netherlands and producing for the Dutch market, is closed down if it is not *demonstrated* that this subsidiary will work at a loss in the forthcoming years?
2. Would their opinion be different, if it could be demonstrated that the profits of the concern as a whole would augment as a consequence of the closure?

13. Translation from Dutch.

3. Would their opinion be influenced, if it could be accepted, that the concern, after closure of the Dutch entity, could continue to produce for the Dutch market and that this production would continue to render a positive contribution to the rentability of the concern?
4. Are the Ministers prepared, in making up their opinion, to take the OECD Guidelines for Multinational Enterprises explicitly into account?
5. Would the issue – taking the OECD Guidelines into account – lead to the introduction of a consultation procedure?

Explanation
An opinion in principle concerning these issues would be important since the intended transfer of the Dutch subsidiary of British American Tobacco Company to Brussels indicates, that the presumed situation could become a reality.

143. The Minister of Economic Affairs, Drs. G.M.V. van Aardenne, and the Minister of Social Affairs, Dr. W. Albeda, have given following *answers*:
Given the general nature of the questions, the answers to questions 1 and 4 will also be general. These answers are, consequently, not to be interpreted as the taking of a position regarding the BATCO case. This case will be dealt with in point 5.
1-2. We consider the closing down of an enterprise, under the conditions set out in the question, regrettable in the light of the envisaged employment policy of the Government.
   In giving an opinion concerning such a closure, one must start from the existing mixed economic order – including the freedom of establishment – which is considered by us as the most acceptable. This starting point has, as a consequence, that the enterprise itself has the ultimate responsibility for a possible closure of the entity in the light of the rentability of the enterprise concerned. This responsibility must be exercised taking the existing legal rules on workers' participation and on the protection of employment into account. We attach much importance to the implementation of these rules. Careful consultation between employer and employees has to have a most important place in the decision-making process concerning a closure.
   The consideration of a possible closing down of a profitable part of a concern or of a whole concern, which is profit-making, engages special societal responsibilities for that concern.
3. A small country, like the Netherlands, so dependable on import and export has traditionally and also for reasons of self interest, always been a protagonist of free commerce and of an optimal international division of labour, following which, production should take place where this – in conformity with the comparative cost advantages – can be done the best. The element mentioned in your question, in our opinion, should, in general not be taken into account.
4. Yes.
5. Given also the explanation, accompanying the questions, we point out that the Dutch Government has forwarded a memorandum concerning the BATCO case to OECD, on the basis of the procedures, which are laid down

in the decision of the Council on Inter-governmental Consultation Procedures on the Guidelines for Multinational Enterprises. The parties concerned have been consulted at the time of the preparation of the memorandum. The Dutch Government asked the IME Committee to indicate the significance of the Guidelines in such cases. A first exchange of views has already taken place. The Government, as well as business — which accepted these Guidelines voluntary — attach a great importance to these Guidelines. The consultation procedures, established in relation to the Guidelines, can in our opinion be improved. The Dutch Government will insist on such an improvement at the occasion of the review of the Guidelines in (1979).

It also means that the Dutch Government will again ask the OECD partners for a fact-finding procedure, in order to prevent, through an examination of the facts on which a complaint is based, this examination of the implementation of the Guidelines, will not remain too abstract.

5. POSITION OF BIAC

144. BIAC insisted at the occasion of the consultations with the IME Committee that economic decisions should not be frozen, even for employment reasons and that companies should be able to move within a given country and from one country to another, taking national rules and the Guidelines into account, especially in the area of information and consultation of employees. Regarding 'general policies' BIAC declared during the meeting with the IME Committee of April 11, 1978, the following:

«Turning now to the section on 'General Policies', BIAC would make the observation, that compliance with the first Guidelines under General Policies and also, perhaps, the Finance Guideline could create difficulties because of the vagueness of the reference to 'established objectives' of a country. BIAC believes enterprises will strive to meet national objectives if they are readily identifiable. Where they are less easy to identify consultation between the competent authorities and the entities concerned should take place.»

6. REPORT OF THE IME COMMITTEE

145. Concerning the problem of the closing down of a subsidiary and of a profitable entity, the Committee concluded as follows:

General policies
Paragraphs 1 and 2 of this chapter of the Guidelines recommend MNEs to take fully into account the established general policy objectives of the Member countries in which they operate' and, in particular, 'to give due consideration to those countries' aims and priorities'. Paragraph 2 identifies a number of areas of aims and priorities. Specific cases have shown that these provisions are of particular relevance when a local subsidiary of an MNE is to be closed down. In

this context a prudent company would be well advised to seek any necessary clarification of government policies through advance consulations with the government concerned. In the view of the Committee, paragraphs 1 and 2 of this chapter of the Guidelines do not affect the right of the enterprise to reach decisions with respect to cutting back or terminating operations in a given plant. But they indicate certain considerations which should be given due weight in making such a decision. If a firm does proceed in this manner, then it clearly follows that the nature of the final decision will be influenced by the considerations set out in paragraphs 1 and 2 whilst respecting the firm's own judgement (paragraph 43).

If MNEs are to take fully into account Member countries' policy objectives and aims as stated in paragraphs 1 and 2, it is understood that governments make such aims and objectives as clear, stable and understandable to management as possible. Where host countries' national legislation or the general framework of their policies may affect disinvestment, *paragraph 7* of the Introduction of the Guidelines is of relevance. Although the right of each state to prescribe the conditions under which multinational enterprises operate within its jurisdiction remains unaffected, such laws, regulations and policies are subject to international law and international agreements and should respect contractual obligations to which a country has subscribed. It also means that these laws, regulations and policies will be consistent with member country responsibilities to treat enterprises equitably (paragraph 44)

The question has been raised whether *paragraphs 4 and 5* of the General Policies chapter have special relevance in cases where the decision to close down a subsidiary and to transfer its activities abroad concerns a subsidiary that can be considered still to be a profitable one. Consideration of this question demonstrated to the Committee how difficult it can be in practice to decide whether a particular entity is profitable or not. Accounting data differ according to differences in valuation and the accounting standards that are adopted and widely diverging estimates can be made, in particular, of the future profitability of the subsidiary. When there is clear evidence of the profitability of a subsidiary, this calls for special consideration by a company when it is contemplating the closure of that subsidiary, although other factors may be of importance and this cannot restrict the right of the company to reach its decision. Paragraphs 4 and 5, read together, can be understood to be in favour of a certain degree of integration of the component entities of an MNE into the economic context of the countries in which they operate. On the other hand, the insertion of the words 'consistent with the need for specialisation and sound commercial practices' in paragraph 5 was intended to provide for giving due consideration to the interests of an MNE as a whole, as well as the situation of any of its entities. The Guidelines do not call for the freezing of the existing structures of multinational enterprises nor do they infringe the freedom of MNEs to take decisions to divest in the furtherance of global strategies judged to be in the best interests of the firm as a whole. But this freedom is circumscribed according to national law and contractual obligations entered into by firms and affected by paragraphs 1 and 2 of the chapter on General Policies as described above.»(paragraph 45)

7. COMMENTS

146. It is clear that the Guidelines as a general proposition do not prevent the closure of a subsidiary, even a profitable one; the responsibility, and the power to do so remains entirely with the management of the multinational enterprise. The multinational enterprise in doing so must, of course, take local law and practices into account, as well as the policy objectives of the Member Countries in which they operate. It is recommended though obligatory, to inform and consult with the Government and with the employees and their representatives, or to negotiate with the representatives of the employees on the matter (e.g. in Sweden). Member States are, of course, free to regulate the closing down of enterprises but must do so, taking international obligations (free flow of investment and capital) into account, as well as the obligation to treat enterprises equitably and not to discriminate between national and multinational companies.

It is at the same time self-evident that a multinational enterprise must respect its contractual obligations, e.g. if an enterprise in return for Government subventions has committed itself to guarantee a number of jobs during a certain period.

IV. The Right of Employees to be Represented

Guideline 1 and 2 of the Employment and Industrial Relations Chapter

«1. respect the right of their employees to be represented by trade unions and other bona fide organizations of employees, and engage in constructive negotiations, either individually or through employers' associations, with such employee organizations with a view to reaching agreements on employment conditions, which should include provisions for dealing with disputes arising over the interpretation of such agreements, and for ensuring mutually respected rights and responsibilities;

2. (a) provide such facilities to representatives of the employees as may be necessary to assist in the development of effective collective agreements;

   (b) provide to representatives of employees information which is needed for meaningful negotiations on conditions of employment;»

---

147 — II. Impact of the Guidelines

A. Respect of That Right by the Employers. The Citicorp Case[14]

1. The Issue. Submission by FIET

WORLD-WIDE ANTI-UNION POLICY BY CITIBANK – CITICORP

147.«Submitted by the International Federation of Employees and Technicians (FIET) and the National Union of Bank Employees (British Union Member of the TUC and FIET)

It is the contention of FIET and NUBE that the international management of Citibank-Citicorp conducts a world wide anti-union policy. Whenever possible, it avoids recognizing trade unions and negotiating with them. To conduct this policy, there is evidence that instructions are given to their local management about the tactics to be used in local situations.

An eloquent example of this hostile approach of Citibank-Citicorp is the enclosed copy of a Guide produced by Citicorp (New-York Headquarters), for the use of the management of Citibank in the United Kingdom, in response to the growing interest in the union among the staff of Citibank-United Kingdom. The Bank's opposition effectively stopped the recruitment of members by NUBE (the National Union of Bank Employees, affiliated to the TUC and FIET) and the hostile environment undermined the support of those who had become members. A recent survey by FIET among its affiliated organizations, has shown evidence of similar difficulties.

On page 11 of the updated version of the 'Managers guide to employee relations', valid for 1977, the international management of Citicorp states: 'The management of Citibank firmly believes that the best interest of all Citibankers are served without the presence of a union. To that end management commits its effort to the maintenance of an environment which renders unnecessary the intervention of a third party.'

'It is further the policy of Citibank that only the President or the Chairman of the Board has the authority to recognise or enter into any agreement, verbal or written, with a union, union representative or group of employees.'

Attention should be paid to the following facts: Citibank U.K. is a wholly owned subsidiary of Citibank International (New-York). Citicorp, which issues the instructions to Citibank International as well as Citibank United Kingdom, is the American mother company. The Chairman of the Board to which a reference is made in the Guide is the Chairman of the mother company Citicorp.»

---

14. See also the Motor IBERICA case and the BLACK and DECKER case, submitted by IMF, Annex II.

174

2. «Managers Guide to Employee Relations (United Kingdom)

148. TABLE OF CONTENTS

INTRODUCTION

As a line manager you are Citibank to the people you supervise. You have the closest, most direct and most frequent contact with them. What you do and what you say, your actions, your words create Citibank's reputation and determine whether it is judged to be a good place to work.

Corporate programs and policies succeed or fail depending upon how you carry them out. It then follows that your people-to-people skills are a major factor in determining your own career progress.

The guidelines in this handbook will help you in employee relations management. They are however not a substitute for good judgement in dealing with the problems and concerns of the individuals whom you supervise.

EMPLOYEE RELATIONS PROBLEMS – COMMON CAUSES

Day-to-day employee relations problems are most frequently caused by:
Inconsistency in the application of Personnel policies and procedures.
Favoritism.
Lack of *fair* but *firm* discipline.
Failure to listen and to follow through.
Failure to keep employees informed, particularly about changes that are going to affect them.

Changes in procedures which appear to be arbitrary.

Sometimes it will seem that employees are imagining that a problem exists. Whether real or imaginary, however, it is your responsibility to recognize the situation and to deal with it effectively. Failure to accept the fact that a problem exists can only result in a more serious situation. Continued denial of the existence of a problem can result in employees turning to alternate sources of leadership, either within their own group or outside the Bank.

From time to time any supervisor will need assistance in solving particularly difficult employee relations problems. There are several sources of help available to you among which are: your own supervisor; your Group/Area Personnel Units; Advisory Service; and Staff Relations.

RECOGNIZING PROBLEMS

Employees who complain may help you in identifying problem areas. However not all employees feel comfortable in discussing a problem, thinking either you can't or won't resolve the situation to their satisfaction. In such cases employees may indicate the existence of problems to you through changes in attitude, behaviour or job performance.

In extreme cases, employees may act in concert to present complaints or effect work stoppages. Finally, if the situation becomes even more critical, there may be signs of union literature; strangers on the premises or loitering outside; new patterns of communications and/or increasing questions about benefits and company policies relating to salaries and overtime pay.

Look for these signs:

A drop in productivity.

Change in peoples' attitude.

Change in the way people work.

Increasing absenteeism.

Increasing turnover.

Many complaints.

Refusal to work overtime.

Resistance to following new instructions.

Destruction of work or equipment.

Unusual groupings of employees at breaks or meals.

Supervisor frozen out of conversations.

The circulation of union literature.

Increasing number of questions about pay and benefits.

Strangers on the premises.

HANDLING PROBLEMS

Once a problem is identified, events tend to move quickly. The following will act as a guideline in the effective handling of a problem.

Complaints from a Single Employee

(a) Discussions should be held in a private area away from the place of work. Listen carefully and attempt to isolate the root of the problem.
(b) If unable to resolve the problem yourself, or if you need further authorization or clarification, end the interview, promise a prompt reply, and follow through.
(c) If a problem cannot be resolved to the *employee's satisfaction*, discuss the problem with your supervisor and/or the Staff Relations Manager. If further action is required, follow the steps outlined in the Problem Review Procedure (see Appendix).

In all of the following situations, contact your supervising officer and the Staff Relations Manager. If they are unavailable have a fellow supervisor present as you follow the prescribed outline.

Complaints from a Group

(a) Under no conditions are you authorized to deal with a group (2 or more people) or committee or anyone purporting to represent a group.
(b) Instead try to talk to members of the group individually. Make it clear that you are talking only about that staff member's individual problem.
(c) If the group is too large or too cohesive to be separated into individuals, do not attempt to deal with them but rather call on your supervising officer and/or the Staff Relations Manager for guidance.
(d) In talking to an individual, follow the same procedures for 'Complaints from a Single Employee'. If an individual refuses to talk to you, direct him/her to return to work and continue with another member of the group.
(e) If the employee refuses to return to work, *advise* the individual that continued refusal may result in disciplinary action.
(f) If he/she continues to refuse, *direct* him/her to resume his/her normal work activities or leave the premises.
(g) If he/she refuses, *advise* the employee to leave the premises immediately and that he/she is subject to disciplinary action up to and including discharge should he/she refuse to do so.
(h) If there is continued refusal, ask Security to remove the employee from the premises. This step should normally be taken after consultation with your supervising officer and the Staff Relations Manager.
(i) Report the incident to your supervising officer and the Staff Relations Manager.

Note: It is very important to avoid dealing with a group, or even giving the appearance of dealing with a group. It is conceivable that such direct dealing may be viewed as recognition of the group for collective bargaining purposes. You may then in effect be dealing with a union.

The determination as to whether you bargained with the group depends on what actually happens and what is said, but you should never put yourself in the position of being unable to prove what you said to a group.

A Group Request for a Meeting

(a) There may be an occasion when an employee group requests a meeting with management and/or a discussion of their complaint. Let the group know that you cannot meet with them, but would gladly arrange meetings with any individual employee who wishes to discuss a problem.
(b) Invite the employee into your office or other private area and attempt to determine the nature of the problem.
(c) If you cannot resolve the problem or need further assistance, authorization, or clarification, promise a prompt reply and follow through.
(d) Report the incident immediately to your supervising officer and Staff Relations Manager.

A Petition or List of Complaints

(a) Do not discuss any petitions or list of grievances with any employee group. If you have knowledge of the existence of such a petition or list, notify your supervising officer and Staff Relations Manager.
 If an individual presents a petition or list and purports to speak for or represent a group, or if the document has more than one signature, treat the matter as you would a group complaint.
 Accept the petition or list, but do not discuss or in any way acknowledge the contents of the document.
(b) Offer to discuss specific complaints with individual employees.
(c) If during the interview the employee is not satisfied, refer him/her to the Staff Relations Manager.
(d) Forward the document to the Personnel Department and report the incident to your supervising officer.

An Unauthorized Work Stoppage

A work stoppage occurs when two or more employees, *acting together*, refuse to perform assigned work; abide by established rules, regulations, or management directives. Some examples of work stoppages are:
(a) Walking off the job without permission.
(b) Refusing to leave the work area at the end of scheduled work time.
(c) Refusing to perform work as directed.
(d) Refusal to work overtime.

Note: It may be difficult to determine if a refusal to work overtime is an unauthorized work stoppage as defined above. The determination relates to whether the refusal results from concerted group activity. You must therefore ask each employee individually to work the overtime and note in writing the reasons for each refusal.

Action to be Taken

(a) If possible, have a management witness present.
(b) Do not deal with a spokesman or committee purporting to represent the employees.
(c) Specifically instruct each employee to resume his/her normal duties.
(d) If the employee refuses, *warn* him/her that continued refusal may result in his/her being permanently replaced.
(e) If the employee continues to refuse, *direct* the employee to resume normal work or leave the premises.
(f) If the employee continues to refuse, *advise* the employee to leave the premises immediately and that he/she is subject to disciplinary action up to and including discharge should he/she refuse to do so.
(g) In the event of continued refusal, *contact* Security and have the employee removed from Bank premises. This step should normally be taken after consultation with your supervising officer and the Staff Relations Manager.
(h) Report the incident to your supervising officer and the Staff Relations Manager.

The Staff Relations Manager should:
(a) Advise and assist supervisors and managers in carrying out this procedure.
(b) Obtain all relevant facts, i.e., time, place, number of employees involved and their names.
(c) Consult with the Vice-President of Personnel to determine the final course of action.

Work Slowdowns

If you determine that a work slowdown is taking place, direct each employee to cease the unauthorised act, and proceed as you would for a work stoppage.

Unidentified/Unauthorized Visitors

You have the responsibility to make certain that strangers who come into the work area are properly identified and that they are on authorized business. If you are not satisfied on either point, ask the Security Department to escort the stranger to the nearest exit.

FNCB POLICY ON UNIONS

The management of Citibank firmly believes that the best interests of all Citibankers are served without the presence of a union. To that end management commits its efforts to the maintenance of an environment which renders unnecessary the intervention of a third party.
It is further the policy of Citibank that only the President or the Chairman of the Board has the authority to recognize or enter into any agreement, verbal or written, with a union, union representative or group of employees.

Union Organizing Drive

Despite their lack of success, various trade unions continue to publicise their intent to organise bank employees. The following situations may occur should FNCB employees be the target of an organizing drive.
(a) Distribution of Leaflets, and/or the encouragement of employees to join a union *by a non-Bank Employee.*
  (1) If an unauthorized visitor is distributing leaflets to or encouraging Bank employees to join a union on Bank property, direct him/her to leave immediately.
  (2) If he/she refuses, ask Security to remove the individual from Bank property.
  (3) Remove all loose literature and cards from premises and forward to the Staff Relations Manager.
  (4) Report to your supervising officer and to the Staff Relations Manager.
(b) Distribution of Leaflets, and/or the encouragement of employees to join a union *by a Bank Employee.*
  (1) If the employee is engaging in such activity during working time, direct him/her to cease immediately and resume his/her assigned duties.
  (2) If he/she refuses, inform him/her that he/she is subject to disciplinary action up to and including discharge.
  (3) If he/she continues to refuse, inform him/her that he/she is to immediately leave the premises.
  (4) If he/she continues to refuse, ask Security to remove him/her from the Bank premises. This step should normally be taken after consultation with your supervising officer and the Staff Relations Manager.
  (5) Report to your supervising officer and the Staff Relations Manager.

Note: If an employee is distributing union leaflets and/or otherwise encouraging employees to join a union, he or she may only do so in time outside of their normal working hours.
It should further be noted that no employee(s) may be approached by these individual(s) during their normal working hours.
Any such activity should be immediately reported to the Staff Relations Manager.

Union Representative's Demand for Recognition

(a) If he/she appears in person:
  (1) Immediately call witnesses equal to or greater than the number of individuals accompanying the union organizer.
  (2) If the union organizer demands verbal recognition, tell him/her that you do not have the authority to discuss this matter. Refer him/her to the Staff Relations Manager.
  (3) If he/she presents union cards and asks you to verify employee's signatures or names, refuse to accept or look at the cards or any other material offered by the organizer. Acceptance of verification of such

material under these circumstances may be interpreted as recognition of the union for the purpose of collective bargaining. Refer him/her to the Staff Relations Manager.
  (4) If possible, make a record of the conversation by whatever means possible.
  (5) Do not argue or discuss the matter. Close the conversation quickly. Ask the union organiser to leave promptly. Do not allow him/her to linger in work areas. Escort him/her to the nearest exit.
(b) If he/she telephones:
  (1) Refuse any request or demand for union recognition.
  (2) Refuse to meet with him/her.
  (3) Refer him/her to the Staff Relations Manager.
  (4) Report to your supervising officer and the Staff Relations Manager.
(c) If he/she sends you a letter or telegram:
  (1) Refer the letter (unopened, if you know it's from a union) to the Staff Relations Manager and report the incident to your supervising officer.

In all situations of this kind where there is the possibility of union involvement, you should make a note of all pertinent facts and report the matter to your supervising officer and Staff Relations Manager. In no case should you discuss these matters with any other individual or group.

Picketing Situations

The presence of a picket line presents both a practical and a legal question. From the practical point of view it is an obstacle to maintaining normal operations. Consequently Staff Relations Manager join with Personnel Department Representatives and line supervisors to effect the following:
(a) Direct employees who are not picketing to go about their normal duties without regard to the picket line activity.
(b) Inform employees that their failure to cross the picket line puts them in the position of strikers.
(c) Keep an accurate count of employees at work each day.

Picket lines frequently give rise to complicated legal problems. You can help to avoid these if you:
(a) Do not speak to any member of the picket line except when directed to do so by proper authorities.
(b) Avoid any arguments or contact with pickets.
(c) Direct other employees to avoid the picket line whenever possible.

The Staff Relations Manager and Personnel Department Representatives will:
(a) Advise and assist supervisors and managers on this matter immediately.
(b) Obtain all relevant facts; course of action, time, place, number of employees involved, etc.
(c) Assist line management in determining impact of picketing on operations.
(d) Assist line management in making whatever changes in operations are necessary to lessen impact of picketing.

181

(e) Assist line management in implementing contingency plan subject to final approval by the senior group operating officer.
(f) Consult with appropriate management representative to determine final course of action.

The Manager's Role in a Union Organizing Campaign

During an organizing drive you will have many things to consider aside from picketing. Primarily, the question of what you may or may not say to employees is most important. Managers are spokesmen for the company and, therefore, what they say can be attributed to the company.
Companies do not, however, win organizational campaigns by remaining silent. Therefore, an understanding of what to say or what not to say is important. Generally you may legally say anything you choose so long as it does not violate one of three general rules.
(a) Don't Threaten an employee with reprisals.
(b) Don't Interrogate an employee(s) about union activities.
(c) Don't Promise an employee any economic benefits.

There follows a more specific listing of the do's and don'ts which must be observed during a union organization drive.
(a) You may tell your employees the following:
    (1) We do not believe a union is either necessary or desirable.
    (2) We believe the best interests of our employees will be served by continuing their direct relationship with the Bank and our management staff rather than through a third party.
    (3) The Bank has and will continue to treat its employees equally and fairly, paying salaries and benefits equal to or better than the industry for comparable work.
    (4) The management of the Bank is always willing to discuss any subject of interest to employees.
    (5) It is important to understand that the union has its own interests aside from the interests of its members. In case of conflict the union's interests come first.
    (6) The individual union member must also abide by the majority decision even when he/she does not agree with the majority.
    (7) The Problem Review Procedure permits employees to voice their thoughts or complaints to management thereby assuring them of personal consideration.
    (8) It costs the employee money to join a union, it costs money to stay in the union week after week, year after year.
    (9) A union member could be fined or 'sent to Coventry' if he does not go out on strike once a strike is called. And, this is so even if he does not want to strike and lose earnings that may not ever be recovered.
    (10) Employees do not have to talk to union organizers.
    (11) Employees do not have to give their name and address to a union organizer.

(12) Employees do not have to attend any meeting called by the union or by employees.

(13) Employees do not have to sign anything distributed by the union and should not do so unless they want to lose their individual rights.

(14) A union cannot guarantee anyone's job – only his own work efforts protect his job.

(15) We believe that employees should not pay dues, and fines for the things they are getting and will continue to get without a union.

(16) We sincerely believe that our employees will not benefit from joining a union.

(b) You must not:

(1) Threaten or otherwise intimidate employees directly or indirectly because of their interest in a union.

(2) Threaten to discharge or discipline employees or lay off employees because of their interest in a union.

(3) Interrogate employees regarding their union feelings.

(4) Promise employees special favours or treatment to stay out of the union or vote against it.

(5) Make statements to employees that they will be discharged or disciplined if they are active on behalf of the union.

CONCLUSIONS

The *Managers Guide to Employee Relations* has been prepared to help you identify and handle employee relations problems and to let you know where you can go for help.

Many of the things you will see or hear may have little meaning by themselves. However, put together with reports of other managers, your experiences may reveal a pattern that will enable management to anticipate employee relations problems. That's why it is important that you report to your immediate supervisor and to the Staff Relations Manager all occurrences of unauthorized visitors, attempts to get employees to join a union, group complaints or requests for a meeting, etc. Of course, picketing and actual demands from a union representative should be referred immediately to the Staff Relations Manager.

We believe you will find the Guide useful in carrying out your day-to-day responsibilities as a manager.

APPENDIX

The prompt and equitable review of employee problems and the resolution of such problems at the lowest possible organizational level is vitally important to the employee relations environment of the Bank. An employee problem exists whenever an employee feels that he has a job-related problem (real or imaginary) that has not been resolved to his satisfaction. In such instances, the employee should be encouraged to use the Problem Review Procedure, and the supervisor is responsible for ensuring that the problem is promptly and fully

183

processed until the employee is satisfied with the decision made or until the procedure is exhausted.

Step 1 The employee should discuss the problem with his immediate supervisor, and if the employee is not satisfied with the results of this discussion, his supervisor must arrange a meeting with the Supervising Officer to take place within 7 days.

Step 2 The employee, his supervisor, and the Supervising Officer will discuss the problem. Subsequent to this discussion, a decision based on the available facts will be communicated to the employee by his supervisor. If the employee is not satisfied with this decision, the Supervising Officer and the Staff Relations Manager should review the problem. If the problem is not resolved to the employee's satisfaction at the Division or Group level, his Supervising Officer and/or the Staff Relations Manager must make an appointment with an officer from Personnel Department within 7 days.

Step 3 The Personnel Officer will discuss the problem with the employee and then with the line supervisors and the Staff Relations Manager. If, after these discussions, the employee feels his problem requires further review, the Personnel Officer will discuss the problem with Senior Management whose decision will be communicated to the employee by his supervisor within 7 days. The personnel Officer will then consult with the employee to determine whether the problem has been satisfactorily resolved.

The processing of the problem will stop at any step where the decision made is satisfactory to the employee. The success of this procedure depends upon the members of the Bank's supervisory staff. They should encourage their employees to use this procedure and must not, under any circumstances, penalize those employees who do so.»

3. Position of BIAC

149. At the occasion of the formal consultation with the IME committee, April 11, 1978, the representative of BIAC made following statement:

«So far as the Guidelines on Employment and Industrial Relations are concerned, BIAC agrees with the Member Governments' very understandable views that their application and interpretation has to be considered within the framework of national legislation and local practice – just as it has been acknowledged in the 'Chapeau' to this section in the Guidelines. For instance, in regard to the first Guideline on Employment and Industrial relations, naturally it has not been possible for the IIME Committee to go into detail on the procedures for the recognition of trade union rights. In some countries a certain number of employees of a firm must indicate a desire to belong to a union before an employer is required and able to agree to negotiating rights. In others, trade unions are recognized for negotiating rights in that country once they are considered to be representative. Practice in these areas varies widely from country to country, and in these situations the 'Chapeau' clause controls the Guidelines and the employer is required to follow local law and prevailing practice. This Guideline also does not go into the question of types of trade unions nor is a distinction made between plant, company wide, industry wide, or national bargaining – all of which re-emphasizes the point that national law and prevailing practice will determine, in each country, the collective bargaining pattern.»

4. The report of the IME Committee

150. Paragraph 60 of the report relates to the right of the employees to be represented by trade unions and other bona fide organizations (paragraphs 1 and 2 of the employment and industrial relations chapter) as follows:

«Paragraph 1 provides that MNEs should 'respect the right of their employees to be represented by trade unions and other bona fide organisations of employees'. The conditions under which these rights are exercised are a matter of national laws, regulations and practices. Thus it was agreed during the drafting of the Guidelines that they would not seek to indicate what organizations in a specific sense should represent employees for collective bargaining or what criteria should be used for the selection of such organizations. It remains, however, that paragraph 1 does provide expressly for management engaging in constructive negotiations with employee representatives on employment conditions and the provision of paragraph 2 adds that enterprises are expected to co-operate with representatives of employees for the specific purposes stated in paragraphs 1 and 2. Thus, the thrust of these provisions of the Guidelines is towards having management adopt a positive approach towards the activities of trade unions and other bona fide organizations of employees of all categories and, in particular, an open attitude towards organizational activities within the framework of national rules and practices.» (paragraph 60)

5. Some comments

151. The report of the IME Committee induces us to the following questions and comment. First, what is the meaning of '*Other bona fide organisations of employees*'? These are works councils, committees for hygiene, union delegations and shop stewards committees, which are set up by national law, collective agreements or practice. The Committee underlines that it is the national law and practice, which will exclusively determine the rules and conditions following which employees exercise their right to organize, to bargain collectively and how bona fide organizations are set up. Multinational enterprises should also in this area, like in other areas, follow and adapt to national law and practice. The Guidelines thus, do not add anything to that. The Guidelines, the

IME Committee states, however, call for *'constructive negotiations'*, a *'positive approach'* and an *'open attitude'*. This means that the employers should not interfere with the right of the employees to organize. An anti-union attitude, policies or instructions to go non-union are contrary to this approach. The employers should, in fact, take a neutral attitude. This does not take away the right of the employer to express his opinion on the matter, but this should not amount to threats or to anti-union policies.

Once organized, the employer should recognize the union and bargain with a view to reaching agreement.

152. The word employees, covers all those working in subordination. This includes blue as well as white collar workers as supervisory personnel. Again, the conditions under which those different groups exercise their rights are subject to national law and practice.

B. THE STATUS OF INTERNATIONAL TRADE SECRETARIATS.

1. The issue

153. The question arises whether the Guidelines give a platform for the International Trade Secretariats to request multinational headquarters to recognize them and to deal with them. The International Trade Secretariats and TUAC claim that the ITS

«are trade unions, certainly bona fide organizations, and that they should be recognized by the multinational enterprises on the basis of Guideline 1 of the Employment and Industrial Relations Chapter.

At the occasion of the consultations of January 29th, 1979, TUAC insisted 'the provisions of the Guidelines must also be interpreted in a way that will not hinder representatives of the International Trade Secretariats to participate in negotiations when necessary'.

To this the employers reply that local law and practice should prevail, that labour relations systems are national and not international, and that they see no reasons, why given this state of affairs they should deal with ITS.»

In its statement on the review, June 1979, BIAC declared . . .

«that while the international trade secretariats have a role to play, within the overall trade-union system itself, they cannot be regarded as organizations of employers in the context of the Guidelines. BIAC questions the suggestion that their recognition might have been within the intention of the Guidelines, since the Guidelines are silent about international trade union bodies and their activities and they were not considered during the negotiations.»

2. The report of the IME Committee

154. The report gives a rather marginal answer to the question of the status of ITS in its paragraph 62:

«The question has been raised, however, whether the Employment and Industrial Relations Guideline could put obstacles in the way of recognition by the management of an MNE, in agreement with the national trade unions it has recognised and consistent with national laws and practices, of an International Trade Secretariat as a 'bona fide organisation of employees' referred to in paragraph 1 of the Guidelines. It is the Committee's view that no such obstacle exists or was intended in the Guidelines.»

3. Some comments

155. Obviously, the Committee's answer is right, but it is not complete. It is self-evident that the Guidelines do not prohibit a multinational enterprise recognizing an International Trade Union as a bona fide organization, provided that national law is respected and the national unions agree. The IME Committee's answer hides a fundamental disagreement, not only between employers and unions but between Governments as well, on the role of the International Trade Unions and International Trade Union Action, especially, as we will see later, concerning international collective bargaining. The fact is, that the Guidelines are neutral on the question of International Trade Secretariats. It is, however, obvious that ITS are Trade-Unions and are bona fide. No one can dispute that. The point is, however, that, as indicated in paragraph 60 of the IME report,[15] the conditions under which recognition or bargaining are exercised are a matter of national laws, regulations and practices. Thus ITS must use the possibilities of national laws and practice to materialize their claims. These possibilities are, however, rather limited. It is, e.g., possible in the USA for a majority union to include in its bargaining team a representative of the International Trade Union; as is already the case in the Federal Republic of Germany that representatives of International Trade Secretariats are sitting on the supervisory boards of corporations under the rules of co-determination as representatives of the employees.

C. The Guidelines and International Collective Bargaining[16]

1. The issue. Submission by IMF

156. Trade unions favour international collective bargaining, which is, in fact, not yet a reality, although several examples could be mentioned, e.g. in the

15. See above no. 150.
16. We use the word bargaining in its broadest and functional definition, . .:«as a process which takes place between, on the one hand, workers acting collectively, usually but not always represented by a trade union – and, on the other hand, by employers or employers' organizations and, in some cases, the public authorities. It is this discussion, this negotiation, this process of give-and-take, with the objective of arriving at an agreed solution, which I have in mind when using the term 'collective bargaining'. In other words, 'collective bargaining' refers to a process of reconciling, of accomodating divergent interests between workers and employers, its outcome is usually a compromise, an agreed compromise.»
(J. Schregle, 'Trends in collective bargaining. General introduction', in: *Bulletin for Comparative Labour Relations*, – Deventer, Kluwer, nr. 10, 1979, 357).

shipping industry, where there are regular meetings between the International Transport Workers' Federation and the International Shipping Federation.

157. *'The need for meetings with multinationals at the decision-making level'* was submitted by the International Metalworkers Federation to the IME Committee, at the occasion of the meeting with TUAC March 30, 1977:

«*The need for meetings with multinationals at the decision-making level*

Numerous cases could be submitted – many of recent date – which would provide continuous proof of decisions affecting employment and social problems and issues raised by trade unions in a subsidiary that are being examined and finally decided upon at international headquarters.

Examples also show that this is a source of conflict that could be avoided if communication from the decision-making centre to the trade unions and the opportunity for consultations and negotiations with the trade unions existed. There are also many issues constantly arising which show that the trade unions must receive timely information, with facts and figures, in order to be able to defend the interests of the workers and co-operate in finding the best possible solutions for safeguarding employment and for working out progressive social agreements to protect workers from the effects of changes occurring in the operations of a multinational company.

A typical example was the conflict in 1976 between SENEFFE in Belgium – a subsidiary of the American multinational BURROUGHS in Detroit – and the Belgian trade unions.

A technological changeover in the product line of this subsidiary, from the manufacture of traditional accounting machines to computer terminals, caused employment problems. This was actually a changeover from electro-mechanical to electronic components, leading to the introduction of shorter working hours and mass dismissals. Some solutions were eventually found to settle the conflict by an agreement which had been negotiated and signed by the Belgian management of BURROUGHS-SENEFFE, in the framework of the Belgian Employers' Federation – Farbimétal on the one hand, and the trade unions on the other hand. However, this conciliation agreement which had been accepted by the Belgian Employers' Federation, was finally rejected by international management in Detroit; thus deciding the fate of the workers in the Belgian subsidiary.

Another multinational company with its parent company in the United States, which creates serious employment problems and disregards the right of trade unions to receive information and negotiate solutions for the workers' protection, is the AMERICAN STANDARD COMPANY. In 1976 its subsidiary in the Federal Republic of Germany – IDEAL STANDARD GmbH – announced the closure of its plant manufacturing radiators in Neuss, making 459 workers redundant, apart from the dismissal of 80 non-manual workers in its regional headquarters in Bonn, and a further 52 workers in another subsidiary plant in Berlin.

The works council of this company and the trade union IGMetall strongly

188

protested that they were confronted with a final decision, leaving merely negotiations about the social measures concerning the dismissed workers. The works council pointed out that there had never even been any attempt to consider ways and means for the reorganization of the plant. The entire decision to fold-up the manufacture of radiators in Neuss was all the more incomprehensible, and met with bitterness and resistance, as this European subsidiary had a strong market position of 37% with regard to cast-iron radiators. Only in December 1975 management had wanted to hire additional workers, strongly urging the works council to give their agreement. There seemed no sign of any structural difficulties ahead for this plant.

There was never any inside information on the profit or loss situation of the company. In the meantime it seems that world central management was following a policy of drastically reducing some of its activities in Europe. Difficulties arising from the rundown of operations had also occurred in France, causing a leading economic journal in France (Le Nouvel Economiste) to comment that the American based multinational never had a comprehensive global strategy, and that its European subsidiary IDEAL-STANDARD could only react with their hands tied. Fears were expressed about further closures in Europe.

There are also issues where works councils, unions and their representatives have to take a position in plants of subsidiaries, which can only be arrived at after full judgement of the case, if the necessary data about developments in other plants and subsidiaries in other countries linked with the same production chains are known.

This is becoming more and more evident in such a sector as the automobile industry. For instance, at the present juncture of recurring demand, works councils are being asked to grant the working of additional shifts with the necessary overtime authorization. Such a decision necessitates knowledge of the trends and developments, and in particular the stock situation in other plants and in locations of final assembly operations. Decisions on possible overtime or new hirings are to be considered in relation to the overall prospects and objectives of the personnel policy and connected problems.

All these factual cases, of present or recent date, bear evidence of the need to bring about contacts, consultations and negotiations between the trade unions and the management level of actual decision-making in multinational companies, as set out as a moral commitment in the OECD Guidelines (Employment and Industrial Relations, paragraph 9).

IMF is pleased to note that this clause has already had some impact. It has contributed to finding a meaningful arrangement for a first time meeting between an IMF delegation and international top management of SKF in Goteborg, at the headquarters of this multinational.

This meeting provided for the presentation of trade union, employment and other social problems encountered by IMF affiliates in various plants of SKF across the world to the Central Management of the whole group, and a discussion and analysis of all these issues. There are expectations on both sides, top management and trade unions, that such a meeting will help to cope with the difficult problems arising at plant level, with a view to employment security, social protection of the workers and progressive collective bargaining in the mutual interests of the entire company.

IMF has specific complaints against certain multinationals, apart from the examples already given, but is holding back from submitting them for the attention of OECD, awaiting an opportunity for multinational companies to enter into contacts between trade unions and the decision-making international management of their multinational groups.

With some multinationals in the watchmaking industry, arrangements for contacts on a small scale are being undertaken with a view to tackling – between the bargaining parties – problems arising for examination at international level. This might lead to interesting developments in line with the principles set out in the OECD Guidelines.»

2. The position of BIAC

158. The position of BIAC on the issue of international collective bargaining is clear: there is no need for international collective bargaining which does not correspond to reality. Multinational enterprises categorically refuse international collective bargaining since it would, a.o., upset the national labour relations systems.

3. The report of the IME Committee

159. The report states as follows:

«The Committee has not considered the question of the conduct of collective bargaining at an international level, for which there are no real examples, although there has been some development of trade union efforts to co-ordinate approaches to multinational enterprises on a cross-country basis» (paragraph 62).

4. Some comments

160. Again, the Guidelines are absolutely neutral on the point of international collective bargaining: they do neither oppose it, nor favour it. This means that the trade unions cannot find a platform in the Guidelines requiring meetings with international management and that the employers find no basis in the Guidelines to refute international bargaining. It simply means that international collective bargaining belongs to the autonomous relationship between labour and management, and will become a reality when two conditions are fulfilled: 1) the necessity to bargain at that level; 2) when the trade unions (at national level) desire to do so and have enough strength to bring the multinational enterprises to the bargaining table. There is no doubt that international collective bargaining is bound to come. The strategy followed by multinational enterprises and by some Governments, which consist in the promotion of a free international economic order on the one hand by trying to constrain labour relations within a national framework on the other hand, is in the long term not realistic. Labour relations, by nature, following economic developments and at the end of the day multinational enterprises will have to discuss their overall investment and desinvestment policies with representatives of workers, at international level, at which ITS' cannot be excluded.

D. PARTICIPATION IN INTERNATIONAL TRADE UNION SEMINARS (THE PHILIPS CASE)

1. The issue – Submission by IMF

161. The issue concerns the granting of leave of absence to employee representatives who wish to attend international union seminars concerned with developments in affiliates of the same enterprise located in different countries.

Submission by the International Metalworkers (IMF) through TUAC

162. «Refusal by central management of PHILIPS to grant permission for leave of absence for participation at an international trade union seminar on developments within Philips, and continued refusal to meet with trade unions at world level.

The Industriebond NKV, one of the bargaining parties with PHILIPS, organized a conference from 25 to 27 October 1976 on the developments within the multinational company PHILIPS, and more particularly PIG – GLASS. This seminar was designed for an exchange of information and experiences about developments in the different GLASS locations of PHILIPS in the Netherlands, Belgium, Federal Republic of Germany and the United Kingdom and, therefore, expected to have international trade union representation from these countries. The conference was also supported by the European Metal Workers' Federation (EMF), which has already had a number of top level contacts with PHILIPS. The seminar also had the co-operation of the Dutch Trade Union Federation for Co-operation and Development; which has the support of the Dutch government.
Permission was asked for leave of absence for one convener and two shop stewards by the British trade union from local management of PHILIPS in Great Britain. The request was refused, no doubt on instructions from central management in Eindhoven, which also refused leave of absence for trade union representatives at its factory in Belgium.
There were strong trade union protests against this incomprehensible attitude of PHILIPS world management, trying to hinder official trade union contacts. The trade unions could not accept such an attempt by PHILIPS to determine –

by its action – what should or should not be discussed by the trade unions at an information conference.

PHILIPS maintained its position. After this incident the matter was brought before the PHILIPS INDUSTRIES JOINT COUNCIL in Great Britain, where it was agreed to explore and attempt to arrive at an agreement in line with the ACAS Code – Advisory Conciliation and Arbitration Service, to avoid such situations in the future.

This interference by PHILIPS in union matters reveals the same kind of policy that PHILIPS has been following so far in refusing to meet a delegation from EMF which would include a representative from IMF. The choice of who should take part in a trade union delegation is a basic trade union right that cannot be infringed upon and it is, therefore, unacceptable that management should decide the composition of a trade union delegation to a joint meeting, and refuse the presence of an adviser from IMF in a delegation of its closely associated EMF.

Unions affiliated to the IMF represent thousands of PHILIPS workers in North America, Latin America, Asia, Africa and European countries outside the European Community.

The attitude of PHILIPS signifies a refusal to enter into discussions with the official international organisation which represents trade unions, who are its authentic bargaining parties in various parts of the world, and to examine problems concerned with decisions at central management level.

This refusal is to be considered as an infringement of the OECD code, as it also concerns the union attempt to bring up matters regarding PHILIPS operations in the area of the OECD member countries.

PHILIPS hampering of trade union participation at an international seminar, is also contrary to the code, preventing representatives of employees – in accordance with local law and practice – from getting information on the enterprise as a whole.

It is hoped that the OECD Guidelines will provide a way to overcome the unfortunate experiences in the past with PHILIPS and that in the future there can be direct contacts between this multinational and the trade unions.»

2. The position of Philips

163. Philips' Eindhoven addressed following letter to OECD:

«N. V. Philips' Gloeilampenfabrieken

PHILIPS' INDUSTRIES

EINDHOVEN, NEDERLAND

RAAD VAN BESTUUR

30th June 1977

De Hoogwelgeboren Heer Jhr. E. van Lennep
Secretaris-Generaal van de O.E.C.D.
2, Rue André-Pascal
Parijs 16

Frankrijk

Dear Mr. van Lennep,

At the conference of the OECD held in Paris on March 30 and 31st our company has been quoted by the IMF as having infringed upon the OECD Guidelines in three cases.

1. Philips is alleged to have refused leave to union representatives from a factory in Great Britain, and another one in Belgium to attend an international meeting in this country held from October 25th – 27th 1976.

2. Philips is accused to have infringed upon the right of the EMF to compose its delegation in a meeting with our company.

3. Philips is accused of failure to inform the trade unions and to co-operate with them on plant closures in the Federal Republic of Germany.

Although these statements have not been submitted to the OECD meeting with the intention to have them dealt with as complaints the accusations have been made public and since they are incorrect we feel we should inform you of the correct state of affairs.

Ad. 1.
The information we received from the responsible Philips Managements in the UK and in Belgium leads to the following conclusion:

In the case of the British factory the national management replied that the 'Industriebond N.K.V.' conference concerning Philips glass activities did not meet the requirement* that the activity relates to and is consistent with the collective bargaining structure within the company in which the employee operates and his role as a representative of the unions within this structure. Therefore the management could not comply with the request to release the 3 persons concerned to attend in Company time.

In Belgium leave may be granted either for training courses or for meetings organized on behalf of co-ordination between the trade union representatives of different establishments belonging to one company in Belgium within the same branch of industry. These various types of leave have been laid down in national collective agreements.
Therefore the Belgian management was not obliged to grant leave for a purpose beyond the scope of these agreements.

We believe that it is incorrect and contrary to normal practice and agreed procedures for the unions to interpret these as having a border-crossing scope, introducing in this way a principle that has nowhere been established i.e. that of granting leave for meetings outside the national industrial relations context.

It is also incorrect to suggest that the decision was taken by the National management on instruction from Central Management in Eindhoven. The decisions were taken by the national managements themselves on the basis of the relevant normal practice and agreed procedures. We are astonished that the unions should not be aware of the actual context of these facilities.

As to the statement of the unions that the refusal has to be considered as an infringement of the OECD-guidelines, we point out that there is no clause in these guidelines that justifies that interpretation.

In this context we should like to recall that the draft declaration of principles which was recently adopted by all parties concerned, including representatives of the complaining union organization, with the International Labour Organization in Geneva, contains the following phrase:

'Representatives of the workers in multinational enterprises should not be hindered from meeting for consultation and exchange of views among themselves, provided that the functioning of the operations of the enterprise and the normal procedures which govern relationships with representatives of the workers and their organisations are not thereby prejudiced.'
It will be clear that the term 'normal procedures' etc. in this connection refers to the national industrial relations' context in the framework of which facilities for granting leave may have been laid down per country.

*which is common in the United Kingdom.

194

Ad 2.
It is surprising that the unions accuse Philips of interference with union matters by refusing to meet a delegation from EMF which would include a representative of IMF, since the company has dealt with this accusation effectively and publicly in the distant past.

For the informative meetings of Philips with the EMF-representatives there was an agreed scope which was confined to the area of the European common market, because the company felt that, in view of the economic coherence of this area, this was the only feasible context for such informative meetings. By introducing the assistant secretary-general of the IMF the unions attempted to extend the agreed scope of the meeting which, of course, the company could not accept. The unions therefore called the meeting off.

We object against the suggestion raised then and again by the EMF and by the IMF that the company would interfere with the composition of a trade union delegation. Against earlier agreement, the EMF at the last minute before an informative meeting, tried to force the company – by introducing an important functionary of the world wide operating IMF – into discussions with international unions on a world scale.

Ad 3.
The reply to this accusation by the responsible management of the German Philips Organization is enclosed.

Finally we should like to observe that we have serious doubts about the effectiveness of the OECD guidelines if they are used as a platform for the realisation of international unions' objectives on the basis of incorrect statements and a false interpretation of the relevant paragraphs.

Yours sincerely,

F. F. Otten   »

164. Philips got following answers:

« OCDE

OECD

ORGANISATION DE COOPÉRATION ET DE DEVELOPPEMENT ÉCONOMIQUES	ORGANISATION FOR ECONOMIC CO-OPERATION AND DEVELOPMENT

Téléphone : 524 82.00   Télégrammes : DEVELOPECONOMIE   2, rue André-Pascal, PARIS-XVIᵉ

Cabinet du Secretaire général
Secretary-General's Private Office

LD-702   Paris, 21st July, 1977

Dear Mr. Otten,

In the absence of the Secretary-General, I acknowledge receipt of your letter of 30th June, 1977, expressing the views of Philips concerning certain presentations made on March 30, 1977, in relation to your company at a meeting of the OECD Committee on International Investment and Multinationals Enterprises (IME).

A substantive response will follow in due course, after the summer recess. In the meantime, however, I would like to make clear that the meeting of the IME Committee, to which you refer, was arranged under the OECD Council Decision that foresees periodical invitations by this Committee to the Business and Industry Advisory Committee (BIAC) and the Trade Union Advisory Committee (TUAC) to enable them to express their views on matters related to the Guidelines for Multinational Enterprises. As such, the presentation made by TUAC during this first encounter – which concerned various other companies as well as Philips – is one for which OECD bears no responsibility and it cannot prejudge of any follow-up action which could be given by the IME Committee. In effect, this Committee is not mandated to reach conclusions on the conduct of individual enterprises and is mainly concerned with problems of a general character related to the implementation of the OECD Guidelines.

Yours sincerely,

Lucien Dantin
Head of the Secretary-General's
Private Office   »

«23rd September, 1977

EL–2382

Dear Mr. Otten,

May I refer to your letter of 30th June, 1977, expressing the views of Philips concerning presentations by TUAC made to the IME Committee on 30th March, 1977. As already explained to you in a letter by the Head of my Private Office, Mr. Dantin, those presentations were made within the context of the OECD Council decision that foresees periodical encounters of the IME Committee with the Business and Industry Advisory Committee (BIAC) and the Trade Union Advisory Committee (TUAC), to hear their views on matters related to the guidelines for multinational enterprises.

I would like to reiterate that any presentation made during such encounters by either of these Advisory bodies cannot be considered as implying a certain responsibility for the O.E.C.D. I would also like to stress once again that the IME Committee is not mandated to reach conclusions on the conduct of individual enterprises. In effect, the Committee is mainly concerned in issues of principle and the presentation by the Advisory bodies of specific cases could only be an illustration of such issues as SIAC or TUAC see them rather than a series of instances where individual enterprises were alleged not to have complied with the guidelines.

. . ./ . . .

Mr. F. F. Otten,
N.V. Philips' Gloeilampenfabrieken,
Eindhoven,
Netherlands.

On this basis the IME Committee has considered the presentation made by TUAC (to certain points of which you refer in your letter) as an illustration and it instructed the Secretariat to analyse this material, distinguishing between issues pertaining to the application of the guidelines and leaving aside cases to which the guidelines clearly did not apply. It also agreed that if there were questions implying possible changes in the existing guidelines, then they would be considered in the framework of the Committee's mandate to review the guidelines within three years of their adoption.

In view of this attitude of the IME Committee which corresponds exactly to its terms of reference indicating that it is not mandated to deal with specific cases and to reach conclusions on the conduct of individual enterprises, I am not inclined to share the concern expressed in the last paragraph of your letter.

Finally, may I take this opportunity to emphasize my hope that the favourable initial reaction of the business community to the O.E.C.D. guidelines will continue and will serve the aim of O.E.C.D. of further encouraging the positive contributions of multinational enterprises to economic and social progress.

Yours sincerely,

E. van Lennep»

3. The position of BIAC

165. In his oral statement to the IME Committee on April 11, 1978 the spokesman for BIAC said the following:

«Similarly, regarding Guideline 2a in this section – in considering such questions as leave of absence to attend union functions, the only possible criteria will be in BIAC's view the practices of the country concerned and the operating requirements of the company in question.»

4. The report of the IME Committee

166. The report reads as follows on this issue:
«While not explicitly addressing the issue, the Guidelines imply that the management of MNEs should adopt a co-operative attitude towards the participation of employees in international meetings for consultation and exchanges of views among themselves provided that the functioning of the operations of the enterprises and the normal procedures which govern relationships with representatives of the employees and their organizations are not thereby prejudiced.» (Paragraph 61.)

5. Some comments

167. It is evident that the Guidelines do not refer to this specific issue and it might have been better to amend the Guidelines to that effect. However, the overall desire to keep the amendments to an absolute minimum prevented such a change of the Guidelines. Reference can, of course, be made to paragraph 46 of the ILO declaration, which reads:
«Representatives of the workers in multinational enterprises should not be hindered from meeting for consultation and exchange of views among themselves provided that the functioning of the operations of the enterprise and the

normal procedures which govern relationships with representatives of the workers and their organizations are not thereby prejudiced.»

Both in the report of the IME Committee and in paragraph 46 of the ILO principles two conditions are set forward for the employees to participate in international meetings:
1. the functioning of the enterprise;
2. the normal procedures, governing the relationship between the representatives and their organizations. This second condition really means that the attendance by employees must be sponsored by the responsible trade union.

V. Provision of information to employees

A. COLLECTIVE BARGAINING. A TRUE AND FAIR VIEW

Guidelines 2b and 3 of the Employment and Industrial Relations Chapter:
«(2b) provide to representatives of employees information which is needed for meaningful negotiations on conditions of employment;

(3) provide to representatives of employees, where this accords with local law and practice, information which enables them to obtain a true and fair view of the performance of the entity or, where appropriate, the enterprise as a whole;»

---

1. The issue

168. Information is, of course, a key issue in industrial relations and does raise a number of important questions, such as what entity (the plant; the enterprise, the multinational enterprise?); *What subjects* (wages-conditions, work organization, investment decisions . . .?); *When* information should be given (before or after the decision has been made . . .?) and to *whom* (the employees, works council members, the union . . .?). Finally, questions arise about the *confidentiality* of the information. There is no doubt that the actual provision of information is still largely dominated by the national labour relations systems. Broadly speaking, two trends can be discerned: where, following the US tradition, information must be given to trade unions, which is 'relevant and necessary to collective bargaining', and the continental European approach, whereby information is given in the framework of workers' participation (e.g. to employee-members of works councils or to employee representatives or to members of the supervisory boards of companies).

199

169. In the case of multinational enterprises there is obviously an additional dimension, since headquarters, which may escape in a sense local legislation or practice, can withhold information, which the local affiliate needs in order to fulfil its obligation under national law and practice and the Guidelines.

2. Submission by TUAC

170. Information on the multinational enterprise as a whole. Information beforehand (in the future and not in history) so as to be able to influence decisions, especially in the investment area is one of TUAC's most outspoken demands. At almost every one of the formal or informal contacts with the IME Committee or its working group TUAC made demands to this end.

a) Cases introduced, March 30, 1977

171. «Lack of information by POCLAIN in a situation of economic difficulties, mass dismissals and possibly of takeover*

Poclain SA faces problems of structural change, due to the serious effects of the present state of the economy on its markets.
After having been a successful competitor worldwide for hydraulic excavators, cranes and other construction material, the company finds its orders are dwindling and that production has had to be reduced drastically. This led to some financial loss. The company now needs financial backing. As a result mass dismissals have taken place in its factories in France, as well as in its two plants in Spain, although there have not so far been dismissals in its production unit in Belgium.
Poclain has also some connection with Volvo. This Swedish company, through its Swedish subsidiary Volvo BM, assists to a certain extent in the marketing of agricultural machinery, soil moving equipment and appliances for forestry work.
In view of the difficulties of Poclain, there have been negotiations for the takeover of this multinational of French origin by another company and rumours about that kind of structural change.
The trade unions have been kept completely in the dark about the financial and economic situation, prospective orders, work on hand and management's basic intentions. Requests for information about the latest state of accounts were refused. The works council and the trade unions were confronted with the announcement of large-scale dismissals, without being able to assess their justification and then negotiate about the need for such dismissals. These rights accorded by French legislation to works councils were ignored.
The trade unions addressed a protest to the French authorities against management policy and its decision-making without giving information and a possibility for negotiations, and even intervened with the Ministry of Labour.
There is no information at all given to the workers and their trade unions in the

two subsidiary plants in Spain. The workers and the trade unions in the Belgian plant also have no way of obtaining information about the situation of the parent plant in France and the state of affairs of the whole group.

This whole position of complete failure of information by this multinational company, particularly in a situation when economic difficulties cause general job insecurity and uncertainty about the company's future, was examined by an IMF meeting with unions representing the workers in the parent company and subsidiaries of Poclain. Subsequently a letter was addressed by the IMF to the Minister of Labour, with a request that the company be obliged to submit all the information required and engage in negotiations with the trade unions on the company's economic and social problems which affect the workers.

This request is in conformity with the principles contained in the OECD guidelines on multinational companies, and IMF reiterates its demand that Poclain respect the relevant clauses on providing information throughout its multinational group and negotiate constructively with the trade unions.

172. International structural reorganization with BENDIX leads to confusing policies and the loss of employment despite job guarantees based on state subsidies

Managers of KIP Kampeerwagenfabriek BV had talks with the Industrial Federations of the Dutch Central Trade Union Organizations NVV and NKV. Director Nilsson of the Swedish camping waggon factory CABBY (which with KIP belongs to Bendix) is to continue KIP operations in Hoogeveen. To that end the KIP caravan factory is separated from the Bendix concern. KIP debts at the bank are to be taken into the Bendix account. At the same time Nilsson is to take over the Swedish plant of Bendix.

The unions refused to give their approval to this plan; first they wanted insight into all the financial repercussions this would have for KIP. Also they wanted information about employment guarantees for KIP workers and the continued operation of the plant.

The week prior to the discussions with the trade unions, during a meeting of KIP management, representatives of the Bendix concern and the major of Hoogeveen at the Ministry of Economic Affairs, it was disclosed that KIP was misusing fl. 1.25 million from the authorities. That money had been loaned to the firm to secure jobs for 151 workers. But meanwhile the personnel at KIP had been reduced to 134 people.

In addition NVV had documents showing that KIP accounts were confused. NVV and NKV have demanded that in as short a time as possible they be fully informed about future plans.

In NVV's opinion, Bendix is slowly withdrawing from KIP; but there is no information from the multinational company on its real intentions. It looks as if the Swedish camping waggon factory would have to continue KIP operations, but as yet it cannot be judged by the trade unions what will really happen. There are indications that the manager of KIP, having some management prerogatives within Bendix, seems to want to withdraw from his links with Bendix.

As to the Swedish camping waggon factory Cabby, industrial relations are satisfactory. The unions were kept informed about the company's negotiations with Bendix and could in every phase express their opinion. There was union approval of the decision to buy Cabby from Bendix, as well as to acquire ESTRUARY Ltd. In England and the Dutch KIP. There is also trade union representation on the supervisory board of the Swedish company. At Cabby they are quite aware of the problems in the Dutch company KIP. The situation in the Swedish company is in flagrant contrast to the management methods and confusion and the adverse repercussions on the employment security of the workers in the KIP plant, which still depends on decisions made by worldwide management of Bendix.

There is a break-off of commitments by the company towards the public authorities with regard to employment security, and there is ignorance in the subsidiaries of management policies and decisions elaborated at the international headquarters, making it practically impossible for the trade unions and public authorities to negotiate in the interests of the workers.

173. Closure of a SIEMENS plant in Belgium and break-off of order and employment commitments between the Government and SIEMENS in Belgium

Of the 4,000 employees in the Belgian SIEMENS plants, 1,000 to 1,200 will be laid off during 1976/1977. The Baudour plant will be closed down and Oostkamp personnel is to be reduced by 800.

In 1970 the Belgian Government and SIEMENS signed a contract, according to which the Government would place orders and SIEMENS would create jobs. SIEMENS committed itself to creating 3,600 jobs. (This would bring the total number employed to 8,000). Since the inception of the SIEMENS plants in Belgium, the number employed has never exceeded 4,000. From 1971 to 1975 the Government placed order with SIEMENS for 5 billion Belgian francs and granted subsidies for some additional 280 million Belgian francs. It is planned that between 1976 and 1979 new orders will be placed. The Baudour plant originally planned to employ 500 workers, but never had more than 344. This plant will now be closed down. The personnel and the trade unions had already been aware for several years that the product lines were technologically somewhat out of date, and that this could have adverse effects on the plant in the future. In spite of this, management continued to affirm that the existence of the plant was secure: first for ten, then for five, and finally for three years.

The Belgian workers find it unacceptable that this plant will be closed down without any attempt being made towards conversion.

The Baudour plant has been occupied by the total staff ever since mid-October. (Of a total of 215 workers, 175 are female.)

There are mutual accusations on the part of SIEMENS and the Belgian Government that the terms of their agreement to provide orders and expand employment had not been kept.

According to the main principles of the OECD Guidelines, due consideration is to be given to the creation of employment opportunities (General Policies, sub-paragraph 2), as well as to the provision of reasonable notice to the representatives of employees of any changes in operations which would have major effects on the livelihood of these employees, and to co-operation with the trade unions so as to mitigate to the maximum extent practicable the adverse effects (Employment and Industrial Relations, paragraph 6).

These various principles are being infringed when agreements made for employment promotion are not being adhered to, trade union warnings about the need for new technology are being disregarded, and in the end when a whole plant is being closed down, the workers and their trade unions are being confronted with a fair accompli.

174. Production transfer with plant closure in Sweden by LITTON INDUSTRIES

The American multinational conglomerate Litton Industries acquired in 1959 50 per cent capital ownership of the Swedish enterprise SWEDA, producing cash registers. The other half of the shares were taken over by Litton Industries in 1963. At the same time, the number of employees at this foreign subsidiary was increased and a Research and Development Department was established in Sweden. The possibility of the development of electronic cash registers in the Nordic market was investigated; and there must have been hopes for finding an expanding market in the future in this region.

At the beginning of the seventies the working conditions at the Research and Development Department were deteriorating due to heavy reductions in the allocations of resources. In 1972 the company still employed 2,600 persons. The situation changed drastically when, in 1975, measures were taken to run down the operations in the Swedish subsidiary. The Research and Development Department was closed and transferred back to the United States but some know-how still remained in Sweden.

Total employment in April 1976 still stood at 1,000 workers, but it had been announced in December 1975 that a total of 425 workers (300 manual and 125 non-manual) would be dismissed during 1976: 350 in the first part and the others in the second part of the year. Furthermore, there was wind of a Litton document of December 1975, according to which Litton intended to close down its Sweda subsidiary in Sweden. There was an announcement by the company board that production would be closed unless a buyer could be found.

The cut-back on the development of cash registers and the intention to move the Research and Development Department to the USA are due to decisions taken in the world headquarters in the United States and determined by the global policies of this conglomerate; without considering any action to safeguard employment in the Swedish subsidiary. There was no background information given to prove the necessity of drastic action and no attempt made to create alternative employment; and there were no real negotiations offered to the trade unions on these issues.

Sweda had never shown a financial loss before 1975 and it is difficult to

understand that market deterioration in a recession should have no other
alternative then pressing action to get rid of the whole subsidiary or otherwise
its complete close-down.
Strong resistance by the Swedish IMF affiliates forced Litton Industries to
consider some solutions. An offer was made by Litton that five top employees
could buy part of Sweda to continue its activities. There is little evidence as to
the validity of such a proposal, which would most likely lead to bankruptcy. The
trade unions insist that some sound projects be elaborated for the reorganization of this Swedish subsidiary which in the past had proved to be financially
solid. To remove research and development facilities away from a factory of
1,000 and once 2,600 workers at a time when there would be need for
adjustments in the product line – without genuine negotiations for a solution on
new activities and without action showing the management's preparedness to
live up to its responsibility for the safeguarding of employment, constitutes an
infringement of principles laid down in the OECD Guidelines (General
Policies, para. 2 stating 'in particular give due consideration to the aims and
priorities of the member countries in which they operate, with regard to
economic and social progress, including industrial and regional development, . . . creation of employment opportunities, the promotion of innovation
and the transfer of technology'; and Employment and Industrial Relations,
para. 6 stating '. . . co-operation with employee representatives and the appropriate government authorities so as to mitigate to the maximum extent practicable adverse effects').

*175. Failure of the PHILIPS Company to inform the trade unions and co-
operate with them on plant closures in the Federal Republic of Germany*[17]

In the framework of the rationalization of its international plant structure,
PHILIPS closed down in the second half of 1976 six of its subsidiary plants in
the Federal Republic of Germany alone. These closures took place despite
strong arguments by the German Metalworkers' Union IGMetall and the
Works Councils; who defend the job security of the workers in these plants.
One of these closures concerned the PHILIPS subsidiary for the manufacture
of condensers at Herborn, with about 300 workers. In this case modern
production facilities were closed down. Not only the trade unions had strong
arguments against the shift of production abroad, even the management of the
German PHILIPS subsidiary and its supervisory board strongly opposed this
central management decision of PHILIPS headquarters in Eindhoven.
The closing down of the PHILIPS plant in Herborn is a striking example of the
lack of information from a multinational to the workers and their trade unions
in the decision-making process, and even after, concerning the actual employment situation of a whole workforce. It is also an example of rigid decision-
making at international level without allowing for any reconsideration of
measures to maintain production, or to provide alternative employment oppor-

17. See further Philips' point of view on this case, Part II, V, A, 4.

tunities in the course of consultations and negotiations with the trade unions on the merits of the whole case.

In fact, the Works Councils and the Metalworkers' Union IGMetall heard, more or less accidentally, about the decision taken by PHILIPS central head-quarters in the Netherlands to close down the plant in Herborn. When the rumours became true, the whole matter had already been definitely settled. Furthermore, public authorities were not approached.

The Works Council and IGMetall confronted with a rigid management posi-tion at a late stage when the fate of the workers had unilaterally been decided upon, tried to bring about a re-examination of the situation. They were able to prove that the subsidiary operation at Herborn was profit making, and that there could be no reasons for closure because of inefficiency or lack of competi-tive power. They also pointed out that there were no other job opportunities available in the region.

These facts were also the reasons which had motivated local management and the supervisory board of the German subsidiary to contest the shifting away of production.

There had never been any reconsideration of the case by international man-agement. The last of the workers leave the plant at the end of February 1977; modern production facilities standing idle.

It has been possible, however, for the trade unions to negotiate and conclude a relatively good Social Plan for severance pay and other social provisions. This will not solve the employment problem in the region concerned and trade unions must be in a position to intervene to safeguard employment, with the possibility of influencing management decisions on the merits of the basic social considerations. Otherwise transfer of production is carried out disregard-ing the interests of the workers and the right of their unions to effectively defend their social concerns.

176. Changes in company structure by INTERNATIONAL TELEPHONE & TELEGRAPH Corporation (ITT) in the Federal Republic of Germany to evade representation, direct information and participation bij trade unions

ITT has decided on changes in its legal company structure in the Federal Republic of Germany, which obviously were not motivated by business reasons, nor by production, financial, commercial or other factors; except the possibility to circumvent – within their existing company structure – their obligations to conform with the new German Law on Co-determination of 1976.

Some ways of escaping this new legislation could be the changing of the legal form of a production company: from its normal structure of a limited liability company (GmbH) to one with limited or special partnership (Kommandit Gesellschaft); the latter being the only form of company that is exempt from the new Co-determination Law. Another measure could be for a company with more than 2,000 workers to be dissolved, with a view to forming two smaller companies with separate management, which would relieve them from setting up a supervisory board with equal trade union representation; which by the new Law affects companies with 2,000 or more workers.

ITT is an example of a foreign multinational changing – in connection with the new legislation of 1976 on Co-determination – its company structure, through the changeover from a 'GmbH' to a 'Kommandit Gesellschaft'. The two ITT subsidiaries in question are GRAETZ GmbH producing radio and TV sets, and TEVES GmbH also producing electrical appliances.

In both cases ITT avoids the setting up of a supervisory board with equal representation by the owners and the trade unions, which at the same time would allow the presence of representatives from the national trade union organizations, ITT's obligations will remain limited to those imposed by the Works Constitution Act (Betriebsverfassungsgezetz).

By using legal loopholes, ITT in the Federal Republic of Germany escapes national legislation which was created to expand trade union rights for companies of the size and nature of its subsidiaries in Germany.

ITT's attitude is to be considered as an infringement of their obligations with regard to representation, direct information and participation of the trade unions.

The spirit of the OECD Guidelines should commit ITT to recognize the new German Legislation. Companies should recognize their moral commitment not to use legal loopholes, particularly in a case where representation of workers and their trade unions – as stipulated by the German Law – is to bring about in foreign subsidiaries the greatly needed protection of the workers against the consequences of central management decisions taken abroad.»

b) Proposals put forward April 11, 1978

177. In its statement to the IME Committee on April 11, 1978 TUAC underlined again its interest in information; it stated as follows:

«Information on activities, results and plans of multinational enterprises as a whole and of their different entities is one of the crucial issues on which the effectiveness of the Guidelines depends. TUAC has noted the work pursued in this field by the UN as well as the efforts of BIAC. The situation is, however, still unsatisfactory and very important problems remain unsolved. This hampers collective bargaining and consultation for the sake of eliminating or reducing adverse effects of changes in operations. The IIME Committee is requested to undertake, in co-operation with BIAC and TUAC, a survey of national laws, rules and practices and their applicability to multinational enterprises both in the home and the host countries in order to formulate adequate general principles. These efforts should not be limited to harmonization of accounting standards. TUAC reflects the problems experienced in this field in the Scandinavian context in a paper and submits it to the Committee as a proposed starting point.»

«ILLUSTRATIVE EXAMPLE – NOT A DEMAND – IN RELATION TO DISCLOSURE AND/OR COMMUNICATION OF INFORMATION BY MULTINATIONAL ENTERPRISES (document presented by LO Sweden)

The text below is written as an example to *illustrate how the technique* for bringing about an international agreement on the right of employees to information, economic and other expertise, exchange of information and consultation can be worked out.

The example is based on demands which can in part be met nationally, in some countries. In some cases they can be made the subject of legislation and in others can be the subject of negotiations and agreements.

INTERNATIONAL AGREEMENT ON EMPLOYEES' RIGHT TO INFORMATION IN INTERNATIONAL COMPANIES

The economic result for a particular subsidiary of an international group of companies, just as the subsidiary's future development as regards production and employment, depends not only on what happens in and around the particular company but also to a great extent on the measures and decisions taken by the international group's executive.

A subsidiary's economic result can be affected by such things as administrative, research and other costs which the company must pay to the group. The result can also be affected by the internal price setting decided on by the group's executive for those goods and services which are exchanged among the various companies in the group and the subsidiary.

The subsidiary's future development is closely related to the decisions on the distribution of investments and production among the various companies of the group made by the group's executive. This applies in particular to subsidiaries which sell their products through other companies in the group or which are sub-suppliers to other group companies. Here the dependency on the rest of the group and on the group's executive is considerable.

In order to make it possible for the union work in international companies to be carried on in a responsible and meaningful way for all parties concerned, the employees and their union organizations need information not only about the conditions within the particular subsidiary, but also about those conditions in the rest of the group which are of importance when assessing the particular subsidiary's economy and future.

This agreement has come about to give the union organisations in international groups the right to information, the right to economic and other expertise, the right to exchange of information among unions and the right to consultations on an international level.

I. *THE RIGHT TO INFORMATION*

1. The employees' representatives in a particular subsidiary of an international group of companies shall be given all the information about the particular subsidiary, parts of the group or the whole group which is neces-

207

sary to enable these representatives to look after the employees' interests meaningfully and effectively as regards the subsidiary's development, terms of employment, working conditions and the employment level.

2. The above applies to information about the situation in the past, in the present and conditions relevant to the particular subsidiary's future, such as the group's investment and production plans. It also applies to information about the subsidiary in question itself and to the conditions in other companies in the group or in the group as a whole or to the relationships between companies in the group which are of importance when assessing the situation and future of the subsidiary in question. It applies to information which is available in the particular subsidiary and to information which can be found in other group companies.

3. The group's executive is responsible for supplying the employees' representatives in each group company with such information continuously and without any waste of time. The employees' representatives are to decide in what form and how often such regular information shall be given.

4. The group's executive shall notify the employees' representatives of their plans in good time before a decision is made, in order to enable the representatives to assess the plans and to enter into meaningful negotiations with the person who is responsible for and empowered to make a decision on the matter in question before the decision is taken. The group's executive is responsible for seeing to it that the employees' representatives in each individual group company are informed about who is responsible for and empowered to make various types of decision.

5. When the employees' representatives request information the company executive shall supply such information. If necessary they shall help with copies of documents and necessary inquiries.

6. The employees' representatives shall have the right to examine books, accounts and other documents which concern the operations of the subsidiary or group in question, to the extent necessary for safeguarding the interests of the employees in relations with the employer.

7. The employees' representatives have the right to make use of the computer which the group of companies has access to, for their own collection and processing of information. The employer shall provide personnel for the systems work, programming and suchlike necessary for utilizing the computer.

8. The local union organizations themselves select, in co-operation and consultation with their central national or international employees' organizations, the person or persons who, as the employees' representatives, shall receive the information. The group's executive has no right to judge or question those appointed by the union organizations to receive the information.

9. The obligation to supply information is, as a rule, to be fulfilled by providing the employees' representatives in the respective companies of the group with information. Where the information is of importance for several companies in the group the union organizations can demand that the information be given to the central national or international employees' organization concerned.

10. The formulation and content of the internal information shall be approved by the employees' organizations. The internal information shall be submitted in the way which the employees' organizations determine.
11. Costs which arise as a result of the employees' representatives being kept informed about the group or parts of the group of companies shall be met by the employer.

II. *THE RIGHT TO ECONOMIC AND OTHER EXPERTISE*

1. The union organizations in a multinational group of companies have the right to call in the economic experts or experts in other fields necessary to enable the union organizations to obtain, interpret or analyse information about their own subsidiary, parts of the group or the whole group.
2. The services of the experts called in can be utilized for longer or shorter periods of time, depending on the type and purpose of assignment.
3. Such an expert has the right to all information, written material, reports, revised material etc in the group of companies necessary for carrying out the assignment he or she was called in for, as decided by the union organizations.
4. The consultant may not disclose to an outsider such information which he or she has received which may damage the company. The consultant always has the right to provide the appointed employees' representatives and the boards of the employees' organizations with all the information he or she has received and the conclusions which he or she has drawn.
5. The consultation costs are to be paid by the employer.

III. *THE RIGHT TO EXCHANGE OF INFORMATION AMONG UNIONS*

1. A prerequisite for a responsible and meaningful union activity in an international group of companies for all parties concerned is that the employees' representatives in the various subsidiaries of the group in various countries are able to contact each other and exchange information.
2. The employees' representatives in various companies within a group shall be given the possibility to contact each other and exchange information to the extent necessary for pursuing an effective union activity in the group.
3. The employees' organizations in an international group are to themselves determine the forms which the union contacts and exchange of information take in the group.
4. This contact and exchange of information shall take place during paid working hours. All costs in connection with this activity shall be paid by the employer.
5. In certain circumstances secrecy is justified so that the group's business operations are not damaged. The employees' representatives should observe great caution with information received when the group's representatives so request. An obligation to observe secrecy should not be an

209

obstacle to exchange of information within the group which the employees' representatives need to pursue an effective union activity in the group.

IV. *THE RIGHT TO CONSULTATIONS*

1. When an international group of companies is considering changes in its operations (including those which depend on mergers, acquisition of other companies or transfer of production) which can effect the level of employment or the employees' living conditions in other respects in one or more group companies or in the group as a whole, the person in the group who is authorized to make decisions on the changes under consideration shall initiate consultations with the representatives of the employees affected before any decision is made.
2. The group's representatives shall in this connection take into consideration the alternatives which the employees' representatives present and co-operate with the employees' representatives in order to alleviate possible unfavourable consequences for the employees of the change which is ultimately made.
3. At such consultations the union organizations themselves decide on their representation, which can be varied according to the type and scope of the change. The employees' representatives can thus come from several group companies in several countries and be co-ordinated by the relevant trade secretariat.
4. The group shall at such consultations be represented by the person who is authorized to make decisions on the questions which are under consideration.
5. International groups of companies shall work towards the development of effective forms of agreement for such questions as the consultations cover.
6. The consultations shall take place during the employees' representatives' paid working hours and the employer shall meet any additional costs incurred in connection with these consultations.

V. *SETTLEMENT OF DISPUTES*

1. In connection with the adoption of this agreement an 'International Council for . . .' is to be set up with the task of settling disputes about the interpretation and observance of the agreement.
2. The 'International Council for . . .' is to be made up of representatives for the governments, employers and the union organizations in . . ./the International organization's, the Nordic Council's, the OECDs, etc area of operation; the representatives are to be selected from all the countries taking part in the agreement or common representatives for groups of countries are to be nominated, depending on the geographical scope of the agreement and on what is practical./
3. The 'International Council for . . .' shall, by declarations on Interpretation and negotiations with the parties concerned in disputes evolve an international practice in those areas which are covered by the agreement.»

c) Meeting with the Working Group, January 29, 1979

178. At the occasion of the meeting with the Working Group on that date
TUAC insisted again on 'information', and this is as follows:

«d. *Right to trade union consultation within multinational enterprises* (paragraph 2 of the employment and industrial relations section). Necessary
facilities must be interpreted in a way to cover facilities for contacts with
employees in other parts of the same multinational enterprise. Information,
to be meaningful, must include information on the enterprise as a whole.
The provisions of the Guidelines must also be interpreted in a way that will
not hinder representatives of the International Trade Secretariats to participate in negotiations when necessary.
e. *Information to employees* (paragraph 3 of the employment and industrial
relations section). This information will have to include future plans, in
order to give a true and fair view of the entity or the enterprise.»

3. Position of BIAC

179. The employers representatives in the line of their overall point of view
are of the opinion that disclosure of information to employees, as a general
proposition, is governed by local law and practice and the circumstances of
each situation. Regarding the third Employment and Industrial relations
Guideline, BIAC observed, at the occasion of the consultations of April 11,
1978:
«that so far as the extent of information on the enterprise as a whole is
concerned, this would appear to be satisfied by the recommendations under the
section on disclosure of information.» (Chapter II of the Guidelines.)

4. The point of view of Philips

180. Management of Philips contested the allegations of IMF on Philips'
failure to inform the trade unions and to co-operate with them on plant closures
in the Federal Republic of Germany, by following statement, which was
forwarded to OECD, and reads as follows:

Information received from the management of the German Philips Organization with regard to statements submitted by the trade unions at the OECD –
meeting of March 30th, 1977

*«Information and consultation with works council and trade unions concerning
the closing down of the manufacture of condensors at Herborn*[18]

In the case of the closing down of a plant the employer is obliged first to inform
18. Translation from German.

the works council and then to consult with them,[19] following the Works Constitution Act.

The closing down of a plant, a so-called 'economic matter', belongs to the competence of the economic committee.[20] The employer has to fully inform this committee, which is elected by the enterprise works council, in due time (§106, Sect. 2–3, 6 Works Constitution Act).

The law says, that information must be given and consultations held the moment the employer has the intention to close the enterprise. The employer is not allowed at that time to implement his intention, since the consultations with the economic committee must leave the possibility open to examine everything and possibly change the employer's intention.

The management of Philips, Germany, informed the economic committee about its intention to stop the manufacture of condensors, during a meeting which lasted many hours. All the members of the economic committee participated at that meeting. These members are elected by the enterprise works council and are, consequently, the legitimate representatives of all employees of the Philips enterprises as far as economic matters are concerned. Taking the information thus given into account the economic committee decided to hold another meeting for the purpose of seeking the intention of management. All the members of the economic committee were present at that meeting, including a representative of the trade union and management representatives from all plants, who might be concerned with the intended closure (Herborn – Wetzlar . . .). That meeting also lasted for many hours.

On the grounds of that meeting the spokesman of the economic committee informed the management of Philips, that the economic committee, even after consultation with the representative of the trade unions, saw no alternative solution to avoid the closure.

In doing so management fulfilled its obligation of information and consultation following the Works Constitution Act.

The Works Constitution Act prescribes as a further step that the employer has to inform the competent works council as well as to consult them about the intended closure (§ 111). This was done in a joint meeting between the management representatives and the works council of Herborn. At that meeting, it was established that due to a need for labour in the Wetzlar plant a large number of the Herborn employees' could be transferred to Wetzlar. On the basis of this decision a joint personnel committee was established, although this

19. Works councils are solely composed of directly elected employees (note).
20. All enterprises with normally more than 100 employees have to establish an economic committee, which is composed of members elected by the works council. The employer has to inform this committee on the economic situation of the enterprise especially the financial situation, the production and marketing situation, the production and investment programs, the rationalization plans, the production techniques and works methods especially the introduction of new works methods, the reduction of operations in or the closing of establishments or parts of establishments, the transfer of establishments or parts of them, the amalgamation of establishments, the changes in the organization or objectives of establishment and any other circumstances and projects that may essentially touch the interests of the employees of the enterprise (§106 Works Constitution Act)»
T. Ramm, *Germany*, in: *The International Encyclopaedia for Labour Law and Industrial Relations*, Kluwer, Deventer, 1979.

is not prescribed by the Works Constitution Act. This committee was set up in order to indicate which workers would be transferred to Wetzlar. This committee held meetings for two consecutive days. The committee was composed of the works council members of Herborn and Wetzlar as well as managers from both the plants and of the enterprise. It was established that 80 employees could be employed in Wetzlar.

On the grounds of the results of the committee work and the joint ascertainments of management, the economic committee, and the Works Council, management decided to stop the manufacture of condensers at Herborn.

Immediately, thereafter, further information was given and consultations held between the management and the works council of Herborn, in which different trade union representatives participated, including a legal adviser, sent by the executive committee of the metal workers union.

Following that meeting, negotiations prescribed by Works Constitution Act, to settle the interests of the workers and the establishment of a social plan were initiated (§112). This settlement as well as the social plan were accepted by both management and the works council in agreement with the representative of the metal workers union.

This settlement reads as follows:

'Taking into account that structural market changes in the sector of electronic condensers on the one hand and unfair competition due to the growing import from low wage countries on the other hand, make it no longer possible for Philips Germany to continue its activity in the field of condensers at Herborn. The same plant will stop its activities in the course of 1976. In order to avert or to mitigate the resulting economic adverse effects for the employees due to the closure, Philips Germany and the works council of Herborn accepted a social plan. The works council agreed to the interest settlement and the implementation measures under §§ 111, 112 of the Works Constitution Act, notwithstanding the legal and conventional rights of co-determination of the works council.'

It shows clearly that the trade union claims have no ground.»

5. The report of the IME Committee

181. The report reads as follows:

«(ii) *Provision of information to employees* (paragraphs 2 and 3)

Provision of information to employees is usually dealt with under national systems of labour relations or, more recently, by legislation and is an area where national diversity is great. Given this diversity, the Guidelines, nevertheless, make some very relevant recommendations in this area (paragraph 63). Attention is drawn, in particular, in this connection to paragraph 2(b) which calls for the provision to employees of 'information which is needed for meaningful negotiations on conditions of employment'. The word 'meaningful' has to be applied of course, to the circumstances of each case; but it is a term which will be of operational value to persons experienced in labour relations.

Again, paragraph 3 speaks of the provision of information, where this accords to local law and practice, enabling representatives of employees to obtain 'a true and fair view of the performance of the entity or, where appropriate, the enterprise as a whole'. A list of items which would be covered by this wording would not be practicable as it would differ from one country to another. This is particularly the case where information on future plans of the enterprise is concerned. As is known, this is still a very controversial area of industrial and social policy in a number of OECD Member countries. Consequently, recourse has to be made to the introduction to the Guidelines referring to the framework of national laws, regulations and practices. Within such a framework, however, and subject to legitimate interests of business confidentiality, management is encouraged by this paragraph to adopt an open and co-operative attitude to the provision of information to employees relevant to the objective of this paragraph, which could include information on future plans (paragraph 64).

Reference is made to paragraph 8 of the Introduction to the Guidelines in which the responsibilities of the various entities within a multinational enterprise are described. If an entity in a given country is not able to provide information to the employees in accordance with paragraph 2(b) and 3, the other entities of the enterprise are expected to co-operate and assist one another as necessary to facilitate observance of the Guidelines. Since representatives of employees may experience difficulties in obtaining such information at the national level, this provision of the Guidelines introduces a useful supplementary standard in this respect» (paragraph 65).

6. Some comments

182. There is no doubt that disclosure of information, not only to Governments and to the public at large but especially to employees, is taking monumentum and constitutes a difinite trend in most countries. The rules to be applied are nevertheless still mainly national. For countries, which do not have specific rules or practice concerning information in general, or on some aspects of it, the Guidelines may be supplementary to the national labour relations system and recommend additional rules. To give one example, Belgian law does not contain the obligation to disclose information in view of collective bargaining. Guideline 2b adds, consequently, a new rule to Belgian law.

It is self-evident that information is only relevant, when it is timely, this at its best, before decisions are taken, so as to be able – taking the specific national labour relations systems into account – to consult or negotiate in due time on the (social) consequences of decisions or the decisions themselves.

183. Guideline 3 foresees, where this accords with local law, to give information on the enterprise as a whole. There are only a few countries, where the law obliges the enterprise to give the employees a true and fair view of the group as a whole. One such case is Belgium. For other countries, where such an obligation is non existent, employees may find the information to the public at large, provided under Chapter II of the Guidelines, useful.

184. Finally, as the report underlines, headquarters must see to it that the subsidiaries get sufficient information in due time in order to be able to fulfil their obligations under national law and practice and the Guidelines.

B. 'REASONABLE NOTICE' IN CASE OF MAJOR CHANGE

Guideline 6 of the Employment and Industrial Relations Chapter:

«in considering changes in their operations which would have major effects upon the livelihood of their employees, in particular in the case of the closure of an entity involving collective lay-offs or dismissals, provide reasonable notice of such changes to representatives of their employees, and where appropriate to the relevant governmental authorities, and co-operate with the employee representatives and appropriate governmental authorities so as to mitigate to the maximum extent practicable adverse effects.»

---

1. The issue

185. Paragraph 6 has been one of the most invoked paragraphs of the Guidelines, at the occasion of the Badger Case, the Batco Case, the Firestone Case . . . all cases involving the closing down of enterprises and where, as indicated, the problem of *reasonable notice* was in the forefront of the discussion.

2. The position of TUAC

186. TUAC wants in the case of major decisions – to be broadly interpreted – to be informed beforehand in order to be able to negotiate, not only concerning the social consequences of the major decisions, but also to discuss the merits of the decision itself.

3. The position of BIAC

187. «With regard to Guideline 6 on Employment and Industrial Relations BIAC recognizes, of course, that worker representatives and managements can differ over what constitutes 'reasonable notice'. This will depend on the circumstances of each situation and on local practice. The Guideline goes on to make the reasonable proposal that there should be co-operation by employers with representatives of their employees and, where appropriate, the relevant governmental authorities, to mitigate to the maximum extent practicable

215

adverse effects. A similar point was made by the International Chamber of Commerce in its Guideline for International Investment in a section on Labour Policies (Guideline VI 1e) and in the ILO Declaration of Principles on Multi-nationals and Social Policy» (paragraph 26).

4. The report of the IME Committee

188. The report reads as follows:

«(iii) *Changes in operations* (paragraph 6)

The management decisions, to which the term 'changes in their operations', in paragraph 6 refers, would cover, in addition to the closure of an entity, which is specifically mentioned in the text, other measures 'which would have major effects upon the livelihood of employees'. The key notions in this paragraph of the Guidelines are the 'reasonable notice' to be given of such changes and actions by management and co-operation with employee representatives and appropriate governmental authorities 'so as to mitigate to the maximum extent practicable adverse effects'» (paragraph 60).
It has seemed to the Committee that there is a link between these two notions. The notice given has to be sufficiently timely for the purpose of mitigating action to be prepared and put into effect: otherwise, it would not meet the criterion of 'reasonable'. It would be in conformity with the general intention of this paragraph, in the light of the specific circumstances of each case, if management were able to provide such notice prior to the final decision being taken» (paragraph 67).

5. Some comments

189. It is obvious that the expression 'changes in operations' must be broadly interpreted and that Guideline 6, as indicated in the IME report, does not only apply to close downs and collective lay-offs, but also to other structural changes, e.g. mergers, provided that they have a major effect on the livelihood of the employees. The wording of the paragraph 'in considering changes' could seem to indicate a stage *prior* to the final decision. Again, specific circum-stances of each case have to be taken into account; especially compelling reasons of business confidentiality that may prevent early information. But this should be the exception rather than the general rule. Following on from the Committee, that reasonable notice has to be linked with the aim of the mitigation of practicable adverse effects, but another point of view could be defended.

190. Co-operation with employee representatives and Governmental authorities does, following the drafters of the Guidelines, not include negotia-tions in the strict sense but means consultation. *Mitigation* to the maximum extent practicable of the resulting adverse effects, includes looking for alternative solutions (no overtime, work sharing e.g.), dismissing of less people, postponement of dismissals, terms of notice, golden handshake, retraining, re-employment and the like. This does, of course, not take away that in certain countries national legislation and practice prescribes negotiations on the decision as well as on the social consequences thereof (e.g. Sweden).

191. Finally, we should bear in mind the fact that the IME Committee has stated that the financial responsibility of the parent company could be of particular relevance in the circumstances set out in Guideline 6.[21] The same could be true in the case of the closing down of a profitable subsidiary: in that case one might accept a special responsibility as far as the mitigation of resulting adverse effects is concerned.

VI. Comparable Standards of Employment. The Warner Lambert Case

---
Guideline 4 of the Employment and Industrial Relations Chapter:

«observe standards of employment and industrial relations not less favourable than those observed by comparable employers in the host country».

---

1. THE ISSUE. SUBMISSION BY IMF

192. Under the Warner Lambert case, introduced by the IMF, through TUAC, March 30, 1977, the issue arose whether Guideline 4 permits an affiliate of a multinational enterprise to pay lower wages than comparable national enterprises because of its particular economic and/or financial difficulties.

«Policy of WARNER-LAMBERT to close down its operations in Sweden

The American multinational WARNER-LAMBERT announced on 8 October 1976 the possible closure of its plant for the manufacture of razor blades, with 240 workers, in Sweden. The final decision would be taken within a year's time, and would depend on whether this kind of production could be concentrated in Halmstad, Sweden or in Amsterdam, Netherlands. New investment in the Swedish operations had been made in 1974, but company accounts showed a loss in 1975.
A meeting was arranged with the Swedish IMF affiliates, when the whole issue was examined. There was assurance from the management of the regional headquarters for Europe – in Brussels, that representation would be made to

21. See above, the Badger case, Part II, I.

the world headquarters in the United States, to bring some alternative employment to Sweden. Nothing has happened and the management has now told the union that no alternative employment can be created in Halmstad. The workers think, however, that WARNER-LAMBERT could have created new jobs in Halmstad – if there had been a real will on the part of the management. On the other hand, already in December 1976, notices of dismissal were sent out to all workers in the Swedish subsidiary and the latest information is that the subsidiary will be closed on 3 June 1977.

The situation for the affected workers is depressed. The local union has paid a visit to the Swedish government, which was not in a position to provide more details nor make any promises for the safeguarding of the workers.

Using the argument of the possible transfer of operations to the Netherlands, the WARNER-LAMBERT subsidiary in Sweden demanded in the course of negotiations that workers should accept a lower wage level than the level of the regional average. Actually, this average for 1976 was more than 12% higher than the wage level of the WARNER-LAMBERT subsidiary.

Here again there was insufficient information to trade unions, and failure to enter into real negotiations with trade unions after some empty pormises had been made. In addition, a contemplated transfer of the production facilities was used as a means of pressuring union representatives during collective bargaining negotiations, when the subsidiary had already paid wages 'less favourable than those observed by comparable employers in the region'. (Employment and Industrial Relations, para. 4.)».

2. SOME COMMENTS

193. The report of the IME Committee is silent on this issue, although I believe that it merits some consideration. It seems in the first place that 'the standards of employment and industrial relations' referred to in Guideline 4 include wages; and that 'comparable' leaves a certain amount of flexibility. In the second place, logic seems to indicate that since a national enterprise is allowed, respecting local law and regulations, to adapt its wages to economic difficulties, that the same must be possible for a multinational enterprise. The Guidelines do not discriminate between national and multinational enterprises and do constitute 'good practice for all' (paragraph 9 of the introduction). Consequently, the Guidelines do not prevent a subsidiary adapting wages when economic and financial difficulties are experienced by the firm if such conduct, under local law and practice is accepted in the country for national enterprises under comparable circumstances.

VII. Transfer of Employees in case of a Labour Dispute. The Hertz Case

> ### Guideline 8 of the Employment and Industrial Relations Guidelines:
>
> «in the context of bona fide negotiations with representatives of employees on conditions of employment, or while employees are exercising a right to organize, not threaten to utilize a capacity to transfer the whole or part of an operating unit from the country concerned in order to influence unfairly those negotiations or to hinder the exercise of a right to organize;
>
> Bona fide negotiations may include labour disputes as part of the process of negotiation. Whether or not labour disputes are so included will be determined by the law and prevailing employment practices of particular countries.»

1. THE ISSUE

194. The question arises, whether the temporary transfer of workers from a foreign branch during negotiations, including labour disputes, in order to influence (unfairly) those negotiations is covered by Guideline 8 of the Employment and Industrial Relations Chapter.

2. «TUAC PROPOSAL TO PROHIBIT THE TRANSFER OF STAFF ACROSS BORDERS DURING A LABOUR DISPUTE

– On the basis of a case concerning HERTZ RENT A CAR, submitted by the International Federation of Employees and Technicians (FIET) and the Confederation of Danish trade unions (LO – Denmark).

A recent dispute between the multinational enterprise HERTZ RENT A CAR and the Danish union HK, a member of TUAC affiliated organization LO – Denmark and of FIET, has shown that the Guidelines, although drawn up in a sufficiently general fashion to cover in principle all possible cases of the abuse of multinational power, reveal loopholes in their wording.

During the labour dispute which took place in November 1976, HERTZ RENT A CAR transferred workers from branches in other countries in order to substitute them to its Danish staff on strike. By doing so, HERTZ management misused the power it had as an employer on its staff *outside* Denmark. Normal labour relations practices in Denmark were clearly disrupted by this behaviour.

HERTZ used this multinational power to transfer staff from other countries in order to undermine a perfectly lawful strike in Denmark and to avoid bona fide negotiations of a collective agreement with their Danish employees and the trade union that represents them. Details of the case are described in a report in appendix by LO – Denmark. Attention should be paid also to the fact that

219

HERTZ international management used the same technique in Belgium, in June 1976, at the occasion of a strike conducted by the employees of Hertz Service Corporation (established in Brussels) on issues of trade union recognition, bona fide negotiations, job security and bonuses. The Belgian trade union involved in the case was the Trade Union of Employees, Technicians and Managers SETCA, affiliated to FIET en FGTB. Recently, in March 1977, Hertz Germany refused to negotiate with the German trade union DAG, also a member of FIET.

The details of the Danish case described in the attached report shows that Hertz management acted in violation of several of the standards set by the OECD Guidelines.

The members of the OECD Committee on International Investment and Multinational Enterprises may wish to study the question on how the behaviour of the international management of HERTZ RENT A CAR is affecting the implementation of the OECD Guidelines for multinational enterprises.

Furthermore, they may wish to explore the possibility of clarifying the interpretation of the Guidelines concerning the abuse of multinational power by a multinational enterprise. The OECD Ministers intended clearly to curb the abuse of multinational power when for example, they drafted article 8 forbidding the threat of the transfer of activities.

In order to avoid in the future any difficulty in the interpretation of the Guidelines in similar cases, TUAC is proposing a paragraph 8 (bis) which should read as follows:

'Enterprises should . . . abstain from transfering workers from affiliates in foreign countries at the time when bona fide negotiations are being carried on (including labour disputes) with the object of undermining these negotiations and the lawful union activities of their workers.' It would not be necessary however, to add a new paragraph to the Guidelines if the interpretation set above could be accepted by the IME Committee as expressing the spirit of paragraph 8.»

 **LANDSORGANISATIONEN I DANMARK**

Rosenørns Allè 14

Telefon 01 - 35 36 41

Telegramadresse: Fagforbond

Girokonto 6 00 05 33

Trade Union Advisory Committee
to the OECD
26 Avenue de la Grande Armée
F–75o17 Paris 17e
Frankrig

Journal dr. SBV/JS/GM.

(Bedes anfort i al konespandanto mid 1D ved-orende denne saq)

Dares ref.

1970 København V. 26 Jan. 1977

Dear Friends,

Report on the conflict between the BK – the Danish Union of Commercial and Clerical Employees – and the Hertz Rent a Car Company in Denmark.

The LO-Denmark wishes with the present report to give an account of a conflict which has taken place in Denmark between the BK, which is an affiliate of the LO, and the Danish branch of the Multinational Company Hertz Rent A Car.

It is the view of the LO that, in connection with the said conflict, the Hertz Company has failed to observe the declaration of the OECD Council of Ministers on international investments and multinational companies. We are therefore of the opinion that the case in question should be discussed by the TUAC with a view to possibly submitting it to the OECD committee on international investments and multinational companies (IME).

1. The conflict between the HK and Hertz Rent A Car

On October 1, 1976, the LO affiliate BK effected a strike and blockade, lawful according to the Danish rules of labour law, against the Danish branch of Hertz Rent A Car.

The background of the union's action was that there had been clear cases of underpayment of the employees of the company.

In the course of negotiations the management of the branch refused to sign an agreement in which the wage level would be in conformity with the minimum wages applying within the field of activity in question.

The European Personnel Manager of the Hertz Company said during negotiations before the conflict that the company intended to close down its branch in Denmark if the HK maintained its wishes.

In agreement with the HK the SID – Union of Special Workers in Denmark – and the Danish Metal Workers' Union effected a sympathetic conflict against the company. This is lawful under the Danish rules.

In a systematic attempt to avoid that the strike became effective the company called in employees from its branches in England, Western Germany, France, Italy, Holland and Belgium.

The foreign employees of Hertz Rent A Car who were transferred to Denmark during the conflict worked in the Danish branch in periods of about ten days at a time. It is the view of the involved unions that the foreign strike-breakers in question knew nothing about the conflict in Denmark before the transfer to Copenhagen.

On November 25 – after just under two months of conflict – the HK signed an agreement with the company and the strike was thereby brought to an end.

At the time of signing the agreement the Hertz company announced that it was unable to employ all the employees of the Danish branch owing to changes in the structure and operations of the company. Nine employees might continue in the company while other nine employees were dismissed.

Immediately after the agreement had been signed it was ascertained that the company continued to employ foreign employees, and this gave rise to a brief stoppage of work in the company.

On January 25, 1977 it has been ascertained that the Danish branch of the Hertz Company does not – at the moment – employ any foreign staff members.

II. Handling of the conflict by Danish authorities, the EC Parliament and the international trade union organizations

During the conflict the LO took the initiative for meetings with representatives of the Danish Ministry of Foreign Affairs and the Danish Ministry of Labour. At the meetings – which were of an informative character – the LO asked the Danish authorities to examine to which extent the Hertz Company made use of foreign strike-breakers. The LO further pointed out that it considered the conduct of the company to be in contravention of the OECD guidelines on multinational companies, and that the trade union movement would be interested, at a later stage, in having this established.

Also during the conflict the *EC Parliament* adopted a resolution – by an overwhelming majority – which clearly denounces the conduct of the Hertz Company, and the EC Parliament invites the Commission to draw up rules that will prevent the repetition of such cases.

The ETUC – the European Trade Union Confederation – at its executive committee meeting on December 10, 1976, adopted a resolution which also clearly denounces the conduct of the company in question. The resolution invites the EC to take measures to prevent repetitions.

In the same resolution the ETUC draws attention to the OECD declaration on multinational companies, pointing out the necessity of making the OECD guidelines legally binding.

In connection with the conflict the FIET – International Federation of Commercial, Clerical and Technical Employees – has fully supported its Danish affiliate.

III. Views of the LO on the conduct of the Hertz Company in relation to the OECD declaration on multinational companies

In connection with the conflict against the Hertz Company the LO and the HK have contended that the company has acted in clear contravention of the guidelines on multinational companies adopted by the OECD.

The organizations are of the opinion that articles (1), (2) (a) and (b), (3), (4), (5), (6) and (8) in the chapter on 'Employment and Industrial Relations' have not been observed by the Hertz Company.

As regards *article (1)* it must be established that the company has not shown any will to engage in *constructive* negotiations with the trade union of their employees – the HK.

The company was unable to accept the minimum wage of *Dkr 4. loo* applying to the field of activity in question and further refused to accept agreements on payment of cost-of-living allowance, employers' contribution to training fund, and compensation for working at irregular hours – arrangements which are generally accepted at the Danish labour market and form part of all Danish agreements.

It is further the view of the trade unions that the negotiators of the Hertz Company before the conflict was effected on October 1 had no authority to make agreements with the trade union of the employees, so that there was no question of constructive negotiations.

The organizations find that the provisions of *article (2)* (a) and (b) have also been violated. The workers' side has at no time before the conflict and in the course of the negotiations received any assistance from the company with a view to the development of an effective collective agreement. Nor have the employees or their organization received any information about the company or any other information that might contribute to making negotations meaningful.

The company has also failed to observe the provisions of *article (3)* – see comments in relation to article (2) (a) and (b).

Until the time of signing the agreement on November 25 the company has not observed *article 4*. As already stated in connection with article 1 the company refused to meet the demand of the employees for cost-of-living regulation of wages, compensation for irregular working hours, etc. The company's wage level was also substantially below what is normal within the field of activity in question.

Article (5) has not been observed either since the company has made use of foreign employees.

Article (6) – provisions to the effect that the employer should provide reasonable notice in the case of changes which would have major effects upon the livelihood of his employees – are considered by the trade union organizations as clearly violated. In connection with the signing of the agreement on *November 25* the company stated – *without any advance announcement* – that nine employees out of a total of eighteen would have to be dismissed. As reason for the dismissals it was stated that substantial parts of the operations of the company were to be transferred to Western Germany. In reply to a question from the representatives of the employees it was stated that the change in question had been planned for six months.

The enclosed advertisement in 'Frankfurter Allgemeine Zeitung' for Saturday, November 27, 1976, confirms that the Western German Branch was to take over the functions of the Danish branch.

In the course of negotiations *before* the conflict started on October 1 the representatives of the company stated that closure of the enterprise in Denmark would be the result if the demands of the trade union for an agreement were maintained. This is in direct contravension of *article (8)*.

Final remarks

The conflict between the Danish HK union and the Hertz Rent A Car company confirms in the view of the Danish trade union movement the need for establishing international *binding* rules for multinational companies within the competence of the OECD.

The LO has further pointed out to the EC that the Hertz Company has abused the intentions of the EC provisions on the free movement of workers. On the basis of this concrete case the EC Commission has accepted to undertake an examination of the prerequisites of adopting regulations that may prevent repetitions.

On behalf of LO-Denmark

Signed: Svend Bache Vognbjerg
Secretary»

«*Stillingsannonce i FRANKFÜRTER ALLGEMEINE ZEITING, lørdag 27.11.1976 'FAZ' or et af Tysklands største dagblade.*

Oversaettelse:
Bliv medlem i HERTZ VIP – klubben
Thi hos HERTZ er alle medarbejder Very Import Persons.
Hertz er en af de store i biludlejningsbranchen verden over.
Markedet er vanskelig. Konkurrenzen sover ikke. Alligevel:
Vi er altid lidt laengere fremme end de andre. Fordi vores medarbejder er fagkyndige, opmaerksomme, ansvarbevidste, venlige og loyale. Netop Very Import Persons.
Hertz – Centralen i Tyskland søger
nogle bogholdere
med mangearig erfaring i finansbogholderi.
Samsbehandlere (kvindelige/mandlige)
til vores debitorafdeling og rykker-afdeling.
En ubetinget forudsaettelse til alle ovenstående positioner:
Meget gode sprongkundskaber i *DANSK* eller *SVENSK* plus *ENGELSK*.
Ideal ville vaere en kombination af disse tre sprog plus gode Tysk-kundskaber.
En kvindelige korrespondent
flydende Tysk/Engelsk, en 'working knowledge' af Dansk eller Svensk ville vaere fordelagtig, er dog ikke forudsaetning.
Deres karrieremaessige, personlige videreudvikling ligger hos Hertz helt alene i deres haender. Gør den første skridt og send Deres korte ansøgning ind.»

«Werden Sie Mitglied im Hertz V.I.P.-Club

Denn bei Hertz sind auch die Mitarbeiter Very Important Persons

Hertz ist einer der Großen der Autovermietbranche in der Welt. Der Markt ist schwierig. Die Konkurrenz schläft nicht. Trotzdem: Wir sind immer wieder einen Schritt schneller als die anderen. Weil unsere Mitarbeiter fachkundig, aufmerksam, verantwortungsbewußt, freundlich und loyal sind. Eben Very Important Persons.

Die Hertz-Zentrale in Deutschland sucht:

BUCHHALTER

mit mehrjähriger Erfahrung in der Finanzbuchhaltung.

SACHBEARBEITER(INNEN)

für unsere Debitorenbuchhaltung und Mahnabteilung.

Muß-Voraussetzung für alle obenstehenden Positionen:
Sehr gute Sprachkenntnisse in Dänisch oder Schwedisch plus Englisch. Ideal wäre die Kombination dieser drei Sprachen mit guten Deutsch-Kenntnissen.

FREMDSPRACHEN-SEKRETÄRIN

fließend Englisch/Deutsch, eine 'working knowledge' von Dänisch oder Schwedisch wäre vortellhaft, ist aber nicht Voraussetzung.

Ihre persönliche berufliche Weiterentwicklung bei Hertz leigt ganz allein in Ihrer Hand. Machen Sie den ersten Schritt. Setzen Sie sich mit einer aussagefähigen, schriftlichen Kurzbewerbung jetzt mit uns in Verbindung.

HERTZ AUTOVERMIETUNG GMBH
Personalabteilung
Mainzer Landstraße 129
6000 Frankfurt a. M.
Telefon (0611) 23 91 21 »

3. THE IME REPORT

195. The report reads as follows:

«(iv) *Unfair influence in bona fide negotiations with employees* (paragraph 8)

Paragraph 8 refers to threats 'to utilise a capacity to transfer the whole or part of an operating unit from the country concerned in order to influence unfairly bona fide negotiations with representatives of employees'. The Committee recalled that this paragraph as drafted was meant to cover only operations involving existing plant and equipment. Nevertheless, future investments, such as replacement of equipment or the introduction of new technology may be crucial to the survival of the enterprises in the medium and long-term and thus may be of interest in this context (paragraph 68).

An important issue with respect to paragraph 8 is the distinction between legitimate provision of information and threats designed to influence unfairly negotiations with employees. It was recognised that the term 'unfair' was the key notion in this context. A distinction should be made between information given to employees on the likely consequences for the future of the firm as a going concern of the eventual outcome of such negotiations and threats which would be an unfair use of the management's negotiating power. If certain demands in the view of management have serious implications on the economic viability of this enterprise, it would be appropriate to point this out to employee representatives in the course of negotiations. Yet, management in such instances should be prepared to provide information in order to support this claim (paragraph 69).

The Committee also considered the question whether the transfer of employees from a foreign affiliate in order to influence unfairly bona fide negotiations with employee representatives on conditions of employment would be contrary to standards set out in the Employment and Industrial Relations chapter and more particularly to paragraph 8. In the view of the Committee, such behaviour, while not specifically mentioned in the Guidelines, certainly would not be in conformity with the general spirit and approach underlying the drafting of the Employment and Industrial Relations chapter. Accordingly, it is recommended that enterprises should definitely avoid recourse to such practices in the future. The Committee, therefore, proposes that this recommendation, which does not imply a major change of the Guidelines, should be made explicit in the text of paragraph 8 by the following addition (amended language underlined): 'Enterprises should within the framework of law, regulations and prevailing labour relations and employment practices, in each of the countries in which they operate, 8. In the context of bona fide negotiations* with representatives of employees on conditions of employment, or while employees are exercising a right to organize, not threaten to utilize a capacity to transfer the whole or part of an operating unit from the country concerned *nor transfer employees from the enterprises' component entities in other countries* in order to influence unfairly those negotiations or to hinder the exercise of a right to organize (paragraph 70).'

*Bona fide negotiations may include labour disputes as part of the process of negotiation. Whether or not labour disputes are so included will be determined by the law and prevailing employment practices of particular countries.»

4. SOME COMMENTS

196. On this point all parties involved agreed, Government as well as business and labour: the use of strike breakers in the sense of transfer of workers from foreign affiliates in order to influence negotiations unfairly or to hinder the right to organize, although not covered by the Guidelines, was not to be tolerated. The Hertz Case indicated a gap in the Guidelines, which had to be filled. Also the European Council of Ministers, at the request of the Danish Government, gave the opinion that the free movement of labour within the Countries of the European Economic Community was only to be used in the positive sense of contributing to the well-being and the promotion of workers . . .[22] Consequently, the Guidelines were amended, in the sense as indicated in paragraph 70 of the report of the IME Committee.

197. It should, however, be borne in mind that this paragraph has definite limits. Guideline 8 refers to threats to transfer the whole or a part of an operating unit from the country concerned in order to influence negotiations . . . 'unfairly'. Thus, this Guideline covers only, as the report indicates, existing plants and equipment. Equally important in this context are the threats not to invest or disinvest, as the impact of such threats on the workers concerns, be it future, job security and employment. Disinvestment is, however, strictly speaking, referring to the wording of Guideline 8 – not covered by the Guideline. The IME Committee recognizes this by stating that disinvestment 'may be of interest'. The transfer of products or materials are not covered by the Guidelines, or the fact that another subsidiary is doing extra 'overtime', or any other measures.

198. The trade unions obviously want to have a broader interpretation of the Guidelines, with the aim of curbing the power of the multinational enterprise,

22. Article 48 of the Treaty establishing the European Economic Community reads as follows:
«1. The free movement of workers shall be ensured within the Community not later than at the date of the expiry of the transitional period.
2. This shall involve the abolition of any discrimination based on nationality between workers of the Member States as regards employment, remuneration, and other working conditions.
3. It shall include the right, subject to limitations justified by reasons of public order, public safety and public health:
a. to accept offers of employment actually made;
b. to move about freely for this purpose within the territory of Member States;
c. to stay in any Member State in order to carry on an employment in conformity with the legislative and administrative provisions governing the employment of the workers of that State; and
d. to live, on conditions which shall be the subject of implementing regulations to be laid down by the Commission, in the territory of a Member State after having been employed there.
4. The provisions of this Article shall not apply to employment in the public administration.»

hindering the enterprise from using its power by installing in the case of a conflict a 'kind of status quo'. Such an interpretation can not, however, be supported by the actual tests of the Guidelines, since 'words mean what they mean'.

199. Transfer of workers, from one foreign affiliate to another is now also covered by Guideline 8. This was already foreseen in paragraph 52 of the ILO Declaration of Principles, which, in its second sentence, makes an explicit reference to the issue as follows '. . . nor should they transfer workers from affiliates in foreign countries with a view to undermining bona fide negotiations with the workers' representatives or the workers' exercise of the right to organize'. International transfer of workers in a case of conflict cannot happen frequently, given the difficulties of obtaining work permits and the like, except in common markets, like the EEC, where there is freedom of labour. It must be pointed out that transfer of workers from one subsidiary to another within the same country does not seem, in the actual status of clarification, to be covered by Guideline 8.

200. The report indicates that the key notion in paragraph 8 of the industrial relations Guidelines is the word 'unfair'.[23]
This term is especially used in USA Labour Law.[24] 'Unfair' indicates employer conduct that tends to coerce an employer; such prohibited action forbids not only physical violence, or the threat thereof, but more subtle means of coercion as well. A difficult problem, Prof. Goldman states, is 'how to distinguish between a threat and a mere statement of information or opinion designed to guide the worker's thinking in reaching an uncoerced conclusion . . .'. Because freedom of expression is protected, the expression of opinions or information cannot be prohibited. The National Labour Relations Board in the USA 'takes the position that whether an employer's statement constitutes a threat must be determined by examining the context in which the statement is made and not just the content of what is said or written.
. . .' The Supreme Court has provided some guidance respecting the distinction that must be made between employer statements that are protected and those that do constitute unprotected threats. The Court has stated that an employer can express his opinion regarding the perceived levels of unionization and can even make predictions regarding the adverse impact of employee concerted activities. However, such predictions 'must be carefully phrased on the basis of objective fact' and not contain 'any implicit or explicit statement of dire consequences that will be brought about by the employer's exercise of its own discretion in responding to the workers' decision to organize'.

23. Following *Webster's Seventh New Collegiate Dictionary*, 1965, unfair means: '1. marked by injustice, partiality or deception; 2. unequitable in business dealings'.
24. Goldman Alvin L., *Labor Law and Industrial Relations in the United States of America*, (1979) in: *International Encyclopaedia for Labour Law and Industrial Relations* (ed. R. Blanpain), Kluwer, The Netherlands, nrs. 299 and following.

VIII. Definition of a Multinational: The European Airline Groupings

---

Paragraph 8 of the Introduction:

«A precise legal definition of multinational enterprises is not required for the purposes of the guidelines. These usually comprise companies or other entities whose ownership is private, state or mixed, established in different countries *and so linked that one or more of them may be able to exercise a significant influence over the activities of others and, in particular, to share knowledge and resources with the others.* The degree of autonomy of each entity in relation to the others varies widely from one multinational enterprise to another, depending on the nature of the links between such entities and the fields of activity concerned. For these reasons, the guidelines are addressed to the various entities within the multinational enterprise (parent companies and/or local entities) according to the actual distribution of responsibilities among them on the understanding that they will co-operate and provide assistance to one another as necessary to facilitate observance of the guidelines. The word 'enterprise' as used in these guidelines refers to these various entities in accordance with their responsibilities.»

---

1. THE ISSUE. SUBMISSION BY ITF

201. «ITF submission to the TUAC and to the OECD Committee on International Investment and Multinational Enterprises on the validity of application of the OECD Guidelines for multinational enterprises in the case of European airline groupings.

ISSUE

Paragraph 8 of the introduction to the Guidelines states that:
'A precise legal definition of multination enterprises is not required for the purposes of the Guidelines. These usually comprise companies or other entities whose ownership is private, state or mixed, established in different countries and so linked that one or more of them may be able to exercise a significant influence over the activities of others, and, in particular, to share knowledge and resources with the others.'
Does this paragraph apply to the case of airlines groupings, such as KSSU or ATLAS?

FACTS

At present, there are two main airline groupings in Europe: KSSU (KLM,

Swissair, SAS and UTA) and ATLAS (Alitalla, Lufthansa, Air France and Sabena). In addition, as a result of existing links between these and other airlines, there are also a number of 'associated companies' (see, for example, page 2 of report on ITF KSSU Group Meeting of 22 May 1975).

The vast majority of employees of the two airline groupings are members of the International Transport Workers' Federation (ITF). The only major group not so represented on an overall basis are the pilots, who belong in part to the International Federation of Airline Pilots' Associations (IFALPA) and in part to the ITF. Since the creation of the two groups, the national unions concerned have held regular meetings under the auspices of the ITF, both separately (KSSU or ATLAS unions) and jointly. It should be stressed here that the problems for the two union groups are largely common ones, due to the consistent refusal of the airlines to meet their union counterparts on a group basis and to engage in consultation and negotiation on decisions taken at group level. The claim that this should be done was submitted at a very early stage, but repeated approaches by both the ITF and its individual affiliates have been without result (see Circ. 50/Ca.7 for copies of letters from three KSSU companies in reply to the most recent ITF approach).

The basic arguments used by the companies are: (a) that the co-operating companies retain their individual autonomy; (b) that no useful purpose could be served by international consultation; and (c) that the co-operation involved is in any case mainly technical in character. For the unions, this is an over-simplification of the existing situation. Decisions taken at group level are, in fact, implemented within the individual airlines, and the unions have little or no possibility of influencing them at that level. They therefore believe that their existing rights of negotiation with the individual airlines must be supplemented by the right to be consulted and to state their views at group level also. Harmonization of working conditions within the grouping is made unnecessarily difficult in the present situation, and there is also the fear that individual negotiating positions and the capacity to take effective industrial action in dispute situations could be immensely weakened by airline group co-operation (See Ground Staff Committee Resolution on Multi-nationals, London, 20/21 May 1975).

It is claimed that the co-operation is mainly technical and therefore of no concern to the unions. the unions believe this to be a naïve argument, since technological developments clearly have very direct effects on working conditions and employment prospects in the industry. This is, in fact, recognised in the systems of joint consultation and co-determination which have been introduced in a number of countries, with changed methods, rationalization measures, and new technologies being considered as legitimate subjects for joint discussion and negotiation. Most innovations in industry nowadays have social implications.

If one looks at the material on KSSU co-operation (see attached ITF document 75/Ca.5/1), it can be seen that there are four main areas of co-operation: *marketing* (including joint ticket offices and handling facilities at airports); *operations* (utilization of a joint Boeing 747 simulator; the provision of identical flight deck lay-outs; and exchange or inter-change of aircraft and crews);

specification (almost identical DC–10 and 747B equipment plus the introduction of joint evaluation of aircraft); and *technical* (joint overhaul of DC–10 and 747 aircraft; utilization of joint manuals). The unions have a strong interest in a number of these items and have been accustomed to negotiate on them nationally – e.g. the implications of joint handling at airports; interchange; flight deck design and other specification; crew training and joint overhaul facilities. The division of maintenance work indicated both here and in APL 75 obviously affects ground maintenance workers, inter alia, in their future job prospects and from the standpoint of training and retraining. In such a situation, the ability to negotiate nationally may not mean very much and needs to be supplemented by an international system of consultation and negotiation. the unions believe this to be in the interests of the companies also if unnecessary friction and conflict is to be avoided.

In its reply, as reproduced in Circ. 50/Ca.7, the management of KLM states that KSSU 'consists of four independent airlines who lend each other – mostly technical – assistance for reasons of efficiency; the KSSU members have each their own corporate objectives and specific policies. Nor do we consider KLM itself a multinational enterprise'. On this, the unions would agree that, taken singly, none of the members is a multinational enterprise. In their group capacity, however, they are engaging in multinational activity which has a very direct impact on employment and industrial relations within each of the individual airline components.

The ITF, after consultation with the TUAC, holds the opinion that the paragraph 8 of the introduction to the Guidelines covers also the case of airline groupings. If it is the case, the Guidelines are to be implemented by the airline groupings including the section on employment and industrial relations.»

2. The KSSU[25]

202. «The KSSU group is an extension of the SAS-Swissair co-operation which began in 1957. The two airlines entered into technical co-operation when SAS ordered seven DC–8s and Swissair, three. The two airline's DC–8s were identical except for livery and interior color schemes. This initially high degree of standardization was not all that easy to achieve, however.

Three aircraft types, in fact, were included in the framework of early SAS-Swissair co-operation. In addition to the DC–8, there were the Caravelle and Coronado, both first-generation jetliners. Swissair overhauled the airframes and engines of both airline's Coronados. SAS did the same for the two carriers' DC–8s and Caravelles. As a result, both airlines avoided duplicating expensive engineering facilities.

KLM formally entered the partnership at the end of 1967 although the Dutch airlines was actually no newcomer to the cooperation. KLM had participated in the original SAS and Swissair DC–8 deliberations and had been overhauling the two carrier's DC–8 engines since 1963. Later KLM had contracted overhaul of its DC–9 engines to Swissair which was already handling SAS's as well

25. *SAS Yearbook* 1976–1977.

as its own. But, until 1967, KLM's role was that of contractor rather than partner.

When the three airlines decided to order identical Boeing 747 in 1968, they signed the KSS agreement. Then they selected the same version of the DC–10 in 1969. So did the privately-owned French carrier, UTA, which also joined the co-operation. Thus, the KSSU group was formed in February of 1970.

The KSSU agreement runs for an initial period of 10 years. It provides for the establishment of an organization to administer the co-operative venture's operations. Staff from all four airlines participate in the organization. The agreement binds the four members to agree upon common specifications for every aircraft type they select, but it does not commit any one partner to buy every type of aircraft the other members might order.

There are numerous practical advantages of an organization of airlines such as KSSU. Most obvious are the savings which the partners make in their initial investments in a new aircraft type. Indirectly, this also benefits the national economies of the airline-members' countries.

Another clear advantage gleaned from the co-operation is the elimination of duplication of maintenance and overhaul facilities. The co-operation also represents potential savings in certain specialized fields – not only in planning engineering activities but also in production planning, material supplies and data processing. As these are all areas with shortages of skilled personnel, the co-operation solves this problem for the airlines as well.

THE KSSU ORGANIZATION

Operation of the KSSU organization is governed by an eight-man Management Committee composed of two top executives from each airlines. Every KSSU committee, in fact, has an equal number of representatives from each participating airlines. The members, however, remain employees of their respective airlines and combine their KSSU duties with their ordinary responsibilities.

The Management Committee sets the overall policy for the organization's activities. Eight executive committees, reporting directly to the Management Committee, are responsible for the execution of the various aspects of the cooperation. One of the most important committees is responsible for the practical details of the maintenance and overhaul agreements.

Reporting to this committee are a number of working groups whose members co-ordinate KSSU activities within their own airlines, among the member airlines, and between their own and other working groups. These groups have a number of sub-committees and teams of specialists working under them.

Reporting to the Management Committee are the Long Term Advisory Group, the Legal Advisory Group, the Finance Advisory Group, the Electronic Data Processing Group, the Specification Policy Conference, the Technical Policy Conference, the Operational Policy Conference, the Marketing Policy Conference, and Management Co-ordinators.

The Long Term Advisory Group deals with the joint evaluation of future flight equipment. The Finance Advisory Group is responsible for, and co-ordinates,

KSSU financial policies and delegates to a joint pricing sub-committee the cost-setting for the exchange of services within the KSSU group.

A team of management co-ordinators act as a secretariat for the Management Committee. The Specification Policy Conference has the important task of ensuring that identical aircraft specifications are met in practice (except for interior and exterior color schemes). The Operational Policy Conference is responsible for functional co-operations.

The entire KSSU operational structure is tightly knit and carefully supervised, with rules and conditions laid down to ensure the best possible co-ordination of every state of the co–operation. The details of the formal agreement are spelled out in the comprehensive KSSU Co-operation Manual.

It is possible that the only serious drawback of a co-operative venture on the scale of KSSU is that the administration is far more complicated than if a single airline were running its own technical services. But the complications arise only at early stages, when a new type of aircraft is selected, its specifications decided upon, and its acquisition completed. Once the allocation of work to the KSSU partners has been decided upon, and the new aircraft type has been delivered, there are few complications.

Whatever the disadvantages of the KSSU co-operation may be, they are outweighed by a wide margin by the advantages. They can be summarized accordingly: considerable savings in initial investments and in annually recurring financial charges; smaller investments when specifications are altered; elimination of duplication of services, especially of overhaul facilities; and, mitigation of problems caused by the shortage of skilled personnel, particularly in such specialized fields as engineering, production planning, acquisition of materials and data processing.

MAINTENANCE AND OVERHAUL SERVICES

		CV–440	DC–9	DC–8	DC–10	747
SAS For SAS and other airlines	COPENHAGEN	Periodic maintenance. All aircraft types. Maintenance of components. All aircraft types.				
	OSLO	Aircraft and engine overhaul (SAS + LIN)	Aircraft overhaul (SAS)			
	ARLANDA			Aircraft overhaul (SAS, SWR, THAI)		
	LINTA			Engine overhaul (SAS, THAI)		Engine overhaul (SAS, SWR, KLM)
KLM For SAS	AMSTERDAM				Engine overhaul (SAS + THAI)	Aircraft overhaul
SWR For SAS	ZURICH		Engine overhaul		Aircraft overhaul (SAS + THAI)	
UTA For SAS	PARIS				APU and landing gear	APU and landing gear

3. THE IME REPORT

203. The report contains following relevant paragraph:

«*Paragraph 8* deals with two aspects of importance to the application of the Guidelines as a whole. First, it reflects the understanding of the Committee of what is meant by the term 'multinational enterprise'. Paragraph 8 is couched in non-legal language and the experience of the Committee has demonstrated the merits of such a flexible approach with an enumeration of some guiding criteria rather than a precise definition which would fit less well the diversity of situations found in the real world. The Guidelines are addressed to entities which can be considered as 'enterprises' (private, state, mixed) 'established in different countries and so linked that one or more of them may be able to exercise a significant influence over the activities of others and, in particular, to share knowledge and resources with the others'. These criteria cover a broad range of multinational activities and arrangements, which can be based on equity participation according to the traditional approach to international direct investment, but the same result could be achieved by other means not necessarily including an equity capital element» (paragraph 39).

4. SOME COMMENTS

204. It is on the basis of the available information really not possible to conclude whether the Airline groupings are multinational enterprises or not. The point made in the report is however clear: 'significant influence and sharing of knowledge and resources is sufficient'. The fact that there is e.g. no chairman or director of such a grouping, neither a secretariat, nor administration and the like may be important indications, but these are in fact not conclusive. The question is: are at that level decisions taken (even informal, by the way of recommendations, which are in fact implemented), which were previously taken at national level and normally discussed with employees. It is, as we stressed over and again, the centralized decision-making structure by which the multinational decision escapes the local grip, which constitutes the 'raison d'être' of the Guidelines. If this is the case, the Airline Groupings are to be considered as multinationals in the sense of the Guidelines.
The IME report however rightly indicates that it should be noted
«that in applying the Guidelines, it is not necessary in every instance to seek to determine whether or not the nature of contractual links of a non-equity character between separate entities leads to the conclusion that such entities viewed collectively constitute an MNE within the meaning of the Guidelines. *Paragraph 9* of the introduction clearly states that the Guidelines, wherever relevant, 'reflect good practice for all. Accordingly, multinational and domestic enterprises are subject to the same expectations in respect of their conduct wherever the Guidelines are relevant for both'» (paragraph 40).[26]

26. See above no. 63.

236

Part III. The 1979 Review: The Follow-Up Procedures

205. One of the elements of the 1976 package was the review of the Guidelines within a period of three years 'with a view to improving the effectiveness of international economic co-operation among Member countries on issues relating to international investment and multinational enterprises'.

The main question was, whether in the light of experience, at national as well as international level, through the exchange of views in the IME Committee, and through the consultations with BIAC and TUAC the text of (1) the Guidelines needed to be amended, as well as the text of (2) the Decision on Inter-Governmental Consultation.

As already indicated there was only one change of the Guidelines accepted:[1] the Decision on Inter-Governmental Consultations was greatly amended while the report also contained a substantial number of improved follow-up procedures.

In the following pages I concentrate mainly on the follow-up procedures. I first give the statements by BIAC and TUAC at the occasion of the review, as well as the Swedish proposal on consultation procedures and the Dutch proposal on fact-finding.

I. Preparing the Review

A. THE POINT OF VIEW OF BIAC

206. This point of view was put forward in a document, dated 21 December 1978.

«BIAC wishes from the outset to emphasize that the Declaration on International Investment and Multinational Enterprises is a carefully negotiated instrument among the OECD Governments combining recommendations to multinational enterprises with the understanding that member countries have responsibilities in the areas of National Treatment and International Incentives and Disincentives. In this statement BIAC is meeting the request of the OECD's Committee on International Investment and Multinational Enterprises to state its views on the review process. In doing so, it will concentrate

1. See above no. 195.

primarily on the Declaration and Guidelines on International Investment and Multinational Enterprises.

The preamble to the Guidelines includes explicit recognition that multinational enterprises through their investment activities bring substantial benefits to home and host countries by contributing to the efficient utilization of capital, technology and human resources between countries and that they thus fulfil an important role in the promotion of economic and social welfare. The preamble states that the Guidelines are designed to contribute to improving the foreign investment climate and to assist in achievement of the common aim of Member Governments to encourage the positive contributions which multinational enterprises can make to economic and social progress, while minimizing and resolving any problems which may arise in connection with their activities.

In relation to codes of conduct, business espouses certain principles which are felt to be fundamental. These are all recognized in the preamble to the Guidelines, but bear repeating. Observance of the Guidelines is and should be voluntary. The Guidelines should be non-discriminatory pertaining equitably to firms whose ownership is private, state or mixed; and not introducing difference of treatment between multinational and domestic enterprises, but reflecting good practice for all. Countries should treat enterprises equitably and in accordance with international law and international agreements, as well as contractual obligations to which they have subscribed.

During the past three years companies in the OECD member countries have demonstrated their willingness and ability to observe the Guidelines, and the activities by member federations to give support to the OECD Guidelines continue. Various examples of such efforts were given in our written Progress Report of 20th March 1978 submitted to the OECD for the Consultation on 11th April, and the number of individual MNE's which have stated their support is increasing.

Some examples of the continuing efforts to promote and support the Guidelines include the following. US-BIAC has prepared and distributed the following series of publications: 'Text and General Review of OECD Guidelines' (1976), 'Disclosure of Information' (1976), 'Competition' (1977), and 'Employment and Industrial Relations' (1978). The CBI in Britain has held a series of seminars to discuss the Guidelines and to pinpoint complexities or problem areas therein. During 1978, Japanese Business has conducted an extensive survey (965 firms, of which 625 have replied) to evaluate compliance with the Guidelines.

Particular attention has been directed by BIAC to the Guidelines on the Disclosure of Information. In July a survey on compliance with those Guidelines was initiated through all BIAC member organizations in the OECD countries. Responses from almost 200 multinational firms in fourteen countries which had been received by mid-December 1978, indicated that the overwhelming majority (90–99 %) of those firms complied in 1979 with the Disclosure Guidelines on structures (i), areas of operations and principal activities engaged in (ii), sales in major lines of business (iii), new capital investment by major lines of business (iv), sources and uses of funds (v) and accounting policies observed (ix). A clear majority either already comply or state their intention to do so in the next year or two with all of the Guidelines on Disclosure.

A full report on the survey on compliance with the Disclosure Guidelines will be included in a separate paper outlining efforts of the business community to promote and support the Guidelines. This will be submitted to the OECD in the first half of January.

The results which have already been received indicate that in some cases application of certain of the Disclosure Guidelines requires adjustment which is in part an educative process requiring time. It seems that most cases of non-compliance are of this temporary nature and that most firms will adapt with time. Conflicting national reporting and accounting requirements are particularly burdensome for those companies whose shares are listed on the stock exchanges of different countries, but may be alleviated by the work of the OECD on harmonization of accounting standards. Similarly the finalization of the proposed EEC Council directive on consolidated accounts will remove some uncertainty and clarify the extent to which further adjustments will be necessary for companies incorporated in the member states of the European Community.

In some cases corporations believe that there will be competitive disadvantages resulting from segmentation as required by Guideline II (the geographical areas where operations are carried out and the principal activities carried on therein by the parent company and the main affiliates) and Guideline III (the operating results and sales by geographical area and the sales in the major lines of business for the enterprise as a whole) as well as from disclosing policies followed in respect of intra-group pricing. This could be the case for example in circumstances where an MNE has only one or perhaps two customers in a particular country or region. However, such complex cases as these are recognized in the text of the introductory part of the Guidelines on Disclosure of Information with its reference to business confidentiality and cost. Nevertheless, for the purpose of providing governments with as full a picture as possible of the field of application of the Guidelines, BIAC has, in the course of its inquiry, asked companies concerned to describe and explain possible situations of this nature.

Inquiries undertaken in order to develop the Progress Report on Support for the OECD Guidelines (March 1978) and the more recent survey to evaluate compliance with the Guidelines on Disclosure (January 1979) have provided the first major opportunities to review the development in the international arena of general awareness and application of the Guidelines. BIAC has concluded as a result of this feedback that the business community is becoming increasingly aware of the existence of the Guidelines. We see evidence that firms are stating their compliance in growing numbers. It should be recognized that this is, however, a process of education and one of adaptation – both of which necessitate time. As indicated earlier, the survey on Disclosure leads us to believe that the vast majority of firms will comply with those Guidelines given sufficient time to adjust.

We believe, therefore, that the further positive response of the international business community to the Guidelines will be facilitated by maintaining the current text. The period since their publication has been far too short to allow for sufficient experience in their operation. Moreover, a change at this time, we feel, would be counter productive to current efforts made by BIAC through its member federations to propagate the Guidelines with industry and to obtain wider support. As Mr. Wagner stated at the consultation on April 11th, 'the success of the Guidelines will have to be judged by the extent to which they become integral in management thinking and practice throughout groups of companies. Implicit or explicit acceptance of the principles of the Guidelines by managers at all levels is the important goal'. The attainment of this goal should not be hampered by changes to the existing text. Furthermore a change of the text would necessitate a review by those MNEs who have either publicly or operationally accepted the text as it currently stands.

It is therefore BIAC's firm view that the text should remain unchanged. This view is strongly held in spite of the exceptional and unique issue involving the transfer of personnel which has come to light and which is apparently not explicitly covered in the wording of the Guidelines. This is particularly so since that matter has been covered by the ILO Tripartite Declaration of Principles Concerning Multinational Enterprises and Social Policy in the following statement: '. . . nor should they transfer workers from affiliates in foreign countries with a view to undermining bona fide negotiations with the workers' representatives or the workers' exercise of their right to organize'. (paragraph 52).

BIAC understands that CIME may write a commentary or an official report on the Guidelines. If this were to be decided, BIAC would request to be consulted and invited to comment on such a document before it is finalized.

In regard to the consultation procedure, BIAC has expressed its preliminary views at the consultation on 11th April 1978 with the OECD's Committee on International Investment and Multinational Enterprises (CIME) and has subsequently amplified those in Mr. Wagner's letter to Mr. van Lennep of 16th June 1978. BIAC considers that every effort should be made to settle specific situations in the country concerned, or if two countries are involved, the matter could be pursued bilaterally through mutually acceptable arrangements. It is only if these efforts have not settled the situation that the principles and issues in debate might be submitted by the Member Government (or Governments) concerned to CIME. CIME in turn may wish to seek the view of BIAC and/or TUAC on issues raised relating to the OECD Guidelines. Under the terms of the Decision of the Council CIME may decide to give the enterprise the opportunity, if the latter so wishes, to express its view concerning the application of the Guidelines. If the enterprise decides to avail itself of this opportunity, it should have the choice of appearing before CIME or communicating in writing. Separate and distinct from situations in which the conduct of an individual enterprise has been referred to, there could be situations where the issue is one which is raised without reference to an individually named enterprise. In such a general context BIAC and TUAC might each be given the opportunity to raise with the CIME questions concerning the application of the Guidelines, but it would be for CIME to decide whether the matter justifies further consideration.

BIAC is cognizant that the promulgation and application of the Guidelines is an on-going or continuing process; on the occasion of the Review, we re-affirm our willingness and our desire to co-operate in this process, commenting upon any issues which may arise and serving as a liaison between business and industry and the Committee on International Investment and Multinational Enterprises.

As the next step along this path, we plan to submit in the next few days a paper containing our update on compliance with the Disclosure Guidelines and highlighting other activities undertaken in our effort to continue to support and promote the Guidelines.»

B. The point of view of TUAC

207. This point of view was put forward into two documents in view of consultations to be held on 29th January 1979 and 27th February 1979 respectively.

1. TUAC views on the occasion of the 1979 review of the OECD Guidelines for Multinational Enterprises, 29th January 1979

«*I. General*

1. Both through the Trade Union Advisory Committee and at the national level, the trade unions participated actively in the preparation of the OECD Guidelines for Multinational Enterprises and the related Decisions of the OECD Council in June, 1976. TUAC has been involved in consultations with the Committee for International Investments and Multinational Enterprises and, lately, its Working Group on the Guidelines. The trade unions have had a major and in some cases decisive role in bringing cases related to the Guidelines to the attention of the Governments and the OECD. They will continue their active involvement in the follow-up of the Guidelines. A basic demand of TUAC is that the methods for doing this and carrying out the necessary consultations be improved both at the company, national and international levels.

2. The trade unions judge the Guidelines from the point of view of their impact on the real world. Their existence created expectations among the unions who hoped that the climate for their relations with multinational enterprises would change for the better. Evidence of this, after almost three years of experience, still is not forthcoming. There is very little to show that the world of the multinational enterprise has been changed. Furthermore, there is very little evidence that the present voluntary set of Guidelines is being vigorously pursued or that there is effective action to create a framework within which their implementation could be ensured.

3. TUAC underlines that even if its involvement in the follow-up of the Guidelines so far has been active and will continue to be so, it is not primarily

241

for the trade union movement to see to the functioning of the Guidelines. They were agreed upon by Governments, who took upon themselves the responsibility to address them to the multinational enterprises. Consequently, they should also ensure their implementation

4. Unless the Guidelines are really implemented, the trade union movement will have to seriously consider their usefulness and also any further support to them. As a compromise, TUAC accepted the Guidelines in 1976 as a first step. At that time, the trade unions clearly envisaged not only their implementation but also further development. If no change to the better has taken place in the real world due to the Guidelines, what was the use of the whole exercise? And if this remains the verdict, all parties will be confronted with a loss of credibility due to a collapse of the discussions. In 1979, OECD must thus be prepared to take the next step.

5. In the context of the present review process, and also looking beyond it, TUAC attaches importance to the implementation, the interpretation and a revision of the Guidelines. Implementation will have to take place both at the company, national and international levels. Interpretation of the provisions of the Guidelines is a *sine qua non* for any meaningful implementation. And a revision of the text itself is necessary in order to make it conform to general developments in other international organizations as well as to respond to cases that have demonstrated lacunae in the present text itself.

II. Implementation

6. TUAC considers that there is a general failure on the part of multinational enterprises to seriously respond to the Guidelines. The trade unions believe that the Guidelines will prove to be a useful agenda for discussing the problems of multinational enterprises at the company level. The major gap in the operation of the Guidelines today is at that level. Too few companies are taking the Guidelines seriously in their day-to-day operations, and few trade unions are aware of the relevance of the Guidelines.

7. In order to secure the implementation of the Guidelines, the Governments should agree to a number of measures which would put certain well-defined obligations on the enterprises. We propose therefore a three stage implementation procedure:

a. Governments should agree, through national legislation, to put an obligation on multinational enterprises based or operating in their territory, or both, to make annual reports on their policies regarding each of the points covered by the Guidelines.

b. Governments should oblige the enterprises to make these reports available to the trade unions and provide that they have the rights and facilities to discuss these reports with the enterprises. These reports would also be available to the representatives of the Governments for similar consultations.

c. Governments should also agree to report to the OECD on steps taken with regard to the above as well as on experiences gained thereof.

8. Governments should submit annual reports to the OECD, taking fully into

account also the views of the trade unions, about any pertinent developments in the countries, including measures taken by the Governments for the
implementation and monitoring of the Guidelines. These reports should
enable the Committee for International Investments and Multinational Enterprises, as well as TUAC and BIAC, to assess the degree of compliance with
the terms of the Guidelines and the action taken by the Governments, the
employers organisation, trade unions and the multinational enterprises
themselves to give effect to them, as well as possible difficulties and inad-
equacies.

9. At the same time TUAC reaffirms that it reserves the right to bring up cases
to the attention of the Committee. This could take place in the event that
national negotiations to settle a question falling within the Guidelines do not
lead into results and if the Government concerned is reluctant to bring the
question up on the international level. Also successfully settled cases could be
brought to the attention of the Committee insofar as they illustrate the working
of the Guidelines. Arrangements should be made to have the multinational
enterprise concerned be heard and participate in the discussions also on the
OECD level.

10. One of the problems of the follow-up hitherto has been the theoretical and
legalistic nature of the discussions. In order to explore the issues involved,
especially where a specific case is concerned, the facts may have to be assessed
through fact-finding procedures. TUAC is favourable to the idea of developing
such procedures and feels that it should be self-evident that such fact-finding
would fully involve the trade unions as well.

III. Revision

11. The experience of the Guidelines has demonstrated a number of needs to
amend their text itself. TUAC fully recognizes that before the questions of
implementation and interpretation have been satisfactorily settled, there is
little point in suggesting extensive revisions. Redrafting, on the other hand, can
come about as a result of the interpretation of the Guidelines, or of the practical
experiences in their implementation. However, there are some questions which
can be addressed already today.

12. There is a clear, demonstrated and recognized gap in paragraph 8 of the
employment and industrial relations section of the Guidelines. This concerns
the transfer of workers in the case of negotiations or labour conflicts. This can
be amended by adding to that paragraph, after the words 'from the country
concerned', the following: 'nor transfer workers from affiliates in foreign
countries'. In the same paragraph, TUAC considers it an omission not to
mention the threat of withholding further investment.

13. In order to make clear the interpretation of the responsibilities of the
parent company (see paragraph 19 (a) below), the following sentence should
be added to the paragraph 8 of the introductory section of the Guidelines:
'This, however, cannot be interpreted as relieving the parent company and/or
the regional management from sharing the responsibility for the policies of any

local entity, to the extent they control the policies and decisions or the entity itself.'

14. In the section on disclosure of information, TUAC considers that the subparagraph (vi) could be replaced by the following: 'the average number of employees by geographic area and, as far as practicable, country by country for the enterprise as a whole;'. After this, a new subparagraph could be inserted with the following wording: 'average nominal wages and fringe benefits by geographical area for the enterprise as a whole, converted in the currency of the home country;'.

15. TUAC also considers that the Guidelines should spell out a specific obligation on enterprises to inform the trade unions concerned, and negotiate with them at an early stage, before final decisions are taken, regarding the economic, social and legal consequences of mergers and other forms of concentration of decision making across the borders within the OECD area. More specifically this concerns the concentration of decision making between companies by the founding of common holding companies, by transfer of activities across borders, by acquiring assets across borders and by concentrating *de facto* decision making power through acquiring assets of another company within the OECD area or also outside the area if enterprises based outside the area carry out activities within the area or affecting it.

IV. Interpretation

16. Unless there is a clear interpretation of the meaning of the Guidelines, the responsibility for observing and implementing them can be evaded. TUAC regrets that despite the discussions on a number of cases by the Committee for International Investments and Multinational Enterprises and its Working Group on the Guidelines, no interpretation of in particular questions of paramount trade union interest have been given. Unless the Governments agree on the meaning and general purpose of what they have collectively adopted, and say so to all parties concerned, the implementation of the Guidelines is seriously impaired. It is the view of TUAC that, as part of the review process, the report to the OECD Council in June 1979 should give a clear interpretation of the Guidelines. Furthermore, arrangements should be made for the further development of the interpretation process. It is only against this background that TUAC has been prepared to participate in the informal discussions with the Committee's Working Group on the Guidelines.

17. Regarding the interpretation of the Guidelines in their present form, there are a number of questions that have to be dealt with urgently. To the extent they are already discussed by the Working Group on the Guidelines, together with TUAC and BIAC, such discussions will have to serve an interpretation by the Summer of 1979. There are important questions, such as the responsibility of the parent company, which have not yet been discussed, and they will have to be taken up in the review process as well, in consultation with TUAC and BIAC.

18. TUAC does not wish to present an exhaustive list of questions where interpretation is asked for. The cases brought forth by the trade unions hitherto

illustrate concerns, and difficulties, that have come up during the first years of experience of the Guidelines. In stressing the need for interpretation, the trade unions are above all concerned about the usefulness of the Guidelines to their own members. Both the Governments and the OECD have recently increasingly solicited the views of the unions and have recognized that the trade unions have a role in following up the Guidelines, both nationally and, through TUAC, internationally. But in the absence of clearer rules and interpretations, the unions, just as Governments, will have to make interpretations nationally themselves. Differences from one country to another in such interpretations only serve confusion and render the Guidelines inefficient.

19. The interest of TUAC at this stage focusses itself above all on the following questions:

a. *Parent company responsibilities* (paragraphs 6 and 8 of the Guidelines). It must be recognized that the parent company has a responsibility for all areas covered by the Guidelines, and a responsibility to inform the local entity of decisions and strategies affecting it. (See paragraph 13 above.)

b. *Local law and regulations* (introduction to the section on employment and industrial relations). The words 'within the framework of law' etc. should not be interpreted so as to enable the enterprises to take a minimalistic line and abstain from their obligations under the Guidelines merely by referring to the absence of specific national legal obligations. The interpretation should at least correspond to the meaning of 'taking into account national circumstances' in the ILO.

c. *Recognition of trade unions* (paragraph 1 of the employment and industrial relations section). An unequivocal pronouncement on this is a precondition for the Guidelines being a useful instrument for the trade unions. It should be clarified that this concerns non-manual workers as well, and especially bank employees. The words 'and other bona fide organisations of employees' should be interpreted in a way to cover the International Trade Secretariats.

d. *Right to trade union consultation within multinational enterprises* (paragraph 2 of the employment and industrial relations section). Necessary facilities must be interpreted in a way to cover facilities for contacts with employees in other parts of the same multinational enterprise. Information, to be meaningful, must include information on the enterprise as a whole. The provisions of the Guidelines must also be interpreted in a way that will not hinder representatives of the International Trade Secretariats to participate in negotiations when necessary.

e. *Information to employees* (paragraph 3 of the employment and industrial relations section). This information will have to include future plans, in order to give a true and fair view of the entity or the enterprise.

f. *Obligation to negotiate future plans* (paragraph 6 of the employment and industrial relations section). Such negotiations should be seen as a mandatory, and they should be introduced immediately when such changes in operations can be anticipated as would have major effects upon the livelihood of the employees. This paragraph, in the view of TUAC, contains both the obligation to give reasonable notice, i.e. notice as soon as the manage-

245

ment becomes aware of an impending situation, and also the obligation to mitigate adverse effects through negotiations. Such negotiations should take place before any final decisions are made, and, whenever necessary, they should enable to alter any decision made without the participation of the representatives of the employees.

g. The Guidelines should also be recognized to cover such groupings as those of airline companies which regardless of their legal structure or the presence or absence of direct investment by the participating companies function as multinational enterprises.

20. TUAC notes that there cannot be conflicting interpretations between those of the OECD Guidelines and other relevant instruments, in particular the Tripartite Declaration on Multinational Enterprises and Social Policy, adopted by the ILO Governing Body. As the ILO instrument will also have its own follow-up procedure, it is imperative that OECD Governments, when interpreting the Guidelines, ensure that there are no conflicts with other relevant international instruments.

IV. Conclusions

21. For the trade union movement, the OECD Guidelines were a first step towards more specific, functioning rules of the game. There has been little progress in making them work, and the follow-up has largely been a theoretical exercise on the level of the Committee for International Investment and Multinational Enterprises. The key question now is their implementation on the everyday working level, in the enterprises themselves. Within this implementation process, the crucial element is the creation of a system of information and consultation at both the company, national and international levels.

22. It is obvious that the review of the Guidelines will have to be seen as an on-going process. For this purpose, the OECD Council should provide for another formal review by 1981 at the latest.

23. TUAC has not addressed itself here to the other parts of the Decisions of the OECD Council in 1976. This is mainly due to the fact that the consultations it has been involved in have concerned the Guidelines. On the other hand, regarding the other Decisions, TUAC is still waiting for the first results of the Government deliberations. TUAC will be in due time interested in pronouncing itself on them, and assumes that work on them by the OECD and the Governments will be of an on-going character.»

2. TUAC presentation to the Committee for International Investments and Multinational Enterprises, 27 February 1979

208. «1. TUAC appreciates the possibility of presenting further views on the review of the OECD Guidelines for Multinational Enterprises. The basic views of TUAC on the current review have been communicated to the OECD earlier. The present paper is an elaboration of some of those views, taking into consideration the informal discussions on 29 January, 1979, with the Working Group on the Guidelines of the Committee for International Investments and Multinational Enterprises, and the fact that the second draft of the OECD review report was made available to the advisory bodies.

2. The trade unions have strongly promoted the notion that it is now necessary to focus on the implementation of the Guidelines at the company, national and international levels. This arises out of the view, expressed by TUAC in 1976, ·that the Guidelines can only be considered as a first step towards more binding rules. The fact that an instrument is characterized as voluntary, when adopted at the OECD level, does not mean that it could not be enforced on the national level, by the governments that have agreed upon it. The emphasis hitherto given to the 'voluntary' nature of the Guidelines tends, in the TUAC view, to encourage passiveness and serves to free governments from the responsibilities they have jointly taken upon themselves.

3. TUAC wishes to underline that, as the Guidelines have been agreed upon by sovereign governments who have addressed them to MNE's, there can be no question of their 'acceptance' by these enterprises. The governments should oblige the MNE's to comply with them, and the purpose of national and international follow-up mechanisms is to see to it that this takes place.

4. In its submission, TUAC addressed itself above all to what the governments should do in order to have the MNE's seriously respond to the Guidelines. The obligations put on MNE's by the governments should lead to a system of reporting annually by the enterprises, regarding the Guidelines. Such reports should be drawn up by the MNE headquarters which would make them available to their subsidiaries. These reports would include an explanation regarding the compliance of the enterprises with the Guidelines as well as declarations about the intents and policies of the enterprises regarding them. In addition to annual reports, special reports could be made when necessary.

5. MNE's would make the annual reports as publicly available policy statements. They should be distributed by the management to the trade unions in each subsidiary. The trade unions concerned could use these reports for consultations with management on issues relating to the Guidelines.

6. As publicly available policy statements, the reports would be transmitted to the competent government authorities. TUAC has no difficulties in agreeing that promotional activities by governments, the business community and the trade unions are needed for making the contents of the Guidelines more widely known. But in order to secure an effective implementation, there should in each country be a focal point (national authority, board, committee or a 'Guidelines ombudsman') with the responsibility of implementing and monitoring the Guidelines nationally. Without such a focal point, there is no basis for either monitoring the compliance with the Guidelines by the MNE's or, indeed, preparing any periodic reports to the OECD. Such an authority would also be available for providing the facilities for the parties concerned on matters arising out of the implementation of the Guidelines. National authorities should also require from MNE's planning new investments in the country a statement on their compliance with the Guidelines.

7. Such an authority should also, in co-operation with national statistical

offices, make brief annual surveys on issues covered by the Guidelines, in order to give general factual information on the situation nationally and to enable an assessment of the situation for the OECD area as a whole.

8. Whenever deemed necessary, special reports from the MNE's on their policies regarding any point covered by the Guidelines and/or arisen in the context of a specific case could be demanded when there are reasons to believe that an enterprise is not fully complying with the Guidelines.

9. Regarding such special reports, consultations should be organized between the responsible government authorities, the MNE concerned, and the trade unions. Special reports should also be made available directly to the trade unions which would have the same rights and facilities to discuss them with the enterprises as they have for discussing the annual reports.

10. Government reports to the OECD should be made annually, taking fully into account the views of the trade unions. Such reports should in particular also cover government action, including institutional developments, for the purpose of implementing the Guidelines.

11. TUAC supports the amending of paragraph 1 of the Decision on Inter-governmental Consultation Procedures to the effect that exchanges of views in the Committee on International Investments and Multinational Enterprises should be arranged also at the request of the advisory bodies. Likewise, TUAC supports proposals for an enquiry into the facts regarding a specific case, stressing the need for full trade union involvement in such fact-finding procedures.

12. In order to have an internationally agreed unified interpretation of the Guidelines, national authorities should work in close co-operation with the Committee on International Investments and Multinational Enterprises. Unclear and/or unresolved cases should be brought to the Committee, and the status of interpretations given should be clarified. The interpretations, in order to be useful to those directly concerned, will have to be clear and not merely consist of a summary of viewpoints. They have to be given timely and reach all parties concerned without delay. If the intention is that this will be done in periodic reports from the Committee to the OECD Council, and if reports to the Council are made only with long intervals, responses can hardly be considered as timely.

13. TUAC has expressed its wish to have a new formal review by 1981 at the latest. Provisions for formal reviews in the future will have to be made; otherwise the value of any implementation procedures nationally and especially internationally can be seriously questioned. If regular reports by the Committee to the Council in fact constitute an on-going review process, the possibility of making necessary and agreed improvements in the text of the Guidelines themselves will have to be provided for, through recommendations made to this effect by the Committee in these reports. They would thus constitute an important element in both increasing the general understanding and knowledge of the Guidelines and in further developing the Guidelines themselves. It is obvious that these reports should specifically include the available information on both government and company action to implement and comply with the Guidelines during the reporting period.

14. TUAC has already earlier noted that unless there is a serious attempt to implement the Guidelines, and unless there is a clear interpretation of their meaning, there is little point in suggesting extensive revisions now. However, regarding clearly recognised gaps (and especially the one concerning paragraph 8 of the Guidelines on Employment and Industrial Relations), the following observations will have to be made:

a. The case of transfer of workers from foreign affiliates has come up during the follow-up procedures within the Committee itself. The existence of a gap has been expressedly recognized by all parties.

b. A reference to the ILO Declaration on MNE's and Social Policy to cover specifically this paragraph could create confusion, as it involves a document with a different focus, adopted by an organization with a scope and composition differing from the OECD.

c. Dealing with the gap merely by an explanatory comment would also create confusion, as a precedent, if later on other omissions are discovered and agreed to or if there is agreement on including new elements under any of the Guidelines. Such explanatory comments could create a 'Christmas tree' effect and lead into a weakening of the text itself through qualifications – which would, in any case, have to be always reproduced with the text of the Guidelines themselves.

15. One of the major concerns of TUAC regarding Information Disclosure Guidelines, in 1976, was that they were worded in such a way that the breakdown of information was not sufficient. Even regarding that, numerous concerns have been forwarded by the MNE's themselves, and it appears that these (which in fact record non-compliance with the Guidelines) seem to be treated with understanding by the OECD. TUAC feels that the governments should at least oblige the MNE's to comply with the present Guidelines. We do not want to see what would amount to an actual weakening of the Guidelines, and have made proposals that underline the necessity of strengthening the existing text so that this section of the Guidelines would commence to be meaningful.

16. For the above mentioned reasons TUAC feels that the only way of dealing with any gaps in the text will have to be by making corresponding changes in the text itself.»

C. Note from the Swedish Delegation on the Consultation Procedures on the Guidelines for Multinational Enterprises, 13 February 1979

209. «1. Matters related to the application and implementation of the Guidelines should primarily be discussed on the national level. Conflicts between states, stemming from the application of the Guidelines, should normally be resolved by consultation and co-operation between the states concerned. Conflicts between states and multinational enterprises with regard to the Guidelines should normally be settled through existing national mechanisms or through other mutually acceptable arrangements.

2. CIME provides a forum for discussion of issues, for which the procedures

indicated under 1. have proven insufficient or inadequate. Having no judicial functions, the CIME's main functions in respect of the Guidelines are:
a. to supply authoritative clarifications of the meaning of the Guidelines;
b. to review continuously the application and implementation of the Guidelines, i.e. with a view to assessing their effectiveness;
c. to serve as a forum for consultations among Member countries on problems arising from situations, in which multinational enterprises are made subject to conflicting requirements;
d. to review the Guidelines at appropriate intervals;
e. to make suggestions to the Council on measures aimed at developing the programme of co-operation among the OECD countries on matters related to multinational enterprises, including the Guidelines.

3. Although OECD is an intergovernmental organization, the specific features of the Guidelines call for a procedure which provides opportunities for BIAC and TUAC to express their views on matters related to the Guidelines directly to the CIME, without necessarily having to go through the governments concerned. The presentation of such views should not be limited to the periodic consultations between the CIME and TUAC/BIAC. TUAC and BIAC should be free to communicate their views to the CIME at any time. The present situation in respect of contacts between the Working Party on the Guidelines and TUAC/BIAC appears to offer adequate opportunities for such communications. A stabilization of this situation should be encouraged by the CIME. The present wording of para. 2 of the decision on consultation procedures on the Guidelines seems to cover such a development of the procedures. Issues raised by TUAC and BIAC should be given the same treatment by the CIME as that accorded to matters raised by governments. This requires a certain discipline, particularly as regards matters related to the conduct of individual enterprises. Before raising such matters, TUAC/BIAC should make sure that the presentation serves the purpose of illustrating unclarities or ambiguities in the Guidelines. They should also inform the enterprise and government(s) concerned before such matters are brought to the CIME.

4. As far as requests for clarification of the meaning of the Guidelines are concerned, it is essential that responses to be given by the CIME on a continuous basis without undue delay. Although it is realized that some matters might require extensive discussions in Committee* before a concrete and final answer can be offered, timely reactions are called for in order to maintain the credibility and effectiveness of the Guidelines. The view that requests for clarification should be seen as merely an input for the periodic reviews of the Guidelines can not be accepted. The CIME should inform all parties concerned, including TUAC and BIAC, of the results of its clarification. It should also refer to such results in its reports to the Council.

5. The collection and presentation of facts are important in identifying issues related to the implementation of the Guidelines. A distinction has to be made between facts pertaining to the general application and implementation of the

---

* References to the Committee in this note also apply to the Working Party on the Guidelines as appropriate.

Guidelines in Member countries and facts related to concrete situations, which serve as illustrations to requests for clarification. As to the first kind, Member governments should report annually to the CIME on their experience in this respect. These reports should be based on information collected in each country mainly from government agencies, trade unions and industry. The reports should include an account of measures undertaken by governments in order to promote the Guidelines. TUAC and BIAC should be asked to produce similar reports. A requirement on multinational enterprises to report specifically on their compliance with the Guidelines does not seem meaningful. The handling of such specific reports would be administratively burdensome. The contents of such reports will necessarily be subjective and provide an oblique picture of the activities of the enterprise concerned. However, multinational enterprises should be encouraged to make a brief statement in their annual reports on steps taken to implement the Guidelines. Such a statement should not be regarded as implying any specific responsibility to observe the Guidelines. The Guidelines are commended to all multinational enterprises, who are expected to observe them, irrespective of whether they have made an explicit statement to that effect or not. As to the second kind of facts, the purpose of drawing the attention of the CIME to concrete situations involving individual enterprises should be born in mind. When fulfilling its responsibility to clarify the meaning of the Guidelines, the CIME can not work *in abstracto*. The activities of the CIME in this respect must be founded on real situations, since only difficulties encountered in the practical implementation of the Guidelines justify a clarification. When considering such a concrete situation, the CIME does not need to collect facts with a view to establishing the veracity of the case, because it is not to pass any judgements as to the behaviour of individual enterprises. The Committee does, however, need to get an all-round and sufficiently complete picture of the situation in order to isolate the issue of clarification. Thus, only facts relevant to the clarification of the Guidelines are required. The CIME, therefore, should invite all parties concerned to express their views. Since normally the activities of individual enterprises are relevant in this context, the enterprise concerned should, as a matter of procedural routine, be given the opportunity to present its opinion. Should an enterprise avail itself of this opportunity, it should have the choice of appearing before the Committee or communicating in writing.

6. So far, the concrete situations discussed in the CIME have been presented by governments and/or TUAC after the situations have occurred. The potentially negative flavour of such a procedure for the business community was pointed out during the negotiations that led to the 1976 declaration. Since the discussion on the conduct of individual enterprises only serves to illustrate points of clarification and no judgements are to be passed, that argument no longer carry much weight. Nevertheless, it seems appropriate to consider measures to attract a positive interest of the business community in the Guidelines. One may well conceive of situations, in which an enterprise wishes to comply with a particular standard in the Guidelines, but has difficulties in interpreting its meaning in a concrete case. Hence, it might wish to get an advance opinion of the CIME before it goes ahead. The enterprise of course

251

could turn to BIAC, which might then raise the matter with the CIME, but such a round would be unnecessarily time-consuming. Furthermore, the enterprise may, for a variety of reasons, with to communicate the particulars of the situation directly to the CIME. The possibility to approach the CIME in such a way is likely to be welcomed by the business community. It may be argued that such a procedure involves difficulties of a legal nature, regarding for instance the status and effects of the advance response by the Committee. Bearing in mind, however, that the Guidelines are not legally enforceable and that the functions of the CIME are not judicial, an advance opinion on the meaning of the Guidelines does not appear to be much different from a response to a subsequent request for clarification.

7. Consistent with the explicit wish of Member countries to co-operate on matters related to multinational enterprises on a continuous basis, the Guidelines should be further developed in the light of experience gained in their application. Consequently, a new review of the Guidelines and the decision on consultation procedures should be undertaken within three years from the adoption by the Council of the report to the CIME. It is to be expected that further reviews are required.

8. The conclusions of the Committee as to the feasibility of letting the results of the review be reflected in actual changes of the text of the declaration should not be prejudicial to the decision on consultation procedures. The arguments against textual changes of the substance of the Guidelines do not apply to the decision, as the latter is not addressed to multinational enterprises and concerns matters of a mainly formal nature.

9. The comments made in this note may to some extent be adequately covered in the report of the CIME to the Council. However, some of them require changes in the decision on intergovernmental consultation procedures as follows:

(Add new sentence at the end of para. 1)

The exchange of views of the Committee shall be based i.a. on reports on the application of the Guidelines, submitted annually by each Member country. The relevant parts of the reports of the Committee shall be drafted for public use and be given a form that serves the purpose of improving the general understanding of the Guidelines.

(New para. 3)

The Committee shall, upon request by a Member country, BIAC, TUAC or a multinational enterprise directly concerned, provide clarifying comments to the Guidelines. Such requests shall be notified to the governments, advisory committees and directly concerned enterprises. The comments of the Committee, being based on concrete situations, where difficulties in interpreting the meaning of the Guidelines have been encountered, should be notified to the parties directly concerned without delay and adequately reflected in the reports of the Committee to the Council.

(Change para. 3 into new para. 4 and change number of paras subsequently)

In order to enable the Committee to get a complete and fair understanding of facts relevant to the clarification of the Guidelines, multinational enterprises directly concerned, should be invited to express their views on the application

of the Guidelines. Should an enterprise avail itself of this opportunity, it may appear before the Committee or communicate with the Committee in writing. The Committee shall not reach conclusions on the conduct of individual enterprises.
(Change first sentence of para. 5)*
This decision shall be reviewed within periods of three years each.»

D. Note by the Netherlands: Factfinding Under The Guidelines, 20th March 1978

210. «**I. Introduction**

At the meeting of the ad hoc Working Party of the Committee on 18th January,1978, the Netherlands Delegation undertook to draft a working paper to serve as a basis for a detailed discussion in the Committee on the need for fact-finding when examining the problems resulting from the application of the guidelines for multinational enterprises. The object of the present note is to consider a certain number of arguments in favour of fact-finding.
At the present stage such fact-finding should in any case come under the provisions of the present consultation procedure.

II. The possibilities and the need for a fact-finding procedure

a. *Is fact-finding possible in the framework of the existing guidelines?*

In June 1976 the OECD Council at Ministerial level adopted a Declaration in the Annex of which was stated, inter alia: 'The common aim of the Member countries is to encourage the positive contributions which multinational enterprises can make to economic and social progress and to minimise and resolve the difficulties to which their various operations may give rise.'
The establishment of guidelines was clearly in itself intended to assist in the achievement of this common aim. According to the Annex to the Declaration 'The guidelines set out hereafter are designed to assist in the achievement of this common aim . . .'
By the formulation of guidelines only, this aim has not however been achieved. In addition to the Declaration, therefore, the Council rightly adopted a Decision providing for a consultation procedure which, as appears from the preamble of the Decision, must be considered to reflect in practical terms the Member countries' wish to establish certain procedures relating to the application of the guidelines.
'Recognizing the desirability of setting forth procedures by which consultations may take place on matters related to these guidelines.'
The main lines of these procedures are set out in three paragraphs which provide for:

* A similar change will have to be made under the heading 'Review' in the introductory part of the declaration.

1. The obligation to hold periodical exchanges of views on matters related to the guidelines and the experience gained in their application and to report periodically to the Council on these matters;
2. The obligation periodically to invite the Business and Advisory Committee and the Trade Union Advisory Committee to OECD to express their views on matters related to the guidelines and to take account of such views in reports to the Council;
3. The possibility, on the proposal of a Member country or of the Committee as a whole, of giving individual enterprises the opportunity to express their views concerning the application of the guidelines.

These three provisions cannot be considered in isolation. For example, Member countries will draw the experience, which is mentioned in paragraph 1, mainly from the opinions expressed by BIAC and TUAC in accordance with paragraph 2. And it is after such exchanges that, on the proposal of a Member country, a particular enterprise may be invited to give its views.

b. *Why facting-finding?*

Concrete and objective data
The task of the Committee with regard to the guidelines is to give as precise an idea as possible of the practical application of the guidelines, to make possible an assessment of the extent to which these guidelines fulfil their purpose.

The Committee obviously should not devote its attention to abstract considerations not based on actual facts.

It is for this reason that the determination and description of an issue to be studied must be established as precisely and objectively as possible and on the basis of facts.

Equitable treatment
In addition to the need to determine the facts as objectively as possible, the principle of equitable treatment constitutes an important argument in favour of the application of a fact-finding procedure. The preamble to the guidelines also refers to this*.

As many enterprises have shown their willingness to comply with the guidelines, enterprises must certainly be given the possibility of making known their views, through the BIAC or directly, on alleged differences in application of guidelines. By enabling both parties to state their case, the Committee can obtain a clear idea of the facts.

The principle of equitable treatment also implies that if a 'case' is raised by one side or the other the parties are entitled to insist that the facts should be established as objectively as possible. Otherwise one party may well be placed in a false position by a unilateral presentation of the facts.

---

* '. . . the Member countries set forth the following guidelines for multinational enterprises with the understanding that Member countries will fulfil their responsibilities to treat enterprises equitably . . .'

Fact-finding at international level (OECD)
Both business and trade union circles have inferred that they would welcome a
set of rules, based on the OECD Declaration, relating to the treatment of
problems arising in connection with the OECD Guidelines, as such rules would
make the guidelines more credible than they are at present. If this proves
impossible at OECD level, governments will probably be obliged to set up
procedures for treatment at national level.
An efficient set of rules at OECD level would however be preferable to
national procedures, which may differ and also give rise to divergent interpretations of the OECD Guidelines. Furthermore, the follow-up to an international guideline necessarily calls for an international procedure. This is especially desirable in the present case in view of the character of multinational
enterprises, since a problem can often arise in more than one Member country.
The effective handling by the Committee of the problems that arise, on the
basis of a balanced fact-finding procedure, would almost certainly reduce the
pressure that is being put on national governments to establish national procedures to deal with these problems.

Review
It may, finally, be noted that for the procedure for review of the guidelines it is
also important to have a precise and accurate picture of the facts with regard to
application of the guidelines up to the time of review.

III. Outline for a consultation procedure with fact-finding

a. *Introduction*

The outline is based on the possibilities indicated in the Council Decision:
1. The TUAC, the BIAC or a Member country may draw the attention of the
   Committee to questions relating to the guidelines.
2. The Committee may give a particular enterprise the opportunity to express
   its views.
3. The Committee shall report periodically to the Council.
Account has been taken of the limitation in paragraph 3 of the Council
Decision: 'The Committee shall not reach conclusions on the conduct of
individual enterprises.'

b. *Outline*

1. The TUAC, the BIAC or a Member country may draw the attention of the
   Committee to certain cases.
2. The Committee shall consider:
   a. whether the case is related to the guidelines;
   b. whether it is sufficiently important.
3. The cases referred by:
   a. the TUAC shall be sent to the BIAC for comment;
   b. the BIAC shall be sent to the TUAC for comment;

    c. a Member country shall be sent to the BIAC and the TUAC for comments.
4. If the Committee considers it necessary, after considering the comments by the BIAC, the TUAC, or both, the multinational enterprise in question shall be invited to express its views on the case.
5. The Committee may decide to obtain information from other sources if necessary.
    This could be done, for instance, by a study carried out by:
    a. the OECD Secretariat;
    b. representatives of the authorities of Member countries;
    c. independent experts.
6. The dossier for the case shall then be sent to the parties concerned.
7. The Committee shall discuss the case in the light of the dossier.
8. The Committee shall report to the Council each year on its findings concerning the cases submitted to it. Such findings shall be formulated as issues without naming the enterprises involved. If possible it shall draw some conclusions from these issues for the application of the guidelines.»

II. The New Follow-up Procedures

211. The follow-up of the Guidelines under the text of the 1976 Decision of the Council on Inter-Governmental Consultation Procedures on the Guidelines for Multinational Enterprises, consisted mainly in *exchange of views between the member countries in the IME Committee and with BIAC and TUAC.* Such an exchange of views shall, following article 1 of the decision, take place periodically or at the request of a member on matters related to the Guidelines and the experience gained in their application. BIAC and TUAC would periodically be invited to express their views on matters related to the Guidelines (art. 2). The Committee would periodically report to the Council of Ministers, taking the views of BIAC and TUAC into account. At the same time individual companies, could also express their views (art. 3), but here two conditions had been built in: (1) there had to be a proposal by a Member Country and (2) the Committee had to agree. Important, of course, was and remains so, the stipulation in article 3 that the Committee 'shall not reach conclusions on the conduct of individual enterprises'.
Articles 1 and 2 have been interpreted by the IME Committee in an evolving and dynamic way and led to the following situation:
1. *exchange of views* have been held between Governments on the one hand and between the IME Committee and BIAC and TUAC on the other hand;
2. these discussions have been held on the basis of the *cases or issues* introduced by Governments, BIAC and TUAC;
3. these discussions have led to an extensive *report* of the Committee to the Council which is made *public;*
4. the report contains answers to the questions put by Governments and social partners and consequently *clarifications* of the Guidelines;
5. *individual companies* did not express their views to the Committee, in

conformity with article 3 of the Decision;[2] one enterprise expressed its views on the case it was involved, in writing.[3]

212. At the occasion of the 1979 Review the text of the 1976 decisions has been changed and brought more into conformity with the IME practice, as this has evolved since 1976. Moreover important changes were introduced as far as follow-up procedures are concerned. Let us consider these as follows: *reporting, problem-solving* and the *review to be held in 1984.*

A. REPORTING

213. Following the report of the IME Committee 'reporting' by multinational enterprises as well as by governments and by the IME Committee itself, is considered as one of the important follow-up procedures.

1. Acceptance and reporting by multinational enterprises

214. In its report the IME Committee (paragraph 77)
«recommends to all enterprises concerned that they indicate publicly their *acceptance* of the Guidelines, preferably *in their annual reports.* Furthermore, enterprises are invited to include in their subsequent annual reports *brief statements on their experience* with the Guidelines, which may contain mentior of steps taken with respect to their observance as well as any difficulties experienced in this respect. Such statements would be particularly useful with respect to the chapter on Disclosure of Information.»

2. Biannual follow-up reports by Governments

215. The IME Committee decided that:
«Member governments will henceforth submit *every two years reports to OECD on experience and pertinent developments at the national level in all matters related to the Guidelines.* These reports will enable the Committee on International Investment and Multinational Enterprises to assess the extent of acceptance and observance of the Guidelines, the action taken within OECD Member countries by governments, business and labour organizations, and the companies themselves to give effect to them, and the areas where problems are being encountered» (paragraph 78).

These reports will be provided then by September 1981 and September 1983.

2. For the Badger case, see the Note of the Belgian Delegation, Part II, I, 2.
3. See Part II, IV, D, 2 and V, A, 4.

3. Mid-term and follow-up report by the IME Committee

216. The IME Committee recognizes in its report:

«the desirability of keeping the interested parties and the general public informed of its activities on matters relating to the Guidelines as well as on the other parts of the 1976 Declaration. One possible vehicle for providing this information, as well as reporting on any further explanatory comments on the Guidelines which the Committee may find it necessary to develop, could be the periodic reports by the Committee to the Council called for in the Decision on Intergovernmental Consultation Procedures. The Committee intends to submit a report to the Council in 1982 with the recommendation that it should be published» (paragraph 87).

The second follow-up report will take place in June 1984, which will also include the report for the review of 1984.

217. The timetable thus set out will, consequently, involve the following action by Governments and by the IME Committee:

September 1981   Follow-up reports by governments
June 1982   Mid-term report by the IME Committee to Council at permanent delegation level
September 1983   Follow-up reports by governments dealing also, as required, with matters related to the next review
June 1984   Follow-up and report by the IME Committee for the Review by Ministerial Council of the Declaration and Decisions on International Investment and Multinational Enterprises.

B. PROBLEM SOLVING

218. It is clear that matters relating to the application and implementation of the Guidelines should in the first place be regulated at national level; this concerns problems involving a multinational enterprise and its relations with a State, or with the business community and with the representatives of the employees. Such efforts should be pursued at bilateral level, i.e., involving the Governments concerned (paragraph 83). It is only when national arrangements are exhausted, that problems should be brought to an international forum, namely, at the level of the IME Committee.

1. At national level

219. The IME Committee states in its report that:
«Member governments which have not already done so will provide *facilities* for handling enquires and for discussions with the parties concerned on matters

relating to the Guidelines. These facilities intend to inform the business community, employee organisations and other interested parties of the appropriate contact point(s) within the government for enquiries on matters related to the Guidelines» (paragraph 79).[4]

2. At international level

a. *The role of the IME Committee*

220. The IME will remain the forum par excellence in which Member Governments will have the opportunity to *exchange views* on all matters related to Guidelines and the experience gained in their application; also to receive the views on these matters of business and labour through the two advisory bodies, BIAC and TUAC. Individual companies can also express their views.

1. Discussion of cases and issues. Information in advance

221. The IME Committee will continue to be 'the' forum to discuss cases and issues introduced either by a Member Government or by BIAC or TUAC. It would indeed, the IME underlined, be detrimental to the credibility of the Guidelines if the Committee were to content itself with only discussing problems in the abstract, using for that purpose purely hypothetical discussions (paragraph 85).
The details of cases, which have been introduced by Governments and TUAC, have been used as illustrations of issues arising under the Guidelines. Issues then are general problems, arising out of a specific case. The IME Committee is mainly concerned with the discussion of issues; cases, should in principle, be settled at national or bilateral level. This is in conformity with the contention of the IME Committee that it is not, and will not, be a semi-court, judging the individual behaviour of multinational enterprises. For the same reason the IME Committee has been reluctant to accept certain proposals for fact-finding, in order to obtain more information on the facts of a certain case, e.g. studies or inquiries carried out by the OECD secretariat, independent experts or the like. The more informal ways in which additional information can be gathered through an involved Government itself, or through one of the advisory organs, or by a voluntary declaration by an individual enterprise itself, seems for the time being to be sufficient. A fact-finding procedure might, following some, bring the Committee too close to a judicial role.

222. When an issue is raised with the Committee, 'the Government(s) and the parties concerned *should be informed in advance of the issues and the points involved*' (paragraph 83).

---

4. See nr. 69 for examples of such facilities.

2. Timely clarification of the Guidelines[5]

223. It is only natural that the IME Committee who drafted the Guidelines and recommended them to the multinational enterprises should, also when problems arise in applying them, clarify given uncertainties. Sometimes these uncertainties are not only due to the fairly general formulation of the Guidelines, which often hides difficult compromises, but are also due to the diversity of the different national systems and practice to which they apply, as well as, to the complexity of the problems and the factual situations involved. The IME Committee simply cannot escape that clarifying role. This role it exercised spontaneously by the publication of its report to the Ministers in which a number of important explanatory comments are given. These comments the Committee reports «should not be considered as modifying the Guidelines. Their purpose is to explain in more detail the meaning of the existing provisions in order to provide guidance to the parties concerned when using the Guidelines» (paragraph 26).

For the future, «the Committee intends to *respond in a timely manner to further requests for clarifications.* Where such responses are possible, they will be given to the interested parties, as appropriate, through informal contacts or in the context of formal consultations as well as in the periodic reports of the Committee to the Council. In order to reflect the Committee's role in clarifying the Guidelines, the following addition to paragraph 1 of the Decision on Inter-governmental Consultation Procedures on the Guidelines is proposed after the first sentence of this paragraph:

'*The Committee shall be responsible for clarification of the Guidelines. Clarification will be provided as required.*'»

224. This new paragraph in the Decision indicates also that next to the IME Committee, others, e.g. national instances can also, through the facilities they provide, give clarification of the Guidelines and that the Committee is not obliged to give answers to all questions which are put to it, but will take into account such criteria as the relevance of the question in relation to the Guidelines.

3. The Committee will not reach conclusions on the conduct of the individual enterprises

225. This principle, which was already set out in paragraph 3 of the 1976 Decision, is reaffirmed by the Committee. «There were good reasons», the Committee reports «for this restriction in 1976, in particular, that the Commit-

---

5. The IME Committee prefers the word 'clarification' to the word 'interpretation'. The latter word seems closer to the activity of courts than the first, although clarification and interpretation have practically, following Webster, the same meaning: clarification (to make understandable); interpretation (to explain the meaning of; to conceive in the light of individual belief, judgment or circumstance).

For TUAC's point of view on the interpretation of the Guidelines, see nrs. 105–110.

tee was not seen as a judicial or quasi-judicial forum, and these reasons still remain valid today. The Committee, therefore, has avoided drawing any conclusions as to the conformity or non-conformity of a certain behaviour with the Guidelines but has used the details of the specific cases as illustration of issues arising under the Guidelines. This approach has proved to be useful for the purpose of clarifying the meaning of the Guidelines in the light of specific problems and resulted in the explanatory comments included in the present report» (paragraph 84).

b. Formal and informal contacts between the IME Committee and BIAC and TUAC

226. The Committee underlined the importance it attaches to the formal and informal contacts with the advisory organs as follows:
«The Committee wishes to acknowledge the great benefit it has derived from the frequent contacts it has had with the two advisory bodies, BIAC and TUAC. Paragraph 2 of the 1976 Decision on Intergovernmental Consultation Procedures reflects the important role BIAC and TUAC are expected to play in the application of the Guidelines. Accordingly, these bodies were provided with the opportunity to express directly to the Committee their views on matters related to the Guidelines. In the understanding of the Committee, the presentation of such views is not limited to periodic consultations; rather, BIAC and TUAC may communicate their views to the Committee at any time» (paragraph 81).
«The Committee and its Working Group on the Guidelines have been fortunate in finding a general willingness on the part of BIAC and TUAC to take a pragmatic and informal approach to the discussion of matters of common interest. As a result, in addition to the periodic consultations between the Committee and the two advisory bodies as are provided for in the 1976 Decision which up to now have been held once a year, a new approach has evolved, based upon more frequent exchanges of views of an informal character between the Working Group on the Guidelines and the two advisory bodies and upon contacts between the secretariats of the OECD and of these bodies. These contacts have proved to be valuable in clarifying issues and in instituting the practice of informal exchanges of views on matters of common interest. Some important results of these contacts are reflected, inter alia, in the explanatory material included in this report on certain questions which have arisen with respect to the scope and meaning of some parts of the Guidelines. The discussions of the Committee on Substantive issues relating to the followup of the Guidelines have also benefited from these informal contacts, and the Committee expects that they will become a permanent feature of its procedures. The Committee and its Working Group on the Guidelines will take a positive attitude to requests by the advisory bodies for holding and exchange of views on any matter related to the Guidelines. The following amendment to paragraph 2 of the 1976 Decision on Intergovernmental Consultation Procedures on the Guidelines is accordingly

proposed to make this understanding more explicit (amended language underlined):
'2. The Committee shall periodically invite the Business and Industry Advisory Committee to OECD (BIAC) and the Trade Union Advisory Committee to OECD (TUAC) to express their views on matters related to the Guidelines. *In addition, exchanges of views with the advisory bodies on these matters may be held upon request by the latter.* The Committee shall take account of such views in its reports to the Council.' (paragraph 82).»

c. The role of individual companies

227. We already indicated earlier that, when an issue is raised with the IME Committee, the Government(s) and the parties concerned should be informed in advance of the issues and the points involved (paragraph 84 of the report). Consequently, an individual company, concerned with a case or an issue, will be informed. It would indeed be unfair «if issues brought to the Committee's attention contained allegations regarding enterprise behaviour concerning the Guidelines without the enterprise which is subject to such allegations being informed when matters of interest to it are likely to be discussed» (paragraph 85).
The enterprise gets now, through a change in the 1976 Decision, also a better opportunity to state its point of view to the Committee. The Committee «will not request an enterprise to make such a presentation but enterprises who wish to present their views without the necessity of government sponsorship may do so. Such views could be communicated through BIAC, government delegations or directly to the Committee itself. Accordingly, the following amendment of paragraph 3 and a new paragraph 4 of the Decision on Intergovernmental Consultation Procedures on the Guidelines is proposed:
'3. If it so wishes, an individual enterprise will be given the opportunity to express its views either orally or in writing on issues concerning the Guidelines involving its interests.'
'4. The Committee shall not reach conclusions on the conduct of individual enterprises' (paragraph 85).»

C. REVIEW AT THE LATEST IN 5 YEARS – JUNE 1984

228. The Committee recommends that it would be appropriate for the next formal review of the Guidelines and the related Decision to be undertaken *at the latest in five years*. This provision of a five-year review period, which is somewhat longer than the initial three-year review period, would have the advantage of providing a stable framework for the implementation of the Guidelines and would allow adequate time for the follow-up procedures set out in this section to develop. It should be understood, however, that this provision does not preclude the possibility of the Organization subsequently deciding, on the basis of future developments, to review and/or make certain modifications to these instruments before the end of the five-year period should this prove necessary (paragraph 88).

III. Statements by BIAC and TUAC on the 1979 Review

A. STATEMENT BY BIAC

229. On the occasion of the review of the Guidelines, BIAC made following statement:

«*Essence of 1976 Principles Unchanged*

In general BIAC believes that the reaffirmation of the principles of the 1976 OECD Declaration by the OECD Council of Ministers represents an important step in continuing intergovernmental discussions on international investment and multinational enterprises. These principles include:
The applicability of the voluntary Guidelines to government owned, privately owned and mixed companies.
The recognition of the responsibilities of government as well as those of enterprises.
The recognition of the importance of national law, regulations and prevailing labor relations and employment practices, which may vary considerably from one OECD member country to another.
A commitment by member countries to treat foreign investors equitably and in accordance with international law as well as contractural obligations to which they have subscribed, and to treat foreign controlled enterprises in like situations no less favourably than domestic enterprises.

Focus on Investment

In addition to a continuing recognition of governmental responsibilities, the OECD Council of Ministers has agreed to place more stress on the issues of national treatment and incentives and disincentives for investment. BIAC feels that consultations on the Guidelines are helpful and notes that the Committee is now empowered to invite the Consultative bodies to give their views on national treatment and investment incentives and disincentives.
The Council of Ministers has again recognized the important role of the international investment process in contributing to OECD economic and social progress and the need for the Declaration to remain a 'positive factor in maintaining conditions favorable to the development of such investment and increasing the basis of mutual confidence between multinational enterprises and states.

Interpretive Comments on Guidelines

The OECD's Council of Ministers considers that experience to date has under-

263

lined the value of the Guidelines and that their further promotion would be best served by providing enterprises with a stable framework. For these reasons, it agreed that only one change be made to the Guidelines at this time in order to cover an issue that was not foreseen when the Guidelines were drafted. This short addition to one paragraph of the Employment and Industrial Relations Guidelines, makes this Guideline generally consistent with a principle adopted by the ILO.

BIAC is also pleased to note that following extensive discussions on the subject of changes in operations, and in line with the acknowledgement of management's final responsibility for decisions, the Ministers recognized that management should be guided by the specific circumstances of each case in determining whether it is possible to provide prior notice.

BIAC takes note of the recognition by the Ministers that while the purpose of the comments in the review report is to explain in more detail the meaning of the existing provisions, they should not be considered as modifying the Guidelines. To illustrate this point it may be mentioned that while the international trade secretariats have a role to play within the overall trade union system itself, they cannot be regarded as organizations of employees in the context of the Guidelines. BIAC questions the suggestion that their recognition might have been within the intention of the Guidelines, since the Guidelines are silent about international trade union bodies and their activities and they were not considered during the negotiations.

BIAC's Activity — Past and Future

National BIAC Organizations have demonstrated their support of the OECD Declaration through extensive efforts including workshops, publication of substantive papers on aspects of the Guidelines and co-operation with efforts by the governments on the subject of national treatment. On the international level those efforts have been complemented by surveys, progress reports and consultations with the OECD Secretariat and with the government delegates to the relevant OECD Committee and its Working Parties. In addition, a significant number of multinational enterprises have supported the Declaration publicly through statement in annual reports, speeches, and other communications approaches.

BIAC is now developing approaches to communicating the results of the 1979 Review of the Declaration to its member organizations and their enterprises. As part of its communications activities, BIAC will circulate not only the OECD Declaration as revised by the Council of Ministers in 1979, but also the Review Report adopted by the Ministers in conjunction with the overall Review. In future BIAC will continue to play its active role as a consultant body to OECD, with particular reference to the planned work program on national treatment and investment incentives and disincentives – a broadening of the OECD Committee's function with which the international business community agrees.»

B. Statement By TUAC

230. At 14 June 1979 TUAC issued following statement:

«The Trade Union Advisory Committee to the OECD notes that, on the whole, the review of the 1976 Guidelines for Multinational Enterprises resulted in a virtual stalemate regarding the contents of the voluntary recommendations to the Enterprises. Consequently, the basic preoccupations presented by TUAC in 1979, underlining the need for more effective and binding rules and regulations in this field, have not been even remotely met. Furthermore, proposals and reports submitted by the Committee on International Investment and Multinational Enterprises to the OECD Ministerial Council should have been accompanied by TUAC views on these proposals.

A positive feature of the review, however, is the recognition by the governments that improved implementation mechanisms are needed both at the national and the international levels. As was pointed out by TUAC in the process of the discussions on the review, there is little point in extensive revisions of the text before there is a clear commitment by the governments to implement it and in cases of conflicts, give interpretations to the parties concerned.

It is now the responsibility of national governments to strengthen their administrative machineries by establishing focal points to deal with matters arising out of the Guidelines. The trade unions associated with TUAC work will closely follow the establishment of such machineries. Trade unions should be involved in their work right from the beginning.

While strongly regretting that the next review will not take place earlier than in five years, TUAC expects that the discussions over that period – noting in particular the mid-term report to be published in 1982 – will enable the governments to draw further conclusions, including revisions whenever appropriate. TUAC also maintains that it is a mistake that governments are expected to report only every second year and not every year on experiences gained and steps taken to implement the Guidelines.

TUAC wishes to remind that national action, including measures on the company level, is crucial if the Guidelines are to have a real meaning for the workers. The review has not taken into account the trade union proposals for consultative arrangements on the company level. The trade unions will continue to work for such arrangements. In the TUAC view, the recommendation to enterprises to publish details of their compliance with the Guidelines is a step in the right direction. It should be natural that facilities be made available for the unions to discuss these reports with management representatives. TUAC insists on the need for developing information rights, especially for the workers. Wherever appropriate, trade unions will also strive to have steps on complying with the Guidelines included in agreements negotiated between the unions and management.

As the OECD now intends to improve the follow-up procedures on the international level, TUAC affirms its willingness to intensify its own activities both regarding the Committee on International Investment and Multinational

Enterprises and its Working Group on the Guidelines. In particular, timely responses from the Committee to requests for interpretations of the Guidelines are indispensable if the follow-up procedures on this level are to have a real part in solving problems arising out of the activities of multinational enterprises.

The importance of interpretations is all the more underlined by the review report which, while giving some answers to cases submitted by above all the trade unions, on the whole fails to give a concise view of the intentions of the governments within the OECD framework. Interpretations on the OECD level are also necessary for national follow-up procedures, as there is otherwise a risk of conclusions that vary from one country to another.

Regarding the one amendment made to the text of the Guidelines, TUAC considers it important in so far as it brings the Guidelines into harmony with other international instruments. It has been, however, more the question of filling a recognized gap than really agreeing upon an improvement in the Guidelines themselves. Further revisions will not doubt prove to be necessary, and TUAC expects that the improvement of both national and international follow-up mechanisms will, besides contributing to a general understanding of them, also assist in convincing above all the governments of the need of further developing the Guidelines in the direction of a truly efficient instrument aimed at eliminating the negative effects of the activities of multinational enterprises.»

Conclusions

231. There is no doubt that the Guidelines live and have an impact on reality, especially in the areas of information and industrial relations and will continue to do so. The reasons are many fold.

Firstly, and this is a necessary condition for any rule of conduct to be implemented, that the Guidelines are a result of a *consensus* – be it a qualified one – between Governments, business and labour. They were drawn up by Governments in close consultation with business and labour who both support the Guidelines. As the latter were seen to be balanced, especially when taken in conjunction with the 'national treatment' commitment, an important number of individual multinational enterprises were able to indicate that they accept the Guidelines and that they will implement them. Thus the Guidelines have the backing of Governments, employers and unions, with all the *moral* weight and authority that this carries. The chance that rules of conduct, what the Guidelines in essence are, will indeed govern the daily life of the multinational enterprise, are greatly enhanced if they are considered by those to whom they are addressed as reasonable and acceptable. But broader support is still needed, including from publicly-owned firms and from the large number of smaller MNE's and it will be the task of Governments and of the Committee to bring them about over the coming period.

Second there is the *political will* of the Governments to succeed, to see to it that the Guidelines are more than a mere scrap of paper and that they will increasingly gain in credibility. In line with the basic idea that the exercise is an evolutionary process, the IME Committee went further than that which a strict narrow legal interpretation of its mandate would allow: the Committee, in fact, clarified a number of questions, brought up by Governments, business and labour, thus giving a number of the Guidelines more meaning; this political will was illustrated by a great sense for compromise which is necessary to reach unanimous consent on a number of important questions. The decision taken in 1979, at the time of the review, now recognizes formally that one of the functions of the IME Committee is to provide clarification of the text of the Guidelines as required. The Governments also decided to publish the report of the IME Committee, thus enhancing the public understanding of the Guidelines. The stress laid in the IME Committee's report on strengthening national procedures fills a gap in the procedures which were foreseen in 1976 and the fact that Governments subscribed to this orientation of the exercise for the future is also a sign of the willingness of Governments to continue to support it.

232. Another factor, favouring an impact on reality, was the excellent *working relationship with the social partners* in the course of 1976–1979 exercise. Indeed, the OECD is not a tripartite organization, like the ILO, and a number of Governments are very sensitive to this aspect of the work of the IME Committee, but the fact is that the advisory bodies, BIAC and TUAC, had easy access to the IME Committee and to the Governments, be it through formal or informal contacts; and had a real impact on the outcome of the Committee's deliberations. The changes that have been made in the decisions on consultation with business and labour as a result of the review carry this process a step further as is indicated below.

Again, the Committee was inspired with a real desire of meeting as much as possible the requests of the social partners.

Thus, the Guidelines, in their clarification and new follow up, on which we will come back later, constitute consequently a realistic framework, relying on the solid groundwork of participative consultation. This continuous involvement of the social partners, who knew from each other, what kind of ideas were put forward to the Committee, brings the Committee's work close to reality, confronting it with concrete problems of those who have to live with them and gives the outcome a stable and more durable nature.

233. The *high quality of the Secretariat* was also an important factor; a Secretariat, which was constantly building bridges between different opinions, looking for areas of consensus and for the language containing a compromise and sometimes hiding a difference of opinion. The Secretariat, also presented that necessary element of daily continuity, between the meetings of the IME Committee, and being in constant contact with the Secretariats of BIAC and TUAC. The report, to a large extent the work of the Secretariat, is a remarkable document for the depth of its analysis and the clear and integrated way of its presentation.

234. To be sure, the Guidelines are *voluntary*; but that does not necessarily diminish their impact, if there is a political will between Governments to make them have an impact. Voluntary does not mean that multinational enterprises are free to choose whether they accept the Guidelines or not. The Guidelines constitute recommended behaviour, since they are recommendations jointly addressed by Member countries to the multinational enterprises and are supported both by business and labour. They are 'the' rules of conduct which society as a whole requires the multinational enterprises to live up to.

In this sense they are *morally* binding, as they indeed relate to societal principles of right and wrong in behaviour, which constitute the essence of public morality. However, the Guidelines are *not legally enforceable*, which means that they cannot as such be sanctioned by the courts, although they could acquire in the course of time the legal character of a custom and become 'as customs' legally enforceable.

235. Difficult questions arise concerning the relationship between these moral obligations and the legal obligations under the law of the land. An analysis of the introduction of the Guidelines, especially paragraphs 6 and 7, clearly shows that national law prevails, confirming the sovereignty of the State and that the Guidelines consequently cannot oblige the enterprises to do anything which would be in conflict with national law. However, the Guidelines do place obligations on multinationals which go beyond what is strictly required by law. This again is self-evident. If the Guidelines only said that multinational enterprises must respect the relevant local law, they would not add anything to the situation as it was previously. The Guidelines are necessary, precisely because national law does not suffice to regulate the 'transnational' character of the multinational phenomenon. It is this which constitutes the very 'raison d'être' of the Guidelines. Consequently, the Guidelines may add obligations and are thus supplementary to national law and the representatives of the MNE's have recognized this in submission to the IME Committee. This is so also for the Chapter on Employment and Industrial Relations. The Guidelines can and do go further than national law and practice, e.g., as in Guideline 6 of the Employment and Industrial Relations Chapter, in that a reasonable term of notice of important future changes must be given to employees and that such a notice would not be obligatory under national law.

236. The fact that the Guidelines are also relevant for *domestic* enterprises (both private and state-owned) makes their possible impact even greater. The Guidelines are indeed 'good practice for all'. Consequently the Guidelines do contain (moral) obligations for national enterprises, when they are taking the domestic character of national enterprises into account, are relevant to them. This rule of equal treatment or of non-discrimination is one of the fundamental principles which made the 1976 package possible.

237. The Chapter on *Employment and Industrial Relations* has occupied most of the IME Committee's attention during the 1976–1979 period. The main reason is, obviously, that one of the advisory organs, namely TUAC, which has its main interests in that area, wants to augment the impact of Guidelines on multinational enterprises and introduced in the IME Committee to that end a number of cases and issues for consideration and interpretation. But these cases were also introduced by Governments. These individual cases, and the general issues they involved, were examined among Governments in the IME Committee and in the Levy Working Group together with BIAC and TUAC during the formal and informal discussions they had with the IME Committee and the Levy Working Group respectively.

238. These discussions enabled the Committee to keep close to real life situations and to avoid getting bogged down in abstract discussions. The cases, and the issues they raised, served as invaluable guides to the key issues that are sources of concern to Governments and to workers. The discussions the Committee and the Levy Group had on them showed the MNE's and the trade unions, even though the latter would clearly have liked to see explicit condemnation of the firms involved, which the nature of the OECD exercise precludes anyway, that Governments were taking the exercise seriously. The comments of the Committee clarifying certain points were given additional weight when it was decided to publish them as part of the 1979 review. The one amendment to the Guidelines also arose as a result of a case submitted to the Committee.

239. The discussions in the Committee and the clarifications in the report can be summarized and commented upon as follows:

240.

1. The Guidelines are addressed to entities which can be considered as enterprises (private, state, mixed), established in different countries and so linked that one or more of them may be able to exercise a significant influence over the activities of others and, in particular, share knowledge and resources with the others. *These criteria cover a broad range of multinational activities and arrangements*, which can be based on equity participation according to the traditional approach to international direct investment, but the same result could be achieved by other means not necessarily including an equity capital element.

241.

2. Multinationals should *adapt to local law and practice* and not try to transplant head office principles which do not respect the local climate.

242.

3. Multinational enterprises should not interfere with the *rights* of the employees *to organize*. An anti-union attitude, policies or instructions by headquarters to go non-union are contrary to this approach. The employers should, in fact, take a neutral attitude. This does not take away from the employer his right to express his opinion on the matter; but this could not amount either to threats or to anti-union policies.

243.

4. The Guidelines are neutral on the question of *International Trade Secretariats*. It is, however, obvious that the ITS' are bona fide organizations. The point is that the Guidelines indicate that the conditions under which recognition or bargaining are exercised are a matter of national law, regulations and practices. Thus ITS' must use the possibilities of national law and practice to achieve their claims in agreement also with the national unions involved.

244.

5. The Guidelines are equally neutral on the point of *international collective bargaining*. It follows that international collective bargaining belongs to the

270

area of autonomous relationships between labour and management and will become a reality when two conditions are fulfilled:
1. the need is felt to bargain at that level;
2. when the trade unions (at national level) desire to do so and can have enough strength to bring the multinational enterprises to the bargaining table.

245.

6. The problem of *'access to real decisionmakers'* goes to the heart of the multinational matter, given the centralized decision-making structure of the multinational enterprise. This decision-making structure may have as a consequence, that strategic decisions affecting the livelihood of the employees, are taken far away at the company's headquarters, with the possibility that even local managers are only informed about decisions which affect the subsidiary they manage when such decisions have already been taken.
The Guidelines are clear in this point and it therefore follows that multinational enterprises will eventually have to adapt their decision-making structure.
Paragraph 9 of the Employment and Industrial Relations Chapter gives two possibilities: the multinational enterprise must either delegate to the local managers authority to conduct negotiations, or send duly authorized representatives from headquarters for negotiations with the employees. What is meant by 'to conduct negotiations on collective bargaining or labour management relations issues', is to determined by national law, regulations or practice, which are prevalent in the entity affected by the decisions.

246.

7. The rules applying to *disclosure of information to employees* are still mainly national, but the Guidelines may be supplementary and recommend additional rules, especially in countries where national law and practice do not contain the obligation to disclose information in view of collective bargaining. Extremely important is, however, the recommendation that headquarters must see to it that the subsidiaries get sufficient information in due time in order to be able to fulfill their obligations under national law, practice and the Guidelines.

247.

8. Paragraph 6 of the Employment and Industrial Relations Chapter has been one of the Guidelines most frequently invoked. According to that paragraph, multinational enterprises should in considering changes in their operations which would have major effects upon the livelihood of their employees *provide reasonable notice . . .* and *co-operate . . . so as to mitigate adverse effects to the maximum extent practicable*. The wording of the

271

paragraph 'in considering changes' would seem to indicate that information should be given prior to the final decision. Specific circumstances of each case have to be taken into account; especially the compelling reasons of business confidentiality which may prevent early information, but this should the exception rather than the rule. *'Co-operation'* means consultation; *'mitigation'* includes looking for alternative solutions, banning of overtime, work-sharing, re-employment, postponement of dismissals, less dismissals, terms of notice, golden handshakes and the like.

248.

9. The Guidelines do not prevent a subsidiary of a multinational enterprise from *adapting wages to economic and financial difficulties* experienced by the firm if such conduct under local law and practice is accepted in the country for national enterprises under comparable circumstances.

249.

10. Managers of multinational enterprises should adopt a co-operative *attitude towards the participation of employees in international meetings* for consultations and exchanges of views among themselves provided that the functioning of the operations of the enterprises and the normal procedures which govern relationships with representatives of the employees and their organizations are not prejudiced thereby. This second condition means that, in practice, the attendance by employees must be sponsored by the responsible trade union.

250.

11. The use of strike breakers in the sense of *transfer of workers from foreign affiliates* in order to influence negotiations or to hinder the right to organize was not covered by the Guidelines. Paragraph 8 of the Employment and Industrial Relations Chapter was *amended* to that end. Paragraph 8 has, however, definite limits. It refers to threats to transfer the whole or part of an operating unit from the country concerned in order to influence . . . 'unfairly'. This paragraph only covers existing plants and equipment; threats not to invest or disinvestment; not covered either are transfers of products, materials, extra-overtime or other measures. The transfer of workers from one subsidiary to another within the same country seems, according to the present status of clarification, not to be covered by Guideline 8.

The key notion in paragraph 8 is the word 'unfair'. 'Unfair', does not take away the employer's right to inform the employees about what he thinks to be the possible effect of certain actions on the viability of the enterprise. Yet, management should be prepared to provide information in order to support this claim.

251.

12. The Guidelines do not prevent a multinational enterprise from *closing down a subsidiary, even a profitable one*; the responsibility and the power to do so remain entirely with the management of the multinational enterprise. The enterprise in doing so must of course take local law and practice into account, as well as the policy objectives of the Member Countries in which they operate. It is desirable, and could eventually be obligatory, to inform and consult with the government and with the employees and their representatives. Member States are, of course, free to regulate the closing down of enterprises but must do so taking international obligations (free flow of investment and capital) into account, as well as the obligation to treat enterprises equitably and not to discriminate between national and multinational enterprises.

252.

13. The problem of the *co-responsibility of the parent company for the action and commitments of its subsidiaries* goes equally to the heart of the multinational matter since it also involves the central decision-making structure of the multinational enterprise, which constitutes, as is stressed time and again, the essence of the multinational enterprise. The IME Committee recognizes that such co-responsibility exists in certain areas. The Committee distinguishes between two kinds of responsibilities: the non-financial and the financial. In the non-financial area, the parent company should see to it, inter alia, that the local affiliate is in a position to live up to local law and practice and to the Guidelines, especially the paragraphs 3 (information), 6 (reasonable notice, co-operation to mitigate . . .), and 9 (access to real decision-makers) of the Employment and Industrial Relations Chapter. As important as these matters of a non-financial nature, if not more so, is the question of the eventual *financial* co-responsibility of the parent and a subsidiary if the latter is unable to honour its liabilities to, for example, governments, creditors or workers. This is a delicate area as governments do not wish to do anything that could weaken the legal responsibility of foreign-owned subsidiaries set up under national law or entities with full legal personality and responsibility. However, the Committee has rated that financial responsibility can also be shared as a matter of moral obligation where national law does not protect the interests of those to whom a foreign-owned subsidiary has contracted financial commitments and in special circumstances according to the relationship between the parent company and the subsidiary and the conduct of the parent company. This responsibility of the parent company is of particular relevance in the cases set out in paragraph 6 of the Chapter on Employment and Industrial Relations, relating to important changes in the operation of a firm and co-operation as to the mitigation of resulting adverse effects.

***

253. Too short a time has elapsed since 1976 – only two accounting years – for the enterprises to fully implement the requirements on *disclosure of information* to the public at large. The business community has, however, indicated that it will undertake further efforts to observe the recommended standards. Especially smaller enterprises will have to be encouraged to do so. The IME Committee is now embarking upon an exercise designed to promote a greater degree of standardization internationally of accounting concepts. The backing already forthcoming for this work from BIAC and the accounting profession suggests that the Committee will be able to make a real contribution to the task of achieving a greater degree of comparability of company reports.

254. The *1979 Review* concentrated on the follow-up procedures. Rightly so! The Guidelines are only at the beginning of their career. If their impact is to grow further, efforts must be made by Governments, business and labour first to *make the Guidelines better known* through publications, the organization of seminars and the like. Of utmost importance in this respect is the recommendation of the IME Committee to all enterprises concerned that they indicate their *acceptance* of the Guidelines, preferably in their annual reports, and to include in those reports *brief statements* on their experience with the Guidelines, which may contain mention of steps taken with respect to their observance as well as any difficulties experienced in this aspect. As important, is the setting up by National Governments of *facilities* for handling enquiries and for discussions with the parties concerned on matters related to the Guidelines. As a matter of general principle such contacts should take place at national level before matters are raised at the international level.

255. The IME Committee, which has in practice interpreted its mandate in an evolving and dynamic way will, also after the 1979 Review, remain the *forum par excellence* in which Governments will have the opportunity to exchange views on all matters related to the Guidelines; the experience gained in their application and receive the views on these matters of business and labour, while individual companies can also express their views.
The Committee is competent to *discuss issues*, introduced by Governments, BIAC or TUAC and intends to respond in a *timely manner* to further requests for clarifications. Exchanges of view with BIAC and TUAC will be held periodically and may now also be held upon request by the latter. Individual companies have a better opportunity to state their points of view since, if they so wish, they can express their views either verbally or in writing on issues involving their interests concerning the Guidelines. Moreover the companies, when a case concerning their behaviour is raised with the Committee, will be informed in advance.

256. The Committee is mainly concerned with the discussion of *issues; cases* should in principle, be settled at national or bilateral level. The cases will be – as in the past – used as illustrations of issues arising under the Guidelines. The Committee is not, and has *no* intention of becoming, a semi-judicial body, judging the individual behaviour of companies. For that reason, the Committee does not intend to request an enterprise to appear before it or to make a presentation in writing. For the same reason proposals for *fact-finding* have not been retained and the word *clarification* is used instead of interpretation, since inviting firms, fact-finding and interpretation might bring the Committee too close to a judicial role. This does not, however, alter the fact that, when issues or questions of principle are discussed, the members of the Committee are informed about the case, have it in mind. Also the way in which a discussion evolves and a clarification is given may well indicate whether a certain behaviour coincides with the Guidelines or not and whether certain enterprises may have to change their conduct.

257. The *clarification process* is obviously more a political than a judicial one. The clarifications are still the result of tough negotiations between Governments, business and labour, each taking their interests into account. This process of give and take, of adjusting fundamental national interests is still too much in the political arena for the interpretation and dispute settlement functions to be handed over to an independent panel of experts. This may become a possibility in a subsequent phase, e.g. after the next review in 1984, if it becomes clearer that clarification is more a matter of interpreting existing texts than the negotiation of refinements to the existing Guidelines or of additional rules for corporate behaviour. For the time being, Governments still want to retain control of that process.

258. Whether the impact of the Guidelines on real life in the enterprises will grow, will depend largely on the *use which the social partners make of the Guidelines* in their negotiations and settlement of disputes and whether they make reference to the Guidelines. Much will depend on whether business and labour, especially the latter, which is a major driving force behind the Guidelines, will make use of the facilities, at national, as at international level now offered for the introduction of cases and issues. The social partners must help Governments to see to it that their exchange of ideas continues to run closely to the facts of life, to the real world. The new follow-up procedures provide more opportunities to that end.

259. The text of the Guidelines was, for the sake of credibility and stability, *only slightly amended*, to cover an issue that was not foreseen when the Guidelines were drafted. It was accepted by most that the 1976 deal constituted a fragile package, the delicate balance of which had to be maintained. The credibility – in the sense of stability – of the Guidelines, required that after such a short period no changes should be made. The one change, obviously again a compromise, since more changes were asked for, indicates that changes which are needed are possible, which is also necessary for the same 'credibility'.

260. Another important element in the follow-up is the *bi-annual reporting by Governments.* These national reports will enable the Committee to assess the extent of acceptance and observance of the Guidelines, the action taken within

OECD Member countries by Governments, business and labour organizations, and the companies themselves to give effect to them, and the areas where problems are being encountered. The Committee itself intends to submit a report to the Council in 1982 – a *mid-term* report thus – and a *follow up report* in 1984, with the recommendation to publish them.

The timetable thus set out will, consequently, involve the following action by Governments and the IME Committee:

September 1981	Follow-up reports by Governments
June 1982	Mid-term report by the IME Committee
September 1983	Follow-up reports by Governments, dealing also, as required, with matters related to the next review
June 1984	Follow-up report by the IME Committee for the Review by Ministerial Council of the 1976 Declaration.

261. The next *formal review* will take place in *1984.* This provision does not preclude – in theory at least – an earlier review or certain modifications to these instruments before the end of the five year period, but this is not likely. Rather, according to the view of TUAC, it was the price which had to be paid for the one amendment of the Guidelines accepted in the 1979 review. Five years has, so the IME report indicates, the advantage of providing a stable framework for the implementation of the Guidelines and will allow adequate time for the follow-up procedures to develop. An earlier date for review would have had the drawback of subordinating the new implementation procedures, and their subsequent evolution, to continued manoeuvering in the Committee with the next review more in mind than a willingness to make the existing machinery work.

262. Since the 1976 Declaration and the adoption of the Guidelines a lot has been accomplished. Important steps have been taken in the area of interpretation and clarification; the Guidelines have proved to be of valuable help in the settlement of certain problems. The Guidelines do indeed offer an efficient and realistic framework for further encouragement of the contribution which multinational enterprises can make to economic and social progress and for the reduction and resolution of the difficulties to which the operations of multinational enterprises may give rise.

Annex I. Declaration of 21 June 1976 on International Investment and Multinational Enterprises as revised on 13 June 1979[1]

THE GOVERNMENTS OF OECD MEMBER COUNTRIES*

CONSIDERING

that international investment has assumed increased importance in the world economy and has considerably contributed to the development of their countries;

that multinational enterprises play an important role in this investment process;

that co-operation by Member countries can improve the foreign investment climate, encourage the positive contribution which multinational enterprises can make to economic and social progress, and minimize and resolve difficulties which may arise from their various operations;

that, while continuing endeavours within the OECD may lead to further international arrangements and agreements in this field, it seems appropriate at this stage to intensify their co-operation and consultation on issues relating to international investment and multinational enterprises through inter-related instruments each of which deals with a different aspect of the matter and together constitute a framework within which the OECD will consider these issues:

DECLARE:

I. *Guidelines for MNE's*

that they jointly recommend to multinational enterprises operating in their territories the observance of the Guidelines as set forth in the Annex hereto having regard to the considerations and understandings which introduce the Guidelines and are an integral part of them.

[1] The amendments are in italic.
* The Turkish Government was not in a position to participate in this Declaration.

Annex I

II. *National Treatment*

1. that Member countries should, consistent with their needs to maintain public order, to protect their essential security interests and to fulfil commitments relating to international peace and security, accord to enterprises operating in their territories and owned or controlled directly or indirectly by nationals of another Member country (hereinafter referred to as 'Foreign-Controlled Enterprises') treatment under their laws, regulations and administrative practices, consistent with international law and no less favourable than that accorded in like situations to domestic enterprises (hereinafter referred to as 'National Treatment').
2. that Member countries will consider applying 'National Treatment' in respect of countries other than Member countries.
3. that Member countries will endeavour to ensure that their territorial sub-divisions apply 'National Treatment'.
4. that this Declaration does not deal with the right of Member countries to regulate the entry of foreign investment or the conditions of establishment of foreign enterprises.

III. *International Investment Incentives and Disincentives*

1. that they recognize the need to strengthen their co-operation in the field of international direct investment.
2. that they thus recognize the need to give due weight to the interests of Member countries affected by specific laws, regulations and administrative practices in this field (hereinafter called 'measures') providing official incentives and disincentives to international direct investment.
3. that Member countries will endeavour to make such measures as transparent as possible, so that their importance and purpose can be ascertained and that information on them can be readily available.

IV. *Consultation Procedures*

that they are prepared to consult one another on the above matters in conformity with the Decisions of the Council relating to Inter-Governmental Consultation Procedures on the Guidelines for Multinational Enterprises, on National Treatment and on International Investment Incentives and Disincentives.

V. *Review*

that they will review the above matters at the latest in five years with a view to improving the effectiveness of international economic co-operation among Member countries on issues relating to international investment and multinational enterprises.

Annex to the Declaration of 21st June, 1976 by Governments of OECD Member Countries on International Investment and Multinational Enterprises

GUIDELINES FOR MULTINATIONAL ENTERPRISES

1. Multinational enterprises now play an important part in the economies of Member countries and in international economic relations, which is of increasing interest to governments. Through international direct investment, such enterprises can bring substantial benefits to home and host countries by contributing to the efficient utilization of capital, technology and human resources between countries and can thus fulfil an important role in the promotion of economic and social welfare. But the advances made by multinational enterprises in organizing their operations beyond the national framework may lead to abuse of concentrations of economic power and to conflicts with national policy objectives. In addition, the complexity of these multinational enterprises and the difficulty of clearly perceiving their diverse structures, operations and policies sometimes give rise to concern.

2. The common aim of the Member countries is to encourage the positive contributions which multinational enterprises can make to economic and social progress and to minimize and resolve the difficulties to which their various operations may give rise. In view of the transnational structure of such enterprises, this aim will be furthered by co-operation among the OECD countries where the headquarters of most of the multinational enterprises are established and which are the location of a substantial part of their operations. The guidelines set out hereafter are designed to assist in the achievement of this common aim and to contribute to improving the foreign investment climate.

3. Since the operations of multinational enterprises extend throughout the world, including countries that are not Members of the Organization, international co-operation in this field should extend to all States. Member countries will give their full support to efforts undertaken in co-operation with non-Member countries, and in particular with developing countries, with a view to improving the welfare and living standards of all people both by encouraging the positive contributions which multinational enterprises can make and by minimizing and resolving the problems which may arise in connection with their activities.

4. Within the Organization, the programme of co-operation to attain these ends will be a continuing, pragmatic and balanced one. It comes within the general aims of the Convention on the Organization for Economic Co-operation and Development (OECD) and makes full use of the various specialized bodies of the Organization, whose terms of reference already cover many aspects of the role of multinational enterprises, notably in matters of international trade and payments, competition, taxation, manpower, industrial development, science and technology. In these bodies, work is being carried

out on the identification of issues, the improvement of relevant qualitative and statistical information and the elaboration of proposals for action designed to strengthen inter-governmental co-operation. In some of these areas procedures already exist through which issues related to the operations of multinational enterprises can be taken up. This work could result in the conclusion of further and complementary agreements and arrangements between governments.

5. The initial phase of the co-operation programme is composed of a Declaration and three Decisions promulgated simultaneously as they are complementary and inter-connected, in respect of guidelines for multinational enterprises, national treatment for foreign-controlled enterprises and international investment incentives and disincentives.

6. The guidelines set out below are recommendations jointly addressed by Member countries to multinational enterprises operating in their territories. These guidelines, which take into account the problems which can arise because of the international structure of these enterprises, lay down standards for the activities of these enterprises in the different Member countries. Observance of the guidelines is voluntary and not legally enforceable. However, they should help to ensure that the operations of these enterprises are in harmony with national policies of the countries where they operate and to strengthen the basis of mutual confidence between enterprises and States.

7. Every State has the right to prescribe the conditions under which multinational enterprises operate within its national jurisdiction, subject to international law and to the international agreements to which it has subscribed. The entities of a multinational enterprise located in various countries are subject to the laws of these countries.

8. A precise legal definition of multinational enterprises is not required for the purposes of the guidelines. These usually comprise companies or other entities whose ownership is private, state or mixed, established in different countries and so linked that one or more of them may be able to exercise a significant influence over the activities of others and, in particular, to share knowledge and resources with the others. The degree of autonomy of each entity in relation to the others varies widely from one multinational enterprise to another, depending on the nature of the links between such entities and the fields of activity concerned. For these reasons, the guidelines are addressed to the various entities within the multinational enterprise (parent companies and/or local entities) according to the actual distribution of responsibilities among them on the understanding that they will co-operate and provide assistance to one another as necessary to facilitate observance of the guidelines. The word 'enterprise' as used in these guidelines refers to these various entities in accordance with their responsibilities.

9. The guidelines are not aimed at introducing differences of treatment be-

tween multinational and domestic enterprises; wherever relevant they reflect good practice for all. Accordingly, multinational and domestic enterprises are subject to the same expectations in respect of their conduct wherever the guidelines are relevant to both.

10. The use of appropriate international dispute settlement mechanisms, including arbitration, should be encouraged as a means of facilitating the resolution of problems arising between enterprises and Member countries.

11. Member countries have agreed to establish appropriate review and consultation procedures concerning issues arising in respect of the guidelines. When multinational enterprises are made subject to conflicting requirements by Member countries, the governments concerned will co-operate in good faith with a view to resolving such problems either within the Committee on International Investment and Multinational Enterprises established by the OECD Council on 21st January, 1975 or through other mutually acceptable arrangements.

HAVING REGARD to the foregoing considerations, the Member countries set forth the following guidelines for multinational enterprises with the understanding that Member countries will fulfil their responsibilities to treat enterprises equitably and in accordance with international law and international agreements, as well as contractual obligations to which they have subscribed:

GENERAL POLICIES

Enterprises should
1. take fully into account established general policy objectives of the Member countries in which they operate;
2. in particular, give due consideration to those countries' aims and priorities with regard to economic and social progress, including industrial and regional development, the protection of the environment, the creation of employment opportunities, the promotion of innovation and the transfer of technology;
3. while observing their legal obligations concerning information, supply their entities with supplementary information the latter may need in order to meet requests by the authorities of the countries in which those entities are located for information relevant to the activities of those entities, taking into account legitimate requirements of business confidentiality;
4. favour close co-operation with the local community and business interests;
5. allow their component entities freedom to develop their activities and to exploit their competitive advantage in domestic and foreign markets, consistent with the need for specialization and sound commercial practice;

6. when filling responsible posts in each country of operation, take due account of individual qualifications without discrimination as to nationality, subject to particular national requirements in this respect;
7. not render – and they should not be solicited or expected to render – any bribe or other improper benefit, direct or indirect, to any public servant or holder of public office;
8. unless legally permissible, not make contributions to candidates for public office or to political parties or other political organizations;
9. abstain from any improper involvement in local political activities.

DISCLOSURE OF INFORMATION

Enterprises should, having due regard to their nature and relative size in the economic context of their operations and to requirements of business confidentiality and to cost, publish in a form suited to improve public understanding a sufficient body of factual information on the structure, activities and policies of the enterprise as a whole, as a supplement, in so far as is necessary for this purpose, to information to be disclosed under the national law of the individual countries in which they operate. To this end, they should publish within reasonable time limits, on a regular basis, but at least annually, financial statements and other pertinent information relating to the enterprise as a whole, comprising in particular:

 (i) the structure of the enterprise, showing the name and location of the parent company, its main affiliates, its percentage ownership, direct and indirect, in these affiliates, including shareholdings between them;
 (ii) the geographical areas* where operations are carried out and the principal activities carried on therein by the parent company and the main affiliates;
 (iii) the operating results and sales by geographical area and the sales in the major lines of business for the enterprise as a whole;
 (iv) significant new capital investment by geographical area and, as far as practicable, by major lines of business for the enterprise as a whole;
 (v) a statement of the sources and uses of funds by the enterprise as a whole;
 (vi) the average number of employees in each geographical area;
 (vii) research and development expenditure for the enterprise as a whole;
 (viii) the policies followed in respect of intra-group pricing;
 (ix) the accounting policies, including those on consolidation, observed in compiling the published information.

* For the purposes of the guideline on disclosure of information the term 'geographical area' means groups of countries or individual countries as each enterprise determines it appropriate in its particular circumstances. While no single method of grouping is appropriate for all enterprises, or for all purposes, the factors to be considered by an enterprise would include the significance of operations carried out in individual countries or areas as well as the effects on its competitiveness, geographic proximity, economic affinity, similarities in business environments and the nature, scale and degree of inter-relationship of the enterprises' operations in the various countries.

Competition

Enterprises should
while conforming to official competition rules and established policies of the
countries in which they operate,
1. refrain from actions which would adversely affect competition in the relevant market by abusing a dominant position of market power, by means of, for example,
   (a) anti-competitive acquisitions,
   (b) predatory behaviour toward competitors,
   (c) unreasonable refusal to deal,
   (d) anti-competitive abuse of industrial property rights,
   (e) discriminatory (i.e. unreasonably differentiated) pricing and using such pricing transactions between affiliated enterprises as a means of affecting adversely competition outside these enterprises;
2. allow purchasers, distributors and licensees freedom to resell, export, purchase and develop their operations consistent with law, trade conditions, the need for specialization and sound commercial practice;
3. refrain from participating in or otherwise purposely strengthening the restrictive effects of international or domestic cartels or restrictive agreements which adversely affect or eliminate competition and which are not generally or specifically accepted under applicable national or international legislation;
4. be ready to consult and co-operate, including the provision of information, with competent authorities of countries whose interests are directly affected in regard to competition issues or investigations. Provision of information should be in accordance with safeguards normally applicable in this field.

Financing

Enterprises should, in managing the financial and commercial operations of their activities, and especially their liquid foreign assets and liabilities, take into consideration the established objectives of the countries in which they operate regarding balance of payments and credit policies.

Taxation

Enterprises should
1. upon request of the taxation authorities of the countries in which they operate, provide, in accordance with the safeguards and relevant procedures of the national laws of these countries, the information necessary to determine correctly the taxes to be assessed in connection with their operations, including relevant information concerning their operations in other countries;
2. refrain from making use of the particular facilities available to them, such as transfer pricing which does not conform to an arm's length standard, for

modifying in ways contrary to national laws the tax base on which members of the group are assessed.

EMPLOYMENT AND INDUSTRIAL RELATIONS

Enterprises should
within the framework of law, regulations and prevailing labour relations and employment practices, in each of the countries in which they operate,

1. respect the right of their employees to be represented by trade unions and other bona fide organizations of employees, and engage in constructive negotiations, either individually or through employers' associations, with such employee organizations with a view to reaching agreements on employment conditions, which should include provisions for dealing with disputes arising over the interpretation of such agreements, and for ensuring mutually respected rights and responsibilities,

2. (a) provide such facilities to representatives of the employees as may be necessary to assist in the development of effective collective agreements;
    (b) provide to representatives of employees information which is needed for meaningful negotiations on conditions of employment;

3. provide to representatives of employees where this accords with local law and practice, information which enables them to obtain a true and fair view of the performance of the entity or, where appropriate, the enterprise as a whole;

4. observe standards of employment and industrial relations not less favourable than those observed by comparable employers in the host country;

5. in their operations, to the greatest extent practicable, utilize, train and prepare for upgrading members of the local labour force in co-operation with representatives of their employees and, where appropriate, the relevant governmental authorities;

6. in considering changes in their operations which would have major effects upon the livelihood of their employees, in particular in the case of the closure of an entity involving collective lay-offs or dismissals; provide reasonable notice of such changes to representatives of their employees, and where appropriate to the relevant governmental authorities, and co-operate with the employee representative and appropriate governmental authorities so as to mitigate to the maximum extent practicable adverse effects;

7. implement their employment policies including hiring, discharge, pay, promotion and training without discrimination unless selectivity in respect of employee characteristics is in furtherance of established governmental policies which specifically promote greater equality of employment opportunity;

8. in the context of bona fide negotiations* with representatives of employees

* Bona fide negotiations may include labour disputes as part of the process of negotiation. Whether or not labour disputes are so included will be determined by the law and prevailing employment practices of particular countries.

on conditions of employment, or while employees are exercising a right to organize, not threaten to utilize a capacity to transfer the whole or part of an operating unit from the country concerned *nor transfer employees from the enterprises' component entities in other countries* in order to influence unfairly those negotiations or to hinder the exercise of a right to organize;
9. enable authorized representatives of their employees to conduct negotiations on collective bargaining or labour management relations issues with representatives of management who are authorized to take decisions on the matters under negotiation.

SCIENCE AND TECHNOLOGY

Enterprises should
(1) endeavour to ensure that their activities fit satisfactorily into the scientific and technological policies and plans of the countries in which they operate, and contribute to the development of national scientific and technological capacities, including as far as appropriate the establishment and improvement in host countries of their capacity to innovate;
(2) to the fullest extent practicable, adopt in the course of their business activities practices which permit the rapid diffusion of technologies with due regard to the protection of industrial and intellectual property rights;
(3) when granting licenses for the use of industrial property rights or when otherwise transferring technology do so on reasonable terms and conditions.

Decision of the Council on Inter-Governmental Consultation Procedures on the Guidelines for Multinational Enterprises

The Council,
Having regard to the Convention on the Organization for Economic Co-operation and Development of 14th December, 1960 and, in particular, to Articles 2(d), 3 and 5(a) thereof;
Having regard to the Resolution of the Council of 22nd December, 1976 on the Terms of Reference of the Committee on International Investment and Multinational Enterprises and, in particular, to paragraph 2 thereof [C(7()209(Final)];
Taking note of the Declaration by the Governments of OECD Member countries of 21st June, 1976 in which they jointly recommend to multinational enterprises the observance of guidelines for multinational enterprises;
Having regard to the Decision of the Council of 21st June, 1976 on Inter-Governmental Consultation Procedures on the Guidelines for Multinational Enterprises [C(76)117];
Recognizing the desirability of setting forth procedures by which consultations may take place on matters related to these guidelines;

Annex I

Considering the Report on the Review of the 1976 Declaration and Decisions on International Investment and Multinational Enterprises [C(79)102];
On the proposal of the Committee on International Investment and Multinational Enterprises;

DECIDES:

1. The Committee on International Investment and Multinational Enterprises (hereinafter called 'the Committee') shall periodically or at the request of a Member country hold an exchange of views on matters related to the Guidelines and the experience gained in their application. *The Committee shall be responsible for clarification of the Guidelines. Clarification will be provided as required.* The Committee shall periodically report to the Council on these matters.
2. The Committee shall periodically invite the Business and Industry Advisory Committee to OECD (BIAC) and the Trade Union Advisory Committee to OECD (TUAC) to express their views on matters related to the Guidelines. *In addition, exchanges of views with the advisory bodies on these matters may be held upon request by the latter.* The Committee shall take account of such views in its reports to the Council.

3. *If it so wishes, an individual enterprise will be given the opportunity to express its views either orally or in writing on issues concerning the Guidelines involving its interests.*

4. *The Committee shall not reach conclusions on the conduct of individual enterprises.*

5. Member countries may request that consultations be held in the Committee on any problem arising from the fact that multinational enterprises are made subject to conflicting requirements. Governments concerned will co-operate in good faith with a view to resolving such problems, either within the Committee or through other mutually acceptable arrangements.

6. This Decision shall be reviewed at the latest in *five years*. The Committee shall make proposals for this purpose as appropriate.

Decision of the Council on National Treatment

The Council,
Having regard to the Convention on the Organization for Economic Co-operation and Development of 14th December, 1960 and, in particular, to Articles 2(c), 2(d), 3 and 5(a) thereof;
Having regard to the Resolution of the Council of 22nd December, 1976 on the Terms of Reference of the Committee on International Investment and Multinational Enterprises and, in particular, to paragraph 2 thereof [C(76)209(Final)];

286

Taking note of the Declaration by the Governments of OECD Member countries of 21st June, 1976 on national treatment;
Having regard to the Decision of the Council of 21st June, 1976 on National Treatment [C(76)118];
Considering that it is appropriate to establish within the Organization suitable procedures for reviewing laws, regulations and administrative practices (hereinafter referred to as 'measures') which depart from 'National Treatment';
Considering the Report on the Review of the 1976 Declaration and Decisions on International Investment and Multinational Enterprises [C(79)102];
On the proposal of the Committee on International Investment and Multinational Enterprises;

DECIDES:

1. Measures taken by a Member country constituting exceptions to 'National Treatment' (including measures restricting new investment by 'Foreign-Controlled Enterprises' already established in their territory) which are in effect on the date of this Decision shall be notified to the Organization within 60 days after the date of this Decision.

2. Measures taken by a Member country constituting new exceptions to 'National Treatment' (including measures restricting new investment by 'Foreign-Controlled Enterprises' already established in their territory) taken after the date of this Decision shall be notified to the Organization within 30 days of their introduction together with the specific reasons thereof and the proposed duration thereof.

3. Measures introduced by a territorial subdivision of a Member country, pursuant to its independent powers, which constitute exceptions to 'National Treatment', shall be notified to the Organization by the Member country concerned, insofar as it has knowledge thereof, within 30 days of the responsible officials of the Member country obtaining such knowledge.

4. The Committee on International Investment and Multinational Enterprises (hereinafter called 'the Committee') shall periodically review the application of 'National Treatment' (including exceptions thereto) with a view to extending such application of 'National Treatment'. The Committee shall make proposals as and when necessary in this connection.

5. *The Committee may periodically invite the Business and Industry Advisory Committee to OECD (BIAC) and the Trade Union Advisory Committee to OECD (TUAC) to express their views on matters related to National Treatment and shall take account of such views in its periodic reports to the Council.*

6. Member countries shall provide to the Committee, upon its request, all

relevant information concerning measures pertaining to the application of 'National Treatment' and exceptions thereto.

7. This Decision shall be reviewed at the latest in *five years*. The Committee shall make proposals for this purpose as appropriate.

Decision of the Council on International Investment Incentives and Disincentives

The Council,
Having regard to the Convention on the Organization for Economic Co-operation and Development of 14th December, 1960 and, in particular, Articles 2(c), 2(d), 2(e), 3 and 5(a) thereof;
Having regard to the Resolution of the Council of 22nd December, 1976 on the Terms of Reference of the Committee on International Investment and Multinational Enterprises and, in particular, paragraph 2 thereof [C(76)209(Final)][1];
Taking note of the Declaration by the Governments of OECD Member countries of 21st June, 1976 on international investment incentives and disincentives;
Having regard to the Decision of the Council of 21st June, 1976 on International Investment Incentives and Disincentives [C(76)119];
Considering the Report on the Review of the 1976 Declaration and Decisions on International Investment of Multinational Enterprises [C(79)102];
On the proposal of the Committee on International investment and Multinational Enterprises;

DECIDES:

1. Consultations will take place in the framework of the Committee on International Investment and Multinational Enterprises at the request of a Member country which considers that its interests may be adversely affected by the impact on its flow of international direct investments of measures taken by another Member country specifically designed to provide incentives or disincentives for international direct investment. Having full regard to the national economic objectives of the measures and without prejudice to policies designed to redress regional imbalances, the purposes of the consultations will be to examine the possibility of reducing such effects to a minimum.

2. Member countries shall supply, under the consultation procedures, all permissible information relating to any measures being the subject of the consultation.

3. *The Committee may periodically invite the Business and Industry Advisory Committee to OECD (BIAC) and the Trade Union Advisory Committee to OECD (TUAC) to express their views on matters relating to international*

investment incentives and disincentives and shall take account of these views in its periodic reports to the Council.

4. This Decision shall be reviewed at the latest in *five years*. The Committee on International Investment and Multinational Enterprises shall make proposals for this purpose as appropriate.

Annex II. MOTOR IBERICA and BLACK and DECKER case, submitted by IMF[1]

Submitted by the International Metalworkers' Federation (IMF) through the Trade Union Advisory Committee (TUAC) on March 30, 1977

Violation of trade union rights by MOTOR IBERICA, Spanish subsidiary of MASSEY FERGUSON

Management at MOTOR IBERICA, subsidiary of the Canadian based multinational MASSEY FERGUSON, has for years taken advantage of the difficult situation in industrial relations in Spain.

Management curbed militant workers belonging to clandestine unions – which being the real representatives of the workers defended their claims. A great number of these militants were fired and management refused to bargain in good faith on wages and working conditions.

The reintegration of such victimized workers was one of the demands put foward by the workers, along with a wage increase of 4,000 pesetas per month for all workers, in an attempt to achieve genuine collective bargaining. This led to a strike of 96 days, from May to July 1976, at the three plants of MOTOR IBERICA in Barcelona, comprising 5,000 workers out of a total workforce of 10,000 employed in all the plants of the MASSEY FERGUSON Spanish subsidiary.

At the end of the strike another 67 workers were dismissed who had defended the claims which the genuine independent trade unions – although not yet legally recognized, openly negotiated for a new collective agreement.

The workers and their unions brought the matter before the Labour Court. This court decided in favour of the workers and declared the dismissals socially unjustified.

Management disregarding this court decision refused to rehire the dismissed workers, and brought the case before the Higher Central Labour Court. As decisions at this level drag on, management of MOTOR IBERICA depriving the workers of jobs and their legitimate claim for reintegration, continues to victimize workers through violation of basic trade union rights.

Refusal of trade union recognition by the multinational subsidiary of BLACK AND DECKER LIMITED in Great Britain

Trade union recognition had been requested by the General and Municipal Workers' Union at the BLACK AND DECKER Spennymoor factory in Great

---

1. See Part II, IV, the right of employees to be represented.

Britain. This request was made after a total membership of 290 employees was reached: 265 general process workers and 25 office staff. This membership extends throughout all areas of the factory, with the exception of the warehouse. The union demands recognition to be granted on a general basis covering all subjects suitable for joint regulation, and that recognition should be granted by the company to duly elected shop stewards of the union at plant level and to Regional and National Officers when their assistance is requested by the factory shop stewards.

A similar claim has been submitted by the Amalgamated Union of Engineering Workers.

In its regional recruitment campaign, the General and Municipal Workers' Union Northern region, gained over 300 workers in autumn 1975. This number has subsequently been slightly reduced, primarily due to lack of management co-operation and refusal to grant recognition. The union claim was put forward by letters to management and in the course of a joint meeting. Management stated at the meeting that the company would give full consideration to all matters raised by elected shop stewards on behalf of their members and that the established company policy and procedures should meet the requirements of representatives, but that the company would not grant recognition and negotiating rights to regional and national offices of the General and Municipal Workers' Union. In the later stage of further union interventions with the company, management refused a further meeting to discuss the matter, indicating that the company held the view that the majority of employees did not wish to be represented by a trade union. The union was advised of a secret company ballot in which the majority of employees at BLACK AND DECKER Spennymoor factory had voted to continue the present company policy.

The union made it quite clear that they did not accept the result of the management-organized ballot for recognition. The union exposed the biased way in which management conducted the ballot, without consultation or participation of shop stewards. It was stressed once more that industrial relations cannot be conducted in an orderly manner without an established procedure for negotiations between management and the trade unions.

Throughout the course of discussions with the company the union have acted in good faith and pursued the legitimate rights of its members for recognition and effective representation. The union deplores the attitude of management for flagrantly disregarding basic principles of industrial democracy – which is a well established local practice in Great Britain – by consistently refusing recognition, discouraging trade union membership and fervently upholding their company policies based on total managerial prerogatives in areas of organizational decision-making.

In view of BLACK AND DECKER LIMITED management attitude in refusing to co-operate with both General and Municipal Workers' Union officials and Amalgamated Union of Engineering Workers' officials (who has membership amongst skilled grades of employees at the factory) and the ACAS – Advisory Conciliation and Arbitration Service – local Newcastle office on this subject, the trade unions requested that the ACAS set up an Enquiry under

Section 11 of the Employment Protection Act 1975, to consider the legitimate rights of union members for recognition and negotiating rights. The trade unions hope that their action, through ACAS, will lead to management acceptance of full trade union recognition at the BLACK AND DECKER LIMITED Spennymoor factory; thus complying with the industrial relations practice that governs the relationship of unions with other subsidiaries of multinational companies in Great Britain, who generally accord full recognition and negotiating rights to the trade unions.

BLACK AND DECKER is known to be a multinational company actively discouraging trade union membership, refusing trade union recognition and bargaining rights across the world. In the United States, however, the International Association of Machinists – an IMF affiliate – has concluded an agreement with the DE WALT division of BLACK AND DECKER at the Lancaster Plant, USA.

The full recognition of trade unions is a basic right that has been set out in the OECD Guidelines, where it states in the chapter on Employment and Industrial Relations that: 'enterprises should, within the framework of the law, regulations and prevailing labour relations and employment practices, in each of the companies in which they operate, respect the right of their employees to be represented by trade unions and other bona fide organizations of employees, and engage in constructive negotiations, either individually or through employers' associations, with such employee organizations with a view to reaching agreements on employment conditions, which should include provisions for dealing with disputes arising over the interpretation of such agreements, and for ensuring mutually respected rights and responsibilities.'

IMF requests, in the name of its British affiliates, that BLACK AND DECKER conforms with this clause in the OECD Guidelines for constructive industrial relations with the trade unions.

Annex III. Note to editors: Press Release, April 11, 1978

The OECD's Committee on International Investment and Multinational Enterprises will meet on 11th–13th April, 1978. During the first day of this meeting, it will hold an exchange of views with the Consultative bodies, the Business and Industry Advisory Committee (BIAC) and the Trade Union Advisory Committee (TUAC) on matters related to the OECD Guidelines for Multinational Enterprises (MNEs).

These exchanges are held under the provision of the 1976 OECD Council Decision on Inter-Governmental Consultation Procedures on the Guidelines for Multinational Enterprises, which calls for the Committee periodically to invite the BIAC and TUAC to express their views on matters related to the Guidelines and for the Committee to take account of such views in its reports to the Council. The first exchange of views with the BIAC and TUAC was held in March of 1977.

The attached note provides information on the recent work of the OECD in the area of international investment and multinational enterprises, in particular, in relation to the Guidelines and the other parts of the 1976 Ministerial Declaration of the OECD countries.

OECD Activities in the field of International Investment and Multinational Enterprises

1. On 21st–22nd June, 1976, the OECD Council, meeting at Ministerial level, agreed to step up co-operation among Member countries in the area of international investment and multinational enterprises. This action consisted of a Declaration of the Governments of OECD Member countries, which included the Guidelines for Multinational Enterprises, and the three related Decisions of the Council on National Treatment, International Investment Incentives and Disincentives, and Inter-Governmental Consultation Procedures on the Guidelines for Multinational Enterprises. The Declaration and the Decisions aimed at improving the international investment climate within the OECD area through joint undertakings by the Governments of Member countries which should strengthen confidence between multinational enterprises and Member states. They aimed further at encouraging the positive contributions of multinational enterprises to economic and social progress and minimizing or resolving present or potential difficulties that may results from their activities, through internationally agreed guidelines, inter-governmental consultations

and review mechanisms. This action was the result of a thorough studies and intensive negotiations among governments as well as consultations with the Business and Industry Advisory Committee (BIAC) and the Trade Union Advisory Committee (TUAC) which publicly welcomed the conclusion of that effort. The consensus reached represents a common approach by the OECD countries, which account for most of the world's international investment.

2. The Guidelines for Multinational Enterprises are recommendations jointly addressed by Member countries to multinational enterprises operating in their territories. These Guidelines, which take into account the problems which can arise because of the international structure of these enterprises, lay down standards for the activities of such enterprises in the different Member countries. Observance of the Guidelines is voluntary and not legally enforceable. Therefore, their effectiveness depends not only on the co-operative action of Member Governments but also to a large extent on wide acceptance by the enterprises concerned and the continuing support of business and labour organizations and the public. To date, the evidence available to the OECD indicates that the Guidelines do have this broad support.

3. The Member countries meet in the OECD's Committee on International Investment and Multinational Enterprises (CIME), to discuss and to review matters relating to the Guidelines and their application as well as other issues relating to multinational enterprises and international investment. Under the procedures established by the 1976 Declaration and Decisions, the CIME also serves as the forum in which any Member country can request consultations on matters related to the Guidelines, National Treatment and International Investment Incentives and Disincentives. In 1979 the OECD Council will review the Declaration and Decisions and the CIME will prepare proposals for that review.

4. At national level, Member Governments have widely disseminated the Guidelines in their national languages and commended them to companies and business organizations. The BIAC and TUAC and various national business and labour organizations have also played a useful role in disseminating the Guidelines. In some countries special arrangements have been made for exchanges of views between the Government and interested parties on the application of the Guidelines and the other aspects of the Declaration and Decisions.

5. At international level, the Guidelines have provided experience which has proved useful for work in other international fora, in particular the United Nations, the International Labour Organization and the Conference on International Economic Co-operation.

6. Within the OECD, the CIME is devoting considerable efforts to matters related to the application of the Guidelines. In particular, the Committee periodically invites the BIAC and TUAC to express their views on these

matters. The first of these exchanges of views took place in March 1977, and the second is scheduled for 11th April, 1978. Exchanges of views among Member governments have taken place both in the meetings of the Committee and its ad hoc Working Group. On the basis of these exchanges the Committee has examined during the past year a number of issues relating to the application of the Guidelines.

7. The Committee has sought to clarify certain issues relating to the meaning or the coverage of the Guidelines as well as to gain experience on their application in concrete situations. It is important to note that, according to the procedures laid down in the 1976 Council Decision for Inter-Governmental Consultation Procedures on the Guidelines, the Committee shall not reach conclusions on the conduct of individual enterprises; in other words, it is not to serve as a judicial forum. The Committee did not seek to investigate further the facts of the individual situations presented to it.

8. The submissions by Governments and by TUAC[1] in the 1977 exchange of views have proved to be very useful to the Committee and served to identify the following seven issues:[2]

   (i) Relations between multinational enterprises and trade unions or other bona fide employee organizations (paragraphs 1 and 2).

  (ii) Application by multinational enterprises of comparable standards of employment and industrial relations (paragraph 4).

 (iii) Changes in operations (paragraph 6).

 (iv) Threats and pressures that might be used by management in order to influence unfairly bona fide negotiations with employees on conditions of employment (paragraph 8).

  (v) Access to decision-makers (paragraph 9).

 (vi) Application of paragraph 1 of the section on 'Science and Technology'.

(vii) Responsibility of the parent company in the context of the application of the Guidelines.

9. In addition to the Guidelines, the 1976 Declaration and Decisions also include provisions on National Treatment and International Investment Incentives and Disincentives. With respect to the National Treatment instruments, the Committee is conducting a comprehensive overview of existing exceptions to National Treatment in Member countries, that is, instances where foreign-controlled enterprises operating in their territories are treated less favourably than domestically-controlled enterprises. This survey is based on notifications

---

[1] The Decision on Inter-Governmental Consultation Procedures on the Guidelines for Multinational Enterprises provides for different procedures governing the treatment of submissions by Member governments and submissions by BIAC or TUAC. Paragraph 1 of that Decision calls for the Committee to hold an exchange of views on matters related to the Guidelines at the request of a Member country. Paragraph 2 calls for the Committee to invite periodically the BIAC and TUAC to express their views on matters related to the Guidelines.

[2] Unless otherwise stated, paragraph citations refer to the section 'Employment and Industrial Relations' of the Guidelines.

submitted by the individual Member countries on the basis of the situation existing when the Declaration was adopted. The notifications described exceptions that exist in such areas as new investments by foreign-controlled resident firms, access to government subsidies and incentives, government contracting and purchasing, taxation and exchange controls. Any new exception to 'National Treatment' which may be introduced by a Member country is to be notified to the Organization with the specific reasons for the measure and its proposed duration. The relevant 1976 Decision also calls for the Committee to act as a forum for consultations at the request of a Member country in respect of any matter related to the National Treatment instrument and its implementation, but to date the Committee has received no such requests.

10. During the April meeting, the Committee will hold a general exchange of views with regard to international investment incentives and disincentives. The 1976 Decision on International Investment Incentives and Disincentives provides for consultations within the Committee at the request of a Member country which considers that its interests may be adversely affected by the impact on its flow of international direct investments of measures taken by another Member country specifically designed to provide incentives or disincentives for international direct investment. The section of the 1976 Declaration relating to this subject calls for strengthened co-operation between Member countries and stresses the need to make such measures as transparent as possible and to give due weight to the interests of Member countries affected by such measures.

Annex IV. Case not considered relevant by the IME Committee:

«Submission by the International Federation of Employees and Technicians (FIET) and the Central Organisation of Salaried Employees in Sweden (TCO) to the TUAC on a proposal to include rules of behaviour regarding the international credit market and the multinational banks in the OECD Guidelines for multinational enterprises on April 11, 1978.

THE INTERNATIONAL CREDIT MARKET AND THE MULTI-NATIONAL BANKS – AN UNREGULATED SPHERE OF THE INTERNATIONAL ECONOMIC ACTIVITIES IN URGENT NEED OF A REGULATORY INTERNATIONAL INSTRUMENT.

During the last twenty years multinational banking and international credits have experienced a phenomenal growth. Almost all OECD countries have experienced an internationalization of their banking systems during this period. In 1965, for example, only 11 US banks had branches in other countries; by 1975 some 125 banks had 732 branches operating in 59 foreign countries[1] Citibank alone has a network of over 2,000 offices in more than 100 countries. Such an international structure enables the bank to arrange loans and take deposits from transnational corporations and governments more or less wherever it chooses.[2]

The Eurocurrency market grew from 65 billion dollars in 1970 to 375 billion dollars at the end of 1977; this rapid expansion corresponds to an average yearly increase of around 28 per cent.[3] The backbone of the expansion of multinational banking over the past two decades has been Eurocurrencies. This specie of quasi-money is simply currencies – mostly dollars – circulating between countries, in Europe as well as other countries, where they are deposited in transnational banks and then recirculated through lending arrangements. During the last years a large accumulation of petrodollars has occurred. In 1974 alone the oil producing countries deposited some 25 billion dollars into the branches of multinational banks.[4] In recent years

1. US House of Representatives, Committee on Banking, Currency, and Housing; Financial Institutions and the Nation's Economy, Book II, Part 4, pp. 809–811. Washington, Government Printing Office, 1976.
2. New York Times, 4 March 1977: Ann Crittenden, 'Citibank Found to Lead in Shift to Tax Havens', p. A1.
3. World Financial Markets, Morgan Guaranty Trust Company of New York; February 1978, p. 12.
4. Salomon Brothers, 'United States Multinational Banking: Current and Prospective Strategies'. New York: Salomon Brothers, 1976; p. 18.

299

these quasi-currencies have become a dominant force in international financial markets.

London, Luxembourg and Zürich are well-known centres of world banking. In recent years an increasing proportion of international loans have been arranged from banking offices in small West Indian islands. The Cayman Islands and the Bahamas are today established as 'banking paradises'. In these financial havens the banking activity is virtually unregulated.[5]

The Joint Economic Committee observed that: 'Banks in London and other financial centres have found accepting deposits in dollars . . . and extending loans in these currencies to be profitable because no reserves are required against such deposit liabilities and because this business could be added to their normal functions at modest cost.[6]

Through 'intrabank transfers' funds need not be made in the countries in which the funds are deposited. The intrabank market includes transfers of funds between branches of the same bank as well as loans between two different banks. Because of the interdependence among the banks in the international financial system a failure of one bank has repercussions throughout the financial system. In a report from the US House of Representatives, Committee on Banking, Currency and Housing, it was reported that: 'one banks problems are inevitably passed on to others'.[7] Further it was concluded that 'the failure of any one of these banks could cause the most serious disruptions in financial markets not only in the United States, but in other countries as well' and that 'the proportions of total funds which these banks provided to other banks in 1974 made them highly vulnerable to failure by other banks'.[8]

The rapid growth of multinational banks can be attributed to a number of factors. The absence of regulations has however had a pervasive influence on the entire development of international banking. In the above mentioned report from the US House of Representatives it was concluded that the growth of multinational banking 'has been encouraged by the absence of regulatory constraints'.[9] In a report from Salomon Brothers it was stated that the 'highly complex, sophisticated and unregulated market where multinational banks take, place, and redeposit Euromonies is larger than any domestic money market in the world'.[10] The Joint Economic Committee of the US Congress expressed that 'the motivation underlying the inception of the Eurodollar market was the desire to avoid regulation, either regulations already in effect or additional restrictions that depositors feared might be imposed'.[11]

The unregulated manner in which the multinational banks are operating today makes the international financial system highly vulnerable to economic disturbances. Simultaneously this unregulated financial system has negative economic impacts which among other things makes the adjustment process

5. US Congress, Joint Economic Committee, 'Some Questions and Brief Answers About the Eurodollar Market'; Washington Government Printing Office, 1977, p. 3.
6. US Congress, Joint Economic Committee, p. 1.
7. US House of Representatives, Committee on Banking, Currency, and Housing; p. 892.
8. Ibid., p. 894.
9. Ibid., p. 883.
10. Salomon Brothers, p. 16.
11. US Congress, Joint Economic Committee, p. 2.

unnecessarily difficult for the individual country. In the present international financial system bank failures could have far-reaching repercussions with disastrous consequences on employment and the living standard. The multinational banks play a very important role in the international economy. The OECD guidelines for multinational enterprises do not include any rules of behaviour for multinational banks which could remedy the problems raised above. This is a severe shortcoming with the OECD guidelines for multinational enterprises. With this memorandum the Trade Union Advisory Committee (TUAC) at OECD wants to draw the attention of the OECD Committee on International Investments and Multinational Enterprises (IIME Committee) to this deficiency and to urge that the IIME Committee in the forthcoming revision of the present guidelines works out rules of behaviour in this important field to be included in the revised OECD guidelines for multinational enterprises.»

Annex V. OECD Information Service: Information Note, 14 June 1979; International Investment and Multinational Enterprises – OECD Ministerial Review

OECD Governments reviewed their co-operation in the field of international investment and multinational enterprises when Ministers met at the OECD on 13th–14th June, 1979. This review was undertaken in the light of the experience with the agreements made by them in June 1976 that included Guidelines for multinational enterprises, national treatment for enterprises under foreign control and international investment incentives and disincentives.

A report, prepared by the OECD's Committee on International Investment and Multinational Enterprises (IME Committee) served as the basis of the review.* It contains a detailed evaluation of the experience obtained in the first three years of the agreements and presents proposals to further improve their effectiveness.

A brief summary of its conclusions and proposals follow:

First, it is noted that, in the context of global interdependence, international investment is a major contributor to economic progress and, in the present economic situation, to stimulating growth, employment and a more efficient allocation of resources. Hence, the need for continuing efforts to enhance the positive effects of the international investment process, including the activities of multinational enterprises, and to resolve problems that may arise.

Experience since the adoption of the Declaration and Decisions on International Investment and Multinational Enterprises at the OECD Ministerial Council on 21st and 22nd June, 1976, shows that:

- they provide a sound and realistic framework for co-operation not only between governments but between governments, enterprises and social partners as well;
- they are an important factor contributing to a favourable investment climate in the OECD area; and
- they have a positive effect on discussion of these matters in other international fora.

With respect to the *Guidelines for Multinational Enterprises*, it is considered that experience to date underlines their value and that their future promotion would be best served by providing enterprises with a stable framework for the period ahead. One change is proposed, however, to cover the transfer of workers from a foreign affiliate in order to influence unfairly negotiations with employees – an issue not foreseen when the Guidelines were drafted.

On the basis of its experience in dealing with issues put forward by govern-

---

* Issued separately.

ments and the two OECD advisory bodies, the Business and Industry Advisory Committee (BIAC) and the Trade Union Advisory Committee (TUAC), it is recognized that there is need for providing supplementary guidance to the parties concerned and the report therefore includes explanatory comments on a broad range of issues. It is proposed that the IME Committee continue to provide such explanatory comments in the future as required.

A number of additional proposals for further promoting reference to and use of the Guidelines are also made. Recognizing the importance of the active and sustained support of the multinational enterprises themselves, it is recommended that enterprises state publicly, preferably in the annual reports, their acceptance of the Guidelines. Enterprises are also invited to include, in their subsequent reports, brief statements on their experience with the Guidelines. This may contain mention of steps taken with respect to their observance as well as difficulties experienced. The Member governments will make arrangements at the national level for handling matters and problems arising with regard to the Guidelines. It is urged that matters first be raised, discussed and, if possible, resolved at the national level. Member governments will report at regular intervals to the OECD on their experience and on developments relating to the Guidelines.

At the international level, acknowledging the benefit derived from the frequent contact with the two advisory bodies, the IME Committee stresses its intention to continue such contacts. In addition, the Committee will give an individual enterprise the opportunity, if it so wishes, of expressing its views to the Committee either orally or in writing on issues concerning the Guidelines involving its interests.

With respect to *National Treatment* for foreign controlled enterprises, that is, treatment no less favourable than that accorded in like situations to domestic enterprises, it is recognized that a notably greater degree of transparency has been achieved with respect to measures existing in Member countries which constitute exceptions to National Treatment.

This is especially true for those exceptions which are formalized in the laws and regulations of Member countries. It is also noted, however, that much still remains to be done in certain areas, particularly with respect to measures which rely upon administrative practices. It is reaffirmed that the process of examination and discussion of National Treatment questions will be used by the IME Committee with the aim of extending the application of National Treatment and provision is made for future association of the BIAC and TUAC with this work.

With respect to *International Investment Incentives and Disincentives*, it is recognized that it would be detrimental to international co-operation and to the efficient allocation of economic resources available for investment if there were increasing conflicts due to an excessive use of incentives and disincentives to influence the international investment decisions of enterprises. The IME Committee accordingly recommends a flexible and pragmatic approach in applying the procedures of the respective Decision to resolve any difficulties which may develop. Provision is being made for periodic exchanges of views with BIAC and TUAC in this area also.

The IME Committee plans to undertake further work on investment incentives and disincentives and on other issues relating to international direct·investment, notably an analytical study of the effects of governmental incentives and disincentives on the international investment process. The aim is to provide indications of the impact of the measures on international direct investment flows and of the effects of competition between governments.

The next formal review by the Ministerial Council of the 1976 Declaration and Decisions on International Investment and Multinational Enterprises will be held within five years. A mid-term progress report to the OECD Council in 1982 is proposed. This report, which will also be published, will cover the experience of the IME Committee and the Member governments in carrying out the proposals contained in the 1979 Review Report and, more generally, the further implementation of the 1976 instruments.

Index

The numbers given are paragraph numbers.

Index